The Hidden Curriculum

NATIONAL BUSINESS EDUCATION YEARBOOK, NO. 30

Editor:
ANNA M. BURFORD
Middle Tennessee State University
Murfreesboro, Tennessee

Assistant Editor:
VIVIAN ARNOLD
East Carolina University
Greenville, North Carolina

Published by:
National Business Education Association
1914 Association Drive   Reston, Virginia 22091

Preface

The hidden curriculum may be defined as *integrated topics often taught or needing emphasis, but having limited coverage in textbooks.* Educators have been talented in selecting information to supplement classroom textbooks, and the theme for this 1992 NBEA yearbook, *The Hidden Curriculum,* acknowledges that an expansion of these topics into the formal curriculum has been and continues to be evident in the classroom. Classroom teachers are among the first to identify the topics that seem most relevant for students; but these same educators sometimes fail to pursue their instincts for lack of confidence, time, or resources. The authors of this yearbook have thoughtfully selected materials to support educators as they attempt to augment and enrich textbook materials.

The hidden curriculum is by no means intended as a panacea for the many problems and needs of education. Improving America's schools will require solutions to a wide range of complex social issues, as well as possible adjustments to curricula. The contents of this yearbook are relevant in that several authors have provided information to help readers envision today's workforce and the skills necessary for survival and promotion. For example, much attention has been directed recently to the problems of functional illiteracy; therefore, separate chapters are allocated to information pertaining to the basics. These topics include: reading, written and oral communications, listening, keyboarding/proofreading, basic business, and learning. The resources provided are not all new, but will be helpful because they are presented as a theme and have direct relevance for the business education curricula.

Part I of *The Hidden Curriculum* calls attention to the subject of excellence versus mediocrity, introduces the reader to current trends in the workforce, and describes the role of the educator as a facilitator of the hidden curriculum.

Part II concentrates on a range of content areas and presents strategies for learning, reinforcing, and evaluating curricula. In addition to ideas for identifying hidden agendas and reinforcing the basics, three chapters in this section focus on the learning process: lifelong learning and learning theories, structure for writing objectives, and structure for grouping students. Education and employment, social/personality development, and ethical behavior are discussed in terms of human relations and career/personal development.

Part III reviews selected features of the hidden curriculum and presents strategies for utilization of telecommunication, youth organizations, and work partnerships as avenues to improve business education.

The content and strategies offered to educators should be directed toward specific student needs as they are apparent to classroom instructors. Since no one knows exactly which skills will be in demand or required for survival in the future, educators must compound and refine the ideas presented. Marketability for future employment may lean more heavily toward a diversity of skills and a desire among individuals to continue learning.

Contributing authors represent all NBEA regions and a diversity of educational backgrounds and experiences at the secondary, postsecondary, and university levels.

The Hidden Curriculum is a refereed yearbook. Chapters were reviewed by at least three persons. Manuscripts for all chapters were divided among members of the NBEA Publications Committee for the first review. Another group of professionals was selected as second reviewers. Members of this group were: Marion Crawford, James Calvert Scott, and Randall Wells. Vivian Arnold also reviewed chapter manuscripts and assisted me throughout the year in planning and executing the details for this 1992 NBEA Yearbook.

I sincerely appreciate the contributions of the 27 authors, members of the editorial review board, and Vivian Arnold. These persons have shared generously their time and expertise to add quality and relevance to this yearbook. Members of the editorial review board were:

Clarice Brantley, Woodham High School
 Pensacola, Florida
Sallie Craft, Prince George's County Board of Education
 Landover, Maryland
Marion Crawford, University of Arkansas at Little Rock
 Little Rock, Arkansas
Wanda Daniel, Fulton County Board of Education
 Atlanta, Georgia
R. Neil Dortch, University of Wisconsin-Whitewater
 Whitewater, Wisconsin
Marie E. Flatley, San Diego State University
 San Diego, California
Donna Holmquist, University of Nebraska
 Lincoln, Nebraska
James Calvert Scott, Utah State University
 Logan, Utah
Randall Wells, University of Louisville
 Louisville, Kentucky

Anna M. Burford, Editor

Contents

PART I
INTRODUCTION AND CONSTITUENT PARTS OF THE HIDDEN CURRICULUM

PART II
THE HIDDEN CURRICULUM: CHALLENGES FOR ACADEMIC REINFORCEMENT

vi

PART III
STRATEGIES FOR MARKETING THE HIDDEN CURRICULUM

Part I

INTRODUCTION AND CONSTITUENT PARTS OF THE HIDDEN CURRICULUM

CHAPTER 1

The Hidden Curriculum: An Opportunity

ANNA M. BURFORD
Middle Tennessee State University, Murfreesboro

VIVIAN ARNOLD
East Carolina University, Greenville, North Carolina

Curricula usually provide a structured framework that permits enough flexibility for educators to interject their personal educational philosophies. These selected agendas create both opportunities and responsibilities for student improvement. The theme for this yearbook was conceived with a mission: to offer business educators enrichment materials that can be incorporated into their lesson plans in a variety of courses. The yearbook authors have provided a myriad of pedagogical strategies for those who wish to promote excellence and discourage mediocrity.

EXCELLENCE VS. MEDIOCRITY

A creeping lassitude regarding responsibility and commitment seems to prevail in American society. For the past decade, many educators and community leaders have expressed their discomfort and concern that students are increasingly more complacent than in previous years. Many students appear to have growing commitments to and preoccupation with things other than education—a trend away from the goal of excellence and toward apparent satisfaction with mediocrity. The same listless and languid attitude seems also to be common among employees. Many business educators have heard the familiar lament: "They don't make employees the way they did in the old days." To those who have encountered this complaint, the thought is discouraging. On a brighter note, however, the work environment has become global and very competitive; therefore, continued growth and excellence are required for both employer and employee survival. These changes in the workplace may magnify any type of mediocrity; nonetheless, independence and progress have their roots embedded in excellence.

Human intellectual prowess is so designed that it may work toward defeat or toward perfection. A first-rate combination for excellence is the capacity to reason and a strong will to achieve. With too little will, the result is mediocrity. Mediocrity is a malady of the will. It is insidious, and no drug can be prescribed as a remedy. The search for the best techniques for motivation to reduce mediocrity is eternal. Classroom procedures for motivation that have been effective in the past may not work today or in the future.

Only after educators have assumed the responsibility to be current, knowledgeable, and flexible are they qualified to make decisions about relevant course content and motivational strategies.

Humans are creatures of comfort and are easily caught up in a program of mental and physical shortcuts. While shortcuts to learning and working are possible and even laudable, ideas about success in the absence of hard work should be purged from the minds of those who lean toward accepting mediocrity. Some drudgery and tedium are facts of life. Too little determination may result in physiological sluggishness and a psychological deterrent. Work has many physiological and psychological benefits. Educators should dispel the notion that working a little and loafing a lot is the good life. Work is both a privilege and a service. Values associated with work, beyond monetary rewards, are frequently only vaguely perceived by high school and college students. The merit of work is better understood when one recognizes its intrinsic aspects. Work provides structure for one's life and has a profound effect on the way one thinks. Work is an opportunity for self-expression and self-reliance. Each person has some degree of control over his or her own destiny. A strong defense against mediocrity is the development of a strong motivation towards productive performance, individual competence, and personal satisfaction with a job well done.

TECHNOLOGY AND EXCELLENCE

Computer intelligence (artificial intelligence) as an advanced technology can be a tremendous asset to neophytes and professionals; however, both students and educators should remind themselves of their mental superiority and uniqueness when compared to machine capabilities. Promoting unrealistic ideas about capabilities of technology may create lackadaisical attitudes that breed mediocrity. No machine can duplicate human mental capabilities. Machines can perform certain tasks faster and with superb accuracy, but inspired human thinking is the highest form of technology. In other words, individuals should never relax or become complacent because they believe that machines will do all of the work. Thinking is still a human responsibility, and thinking skills have never been in greater demand.

QUEST FOR EXCELLENCE

No exact set of rules exists to motivate performance. Nevertheless, some thoughtful recommendations for nurturing excellence in teaching are presented in this yearbook. Two topics, (1) visualization and imagination and (2) networking, were not included as chapter topics. These topics, however, have potential for opening doors and encouraging students to attain excellence; thus, a brief discussion of each follows.

Visualization and imagination. Visualization is the ability to picture clearly a given object or situation. Imagination is a broader concept. A person who has an active imagination can create an inner world that consists of many mental images, preferably worthwhile events. These creations of the mind may spawn challenging thoughts and creativity. Creativity is an element for success in a competitive, global work environment, and most persons have far more imaginative and creative powers than they have used and more than they suspect they have. Visualization and imagination are relatively unexplored except in the areas of drafting, visual arts, drama, solid geometry, and sports. Nevertheless, many more possibilities exist to encourage actions. Business leaders are often asked to envision the future for their respective companies. "Vision is the link between dream and action" (Naisbitt and Aburdene, 1985). Vision is practical for both business educators and students as they visualize (a) the successful performance of a difficult task; (b) employment in a career congruent with talents; (c) a reader's or listener's response before selecting words for written or oral communication; and (d) ways that computer technology can refocus curricula. Just imagine the additional possibilities that bright, creative students could originate in a small-group class arrangement!

Winners are people with vision and focus for the future. They often create new ideas by combining previous experiences with new impressions. Visualization and imagination are components that help guide human growth. The fulfillment of human potential depends somewhat on a growing awareness of possibilities. There is a growing problem in the 20th century: Most people's schedules are so fragmented or overloaded that no time remains to think about or experiment with possibilities. Personal research and research of others are powerful and necessary tools to enrich one's own imagination and to enhance the visions and imaginations of students. Innovation is stifled by always retreating to the known and familiar.

The resourcefulness of students may be either encouraged or discouraged by the wealth of information available—access to numerous TV channels, to computer software, to term papers by mail, and to major literary works, from *The Iliad* to *The Old Man and the Sea*, on the shelves of college book stores for approximately $2.98 each. One would have to ask whether the resources are aids or crutches.

Today's students should be led by visionary educators who applaud the resources available to them and to their students. Quality decisions are usually based on multiple factors such as imagination, heuristics, primary research, secondary research, and knowledge gained via networking.

Networking. Networking provides opportunities for interactions with like-minded people who are in pursuit of similar goals. Networking may represent interactions between individuals, small groups, large groups, or a hierarchical arrangement between small and large groups. In America the business card also symbolizes networking. Each card exchanged has potential for future networking. No restrictions normally exist as to the number of interacting arrangements possible.

Networking encompasses several concepts for students, educators, and business persons: (1) group influence in setting short-term and long-term goals, (2) giving support to other capable persons and not taking all of the credit for self, thereby helping each other grow, (3) communicating with poise and efficiency with all persons who may impact one's future, and (4) using

3

computer technology as a network for information exchange. Networking as a teaching-learning device may occur in any one of the following settings: intradepartmental, interdepartmental, community-business exchange, home-community exchange, and national-international exchange. Some expected benefits of networking for educators and business persons follow:

- Knowledge of trends and issues in education
- Knowledge of competencies most needed for the workplace and recruitment strategies of employers
- Standards for employability and promotability
- Information about suppliers and distributors
- Benefits of training and development
- Self-confidence for planning and executing objectives
- Self-assurance to become an enthusiast and a facilitator
- Technology updating: hardware/software resource awareness and availability
- Appreciation for America: workforce diversity, information capabilities, technological superiority, free press, stable political environment, and one of the world's largest consumer markets
- Appreciation for a global environment: knowledge of other cultures, educational curricula, and economic systems

Mentoring is also a form of networking. A network of supporters provides visibility and can even be a means of survival. The list could be expanded, but the power of networking as a tool for personal, social, business, and educational competencies should be obvious. Remember, though, that networking is a two-way street. If benefits are to be derived, it may be necessary to get outside one's comfort zone and to be proactive rather than passive.

QUEST FOR FIRE

The idea of "quest for fire" was expressed by Saunders when he gleaned from Ezekiel 1:27-28 that the fire spoken of in this Biblical reference suggests a quest that burns deep within us—a spark that gives life, a search for significance, and a drive for self-actualization.

If within us all there exists an innate "fire," educators have fewer reasons to despair as they encounter mediocrity than they might have imagined. Instead, all educators should strive to ignite or rekindle this heritage that adds uniqueness, warmth, and meaning to life. Words form symbols of communication that express meaning, wisdom, love, and deep feelings. Educators are in strategic and honored positions to choose words that give guidance and direction for the journey ahead, much the same as the tour guide determines the success of the tour. Leaders in education could just possibly be some of the "points of light" that President Bush mentioned in his inaugural address in 1989.

Excellence in teaching or in performance is not a single act or a static concept. Excellence is a state of mind, an attitude, and a force that requires constant use and has a passionate impatience with mediocrity among those who are competent and talented. (Not all persons are capable of high-level performance.) Personalities possess mystery, and educators can not always unravel that mystery; but educators must stay convinced that a caring attitude and carefully selected teaching agendas can make a difference. *Footnote:* Teachers should adopt high standards that are fair, understood, and enforceable.

SUGGESTIONS FOR EXCELLENCE

Consider the following thoughts as a means of comprehending and applying the concepts of excellence, some of which were influenced by *Bravely, Bravely in Business* by Conarroe (1972):

- Tell the truth. This makes one special and rare.
- Strive for perfection. Mistakes are costly. One can learn from mistakes, but it is better to learn from victories.
- Reach for success in areas where talents and personality are congruent with job responsibilities.
- Be resourceful and rely on persons who have strengths in areas of one's personal weakness.
- Build on successes and strengths and work to improve weaknesses.
- Practice a solid code of self-management; this code should hold even in everyday activities.
- Think of self as a salesperson, no matter what the job is. Everyone must sell ideas and concepts.
- Express thanks and give praise when appropriate. Acknowledging others creates motivation for continued success.
- Always consider the future significance of one's actions and words.
- Decide on the price of compromise; if too costly, find a way to replace compromise.
- Maintain a healthy enthusiasm—attitude is always on display.
- Avoid toxic and jealous people as much as possible. These people often spend time trying to bring others down to their level.
- Establish clear, attainable goals and review them periodically.
- Be persistent. Personal charisma is helpful, but sincere, sustained commitment is needed to accomplish visions.
- Show evidences of being inner-directed rather than other-directed. Self-reliance is a leadership quality.
- Establish relationships and charisma by favoring results over politics.
- Maintain a learning attitude. Change and adaptation are easier when one continues to learn.
- Accept the need to change and to adapt to unfamiliar situations. Change is inevitable.
- Measure personal success on personal capabilities instead of comparing to the success of others—individual talents differ.
- Remember that life is more enjoyable when doing one's best.

Just as education is costly, excellence is costly; but it is not as costly as mediocrity! Mediocrity can be an adopted practice by persons of all ages, and the personal practice of such is influenced by organizational policies and the environments in which one lives and works. One can surmise, however, that a result of observable mediocrity in a society will mean a decline in the quality of education and ultimately in the quality of life.

The decision to assume responsibility for excellence rests within us all. The authors of *In Search of Excellence* made numerous observations about excellent corporations that also apply to education. Among their thoughts are the following:

> Excellent companies are learning organizations . . . they experiment more, encourage more tries, and permit small failures (p. 110). Excellent companies seem to abound in distinctly individual techniques . . . (p. 121). (Peters and Waterman, 1982).

These ideas and others suggest that if one desires change or results, one may need to experiment with strategy. *The Hidden Curriculum* offers strategies and opportunities. Each in his or her own way must select strategies to optimize results.

REFERENCES

Conarroe, Richard R. *Bravely, Bravely in Business,* American Management Association, New York, 1972.

Peters, Thomas J., and Robert H. Waterman, Jr. *In Search of Excellence,* Harper and Rowe, New York, NY, 1982, p. 110 and p. 121.

Naisbitt, John, and Patricia Aburdene. *Re-inventing the Corporation,* Warner Books, Inc., New York, NY, 1985. p. 21.

Saunders, Landon. "Hearts of Fire Series." *Heartbeat,* Hanover, NH 03755.

CHAPTER 2

Defining the Work Force of the 1990s: Implications for Curriculum Development and Instructional Practice

THOMAS HAYNES

Illinois State University, Normal, Illinois

Johann Wolfgang Von Goethe said, "Life belongs to the living, and he who lives must be prepared for change." Americans, as well as citizens of other developed economies, pursue happiness, well being, and fulfillment through their ability to be productive in their personal and work endeavors. Most would agree that the ability to have a full, happy, and challenging life is highly correlated with the ability to be economically productive for ourselves, our employers, and our country. Generally speaking, we attempt to improve our standard of living through our involvement with school, work, home, and social/cultural activities. Our desire for an improved standard of living, as measured by growth in the GNP, gains in productivity, improvements in the balance of trade, and expanding sales in international markets, is an economic canon that reflects our hope for a better future. These economic statistics impact all of us that make up the United States economy: Articles, reports, symposia, journals, and mass-produced communication events and programs have highlighted these issues and have raised them to a level of interest that has rarely been experienced in our history.

With relative ease since the Industrial Revolution, U.S. citizens have experienced a trend in better living through gains in productivity. But, since the late 1970s, we have witnessed a tremendous turnabout in the results from our economic efforts, the nature of our work, and in the roles that individuals play in workplaces. We have seen our ability to easily increase GNP become a struggle. Two-career families are common today as compared to peacetime eras of the past. Yet standards of living are not increasing dramatically. Since the mid 1970s, our balance of trade has been negative, although our previous history produced quite opposite statistics. Once we were considered the only true source for high quality goods and services in the world. Today, our products struggle to compete in price and quality with products and services from developing economies. Simply put—business isn't an easy game to play anymore now that we aren't the only ones playing. Much of the concern over our economy's performance hinges on the abilities of the work force, the nature of the work place, and the interaction between the former and latter.

7

The intent of this chapter is to focus on the nature of the work force and workplace for the 1990s and the implications this has for curriculum development and instructional practice in business education. In analyzing the work force and workplace of the 1990s, it is essential to establish a baseline of current information reflecting the path of change leading to the basic foundations necessary for a productive work force in the 1990s. This evaluation will identify some major developments and projections for the work force and workplace. The identified developments and projects will highlight a variety of needs that should be addressed if our economy is to take advantage of the opportunities of the 1990s. From this synthesis, implications for curriculum development and instructional practice in business education will be delineated. The identified implications will focus on activities that business educators can pursue to positively impact their students—the work force of the 1990s.

TECHNOLOGICAL AND EDUCATIONAL ADVANCEMENT

Dwight D. Eisenhower predicted, "As technological achievements continue to mount, the normal life span will continue to climb. The hourly productivity of the worker will increase." The application of technology to work settings has provided opportunities for geometrically improving our productivity and hence, our standard of living. But, technological developments have had other effects, such as worker displacement, job extinction, and job deskilling (a reduction in job duties, skills, and responsibilities) and has been the focus of much concern since the early 1970s. Bell (1973) and Braverman (1974) deduced that the nature of work would become dehumanized and require fewer higher order skills and activities, except for the activities of managers and executives. Both of these authors' works were published at a time when the United States was becoming increasingly challenged in the world marketplace and losing its luster as an economic juggernaut. Yet, little analysis was completed in the opposite vein—reviewing the need for expanded, higher order skills in existing jobs and the broadening or enriching of job duties in occupations that were becoming highly automated. During this period average educational levels in the United States were increasing.

Several researchers supported the position that Americans were receiving more education than they needed for the jobs that were available. Due to the "baby-boom population" entering and completing higher education, more and more jobs were being filled by those with a variety of postsecondary education. Also, there appears to have been a decrease in the earnings differential between those with college degrees and those without during the 1970s. For example, Rumberger (1984) found that college enrollments tripled between 1960 and 1980, but the number of jobs requiring college education only doubled. Thus, an overpopulation of college-educated individuals entering the labor market led to many accepting positions for which they may have been overqualified.

Parallel to the "overeducation" of the population, investigators have indicated that as new technologies were developed, the skills needed to enter

8

the work force and to advance in a career were of a higher level. But as these technologies matured, the skills necessary to function effectively began to fall (Johnston and Packer, 1987). It wasn't until the Department of Labor's *Workforce 2000* that the idea of deskilling declined in acceptance. This report indicated that there was faster growth in occupations that required more highly skilled workers and that utilized technology than in those jobs that did not use technology. During the last half of the 1980s the deskilling notion came under increasing review and analysis. As researchers attempted to get an intellectual grasp on the changing needs of the work force due to changes in technology and occupations, they came to understand the problematic nature of reviewing data that had many research methodology problems. Part of this problem was that the research did not consider the changes in the environments surrounding the introduction of new technologies. Although it had been argued that advancements in technology will deskill the nature of the work to be completed, often these advancements increase the number of worker operations, duties, and responsibilities, thus, creating a need for higher level skills. In addition to the skills needed to use new technologies, machine repair and maintenance functions require higher level skills that may require a postsecondary technical degree program or certificate.

In utilizing new technologies, such abilities as problem solving, creating new procedures, directing one's own job-related learning, and communicating effectively with others are critical to worker success and productivity. This is due mainly to a more uncertain and less well defined environment, to the need to manage greater and more complex interactions with a variety of individuals in a more collaborative environment, and to utilize new technology in new situations. For example, in view of the use of technology and automation in the workplace over the last twenty years, it is evident that most organizations have used computers and advanced equipment to improve production efficiency and the quality of their products and services. According to Bailey (1990), in 1960 the textile industry ranked 48th out of 61 manufacturing industries in terms of its average equipment age (the industry that ranked first had the newest equipment). By 1980 the industry had risen to second. This modernization led to impressive gains in productivity. While total productivity in the manufacturing sector grew 2.4 percent a year between 1975 and 1985, textile's productivity grew by 5.6 percent. But, it is unclear how the infusion of technology into the textile industry impacted the skill requirements of workers. The skill requirements for workers may be dependent upon the intentions and actions of managers and executives who are in control of the application of technology in the workplace. If technology reduces routine and hazardous tasks, while expanding the duties and responsibilities of workers, then the technology, through management, enriches workplace activities. But, if technology reduces the quality of worker activity to a minimum, then it deskills positions. This deskilling or enriching manifests itself in dynamic fashion. Technology, jobs, and worker skills don't change in lock step, proportional increments. Sometimes these changes occur in unusual patterns, leaving jobs deskilled for a time; then after technical or human resource adjustments, these jobs are dramatically enriched.

9

BUSINESS AND ECONOMIC ENVIRONMENT

Adlai E. Stevenson said, "On a shrunken globe, men can no longer live like strangers." Although technology has advanced at what appears to be 1,000 percent in just 20 years, a look at the business and economic environment surrounding technological change provides a clearer picture of the myriad of factors that are impacting us today. According to popular press books, such as *Megatrends 2000*, by Naisbitt and Auberdene (1990), the business environment over the last 20 years has become global instead of completely domestic. According to the Office of Technological Assessment, the share of the United States Gross National Product accounted for by imports and exports increased from 10 percent in 1960 to almost 22 percent in 1984. Not only has trade increased, but also the direction of trade has shifted. Prior to the early 1980s, the United States had a significant world leadership position in terms of a positive balance of trade; but at the time of this writing this situation has shifted 180 degrees to place the United States as the leading importer of goods and services in the world.

Parallel to the development and expansion of international business, the nature of the marketplace has changed. Companies that had been comfortable with the mass production of "white appliances" since the post-World War II era have learned that customizing and finding market niches were common strategies for successful companies during the 1970s and 1980s. One look at the changes in the banking system in the United States over the last 20 years illustrates the changes in the marketplace and the customizing of services. Rising household incomes not only created a demand for very basic banking services but also increased the market for many more consumer financial instruments and services. Whereas 15 years ago consumer banks in the United States offered six basic products, today, customers of most progressive retail banks can choose from over 100 different products. In addition to change in the marketplace, new technology assists in the timely delivery of customized services and products.

Accompanying the use of technology and automation, improved patterns of work have been developed that have had a positive impact on the speed and direction in which producers can react to market needs. As an example, one may look at the number of fashion and apparel catalogs that are received through the mail on a regular basis. Even the stalwarts of the industry, Sears and J.C. Penney, have moved to more precise and segmented marketing. Today you may not receive just one Sears catalog but two or three within several weeks. These will focus on different merchandise and services, as well as different styles and features, to accommodate more than the standard four seasons of the year, i.e. white sale season, lawn and garden season, early spring season, late spring season, and back-to-school season. Cataloging has become so customized and competitive that Sears is contemplating discontinuing their large mass merchandise *Wish Book* because of its recent lack of profit generation.

CHANGE: SPEED AND POWER

According to Lyman Lloyd Bryson, "We are restless because of incessant change, but we would be frightened if change were stopped." With increased competition from overseas firms, as well as the application of technology in producing goods and services, the swiftness and quantity of change that is taking place in business settings is incomparable to any other time in our history. These changes exert pressure on business leaders to reconceptualize the very structure and alignment of their business firms. For example, in analyzing site location decisions for the Diamond Star Motor Car Corporation in Normal, Illinois, two of the top concerns were transportation and proximity to suppliers of component parts. Management's understanding of the nature of change and need to respond quickly to it made these priority concerns. The ability to acquire parts, sometimes newly engineered, as quickly as possible for their just-in-time inventory system was high priority. Their location allows them to make adjustments in component parts quickly so that production schedules are not delayed. Further, at this "factory of the future" operation, highly skilled, flexible employees can change body stamping dies in a matter of seconds with the help of computers. International competition is one of the reasons why companies are focusing on the ability to change quickly. According to Clark, Chew, and Fujimoto (1987), Japanese automobile firms completely design projects in two-thirds of the time, with one-third of the engineering hours, of U.S. firms. This obviously reduces costs and allows them to react more quickly to changes and market demands.

ORGANIZATIONAL AND STRUCTURAL CHANGES

Alfred North Whitehead said, "The art of progress is to preserve order amid change, and to preserve change and order." In the mass production, standardized product firm of the post-World War II era, a multi-level, hierarchal organization with structured policies and definite procedures dominated business and industry. Due to the speed at which markets, competitors, and processes currently change, this type of organizational pattern does not fit the demands of the 1990s. From the mid 1970s to the present, company after company has flattened its organization, transferred authority, responsibility, and decision-making down the hierarchy of the organization, and become more dependent upon team work and team building activities. New supervisory and managerial skills are being implemented where managers are abandoning general autocratic, direct authority styles for more cooperative, facilitative practices. In these situations, employees and managers alike need to acquire a clearer understanding of how these new and less understood managerial roles should be best handled and utilized. Such concepts as quality circles and work teams are no longer pilot studies and experiments, but typical of many of the high-skill, high-technology companies in the marketplace. For example, most American banks have a turnover rate among tellers that averages more than 40 percent a year.

11

Pressures to perform one's duty accurately and quickly and the limited opportunities for advancement are cited as reasons for this level of turnover. Training for these jobs consists usually of four to six weeks of orientation. But, in a number of European banks, workers are now being reorganized and assigned greater responsibility. These individuals do much more than just complete the duties of a teller. They perform much of the "front office" work—opening new accounts, granting mortgages and loans, processing commercial, foreign, and consumer transactions, providing investment advice, and selling stocks and bonds. In America these functions are usually performed by specialized departments.

CUSTOMERS AND SUPPLIERS

Martin Luther King said, "We must learn to live together as brothers or perish together as fools." During the supremacy of post-World War II industrial America, the focus upon customers was not a concern. Post-war consumer demand was so great that many felt that whatever was produced by business and industry would be gobbled up by consumers. This scenario has changed dramatically with the progress of marketing concepts, especially marketing research related to consumer or buyer behavior and the international marketplace.

Gaining in importance is the concept of the business "client." Clients are usually thought of as the people who purchase a firm's goods and services, but today this concept is much broader and includes those individuals and groups within and outside the organization that interact and exchange communications and support. These clients are oftentimes just as critical to the firm's productive abilities as their purchasing customers. At Saur-Sunstrand Corporation, Freeport, Illinois, for example, front-line workers have been trained to understand how the client relationship impacts their production activities. They are helped to see that they are a client for other production workers in their own facility and that they will be developing or working on products on the assembly line for other clients within the same building. They also understand that suppliers of parts and services to their organization should have the perception that Saur-Sunstrand is their client, that they have needs, and they should be willing to communicate these to suppliers. The firm's philosophy is that companies outside their organization are customers and clients and that they are the ultimate source of success for the company. Furthermore, the company is engendering a notion that the community in which Saur-Sunstrand operates is a client of the company, since many of the employees are active in civic organizations and participate in the local economy. Management's purpose is to develop ownership of and commitment to the production process by front-line workers. The objective is to raise the concern for quality production through dynamic, two-way interaction.

Treating suppliers as customers and clients is a change in the traditional nature of how organizations view the process of purchasing component products and services for their business venture. Historically, purchasing agents have worked behind the scenes to have competing firms bid against each other. The firm with the lowest price for goods or services is the usual winner of the competition. Today, the single-sided, price competitive bid process is slowly dying. Replacing it is a form of purchasing that is multi-faceted, developmental, and based on relationships. Companies today seek out vendors who are not only price competitive, but deliver in a timely manner high quality goods that are cooperatively designed and engineered by the vendor and the customer company. The intent is that the closer the relationship between the companies, the more success and flexibility these organizations will be able to enjoy in the future.

WORKPLACE DEMOGRAPHICS

According to Walt Whitman, "Other lands have their vitality in a few, a class, but we have it in the bulk of our people." Popular press and professional research publications have documented the changing nature of the work force (Cetron, 1989; Johnston and Packer, 1987; Kutsher, 1987; Silvestri and Lukasiewicz, 1987). Recent research literature has focused on three major strands of change in the characteristics of the work force: 1) the decreasing numbers of young adults entering the work force; 2) the cultural diversity of workers; and 3) the retraining of older workers (Bailey, 1990; Raizen, 1989; Schwartz and Turner, 1990).

The number of new workers entering the labor force will continue to decrease, even taking into account immigration, until the children of "baby boomers" begin to enter the work force. Due to slow population growth, the work force will expand by only one percent annually during the 1990s, thereby slowing the economic growth of the nation. This slow growth will likely require employers to recruit, hire, and train nontraditional groups that have typically faced the greatest barriers in becoming productive workers. Projections by Johnston and Packer (1987) indicate that five-sixths of the net additions to the work force in the 1990s will be nonwhite women and immigrants. The work force will become increasingly multi-lingual and multi-cultural. This will have a considerable impact on employee-employer relationships related to values, life styles, and the skills needed for the workplace.

According to Bailey (1990), minorities (Blacks, Hispanics, and Asians) are projected to account for nearly 60 percent of the labor force in the 1990s, while women will make up nearly 60 percent of the net increase. Unfortunately, data have shown that, historically, these populations have done poorest with educational attainment. To address this, the thrust of the Carl Perkins Vocational and Applied Technology Education Act of 1990 targets these populations to assist them in entering and being successful in the workplace. With the projected change in the makeup of the work force, employers and educators will have to make a concerted effort to help these groups prepare for successful workplace participation if our economy is to be globally competitive.

According to Schwartz and Turner (1990), we will see the median age for the U.S. population continue to increase due to increased life expectancy, lower birth rates, and the aging of the "baby boomer" generation. But this is true mostly for white Americans. A review of minority populations presents a different picture. Although the median age for white Americans is 31 years, African Americans and Hispanics average 25 years and 22 years respectively. When taking into account U.S. immigrant populations, the median for minority groups is reduced even further. Although there are large numbers of minority youth, television commercials over the last ten years have illustrated an obvious trend toward societal values focusing on the middle-aged culture, including stronger minority representation. This perspective should continue as we drift away from a somewhat ingrained "white youth" perspective to a more multi-cultural, middle-aged focus. With this backdrop, firms will likely seek out and employ older workers, as well as retrain older workers for new types of occupations that require different skills than they may possess. In addition to skill deficiencies, employers will have to consider the older workers' different personal and cultural values.

Another population-related issue is mobility and the configuration of the population. In the recent 1990 census, such states as California, Florida, Texas, and Arizona have increased their population to such a degree that political analysts have indicated that in the next presidential election, these four states could dictate who will be the next president. This trend of major growth in the Sun Belt should continue throughout the 1990s. Also, within geographic regions, people are tending to live in metropolitan areas as major cities continue to provide a hub-and-spoke network for jobs, culture, services, and entertainment.

CHANGES IN FAMILIES, RELIGION, AND SCHOOLS

Other major forces affecting work situations are changing the structure of the American family, the role of religion and spiritualism, and the role, place, and structure of education. To many, one of the most troubling and significant changes is the metamorphosis of the traditional family. Definitions of family today include traditional nuclear families; singlehood; non-marital, heterosexual, and homosexual cohabitation; single-parent families; remarried couples and step-families; foster and adoptive families; child-free households; and multi-adult households. Although families have reached higher levels of affluence in the 1980s, it has been because both parents are working and not because of increased standards of living based on one individual's salary. Interestingly, although women have taken a stronger role in the work force over the last 20 years, many two-earner families would be considered in the poor category if they were to rely only on the father's or mother's income.

Unfortunately, two-thirds of new marriages will end in some form of dissolution, with the highest rates among minorities. The increases in single-parent families due to divorce and out-of-wedlock births have a troublesome impact on our society in general, and the work force specifically. The needs of women caring for children as well as maintaining a livelihood, in conjunction with the increasing participation of minorities in the work force,

14

will require dramatic and possibly systemic changes in the organization of the workplace.

The changes in family structure and composition have placed an enormous burden on individuals and institutions to provide support. Neighbors, employers, schools, day care centers, government agencies, and churches have all assisted families in coping with the dramatic changes taking place in the 1980s. And based on current projections, this will continue in the 1990s. The level of concern for family development, as a positive means to combat the malaise resulting from broken homes, has been espoused by some school principals through their support for parenting education for junior and senior high school students. They believe that students need to receive this training prior to leaving high school. Some educators say that the junior high school level may be the most appropriate place to start so that adolescents are prepared for parenting-related decisions while they are in high school.

A review of the amazing events of the 1980s, including massive failures in the savings and loan industry, ethical improprieties among the leaders of Congress, the mishandling of funds by brokerage firms, and the fracturing of families have all led to increased levels of concern for our society's ethics and morals. People are less willing to trust public and private institutions and individuals. To combat this lack of trust, Naisbitt and Aburdene (1990) have indicated that people are becoming more spiritual and religious, trying to find a stronger foundation on which to base their decisions. Much of this new spiritual movement is being provided by new, more evangelical denominations that are not necessarily the traditional Catholic, Protestant, and Jewish churches. In addition, there is a wealth of periodicals and support groups that provide spiritual instruction and insight not associated with formalized religions.

The largest segment of the American work force consists of high school graduates who have not graduated from college; the nation's economic survival depends heavily on their performance. It will be the front-line workers of America, their ability to produce effectively and deal with a changing environment that will be a paramount concern in the 1990s. For without a productive front-line work force, our ability to remain economically powerful will be in jeopardy.

The 1980s saw an unprecedented review and analysis of educational institutions in the United States. This analysis has had the aim of improving the quality and effectiveness of the schools in educating the traditional population of students, not the type of population discussed earlier. At least the majority of these reforms have centered on the effectiveness of public school education in the United States in terms of the gap between what students can do and what they should be able to do when they receive their high school diplomas. The school reform movement has resulted in a number of legislatively mandated measures to attack this gap, including increasing academic study, changing teacher certification and recertification, longer school days, more frequent and broad-based testing and assessment, and increased standards for admission to higher education. But many of the proposed changes have focused on the 25-30 percent of the student population

15

who are planning to attend college. Reviewers, for the most part, blindly disregarded the majority of students attending school. *The Neglected Majority* (Parnell, 1985) have now become a target for much of the current reform of vocational and general education. Since 70 percent of the school population will become the front-line work force of the 1990s and the 21st century, efforts are being made to change the structure and delivery of education in order to help this population become more effective as citizens and workers. Hence, the Carl Perkins Vocational and Applied Technology Education Act pinpoints students with special needs, integrates academic with vocational instruction, and develops Tech Prep programs.

SKILLS FOR THE 1990S AND BEYOND

Benjamin Franklin said, "Forewarned, forearmed." There appears to be a changed perspective on what skills potential employees will need to be effective in work activities. Below in Table 1 is a comprehensive listing of skills that workers will need if our country is to be productive and competitive in a global environment.

Table 1.

Basic Workplace Skills for the 1990s and Beyond

The workplace will demand that workers will need to be able to:
- Speak, listen, write, read accurately
- Compute basic arithmetic and statistical calculations accurately
- Acquire understanding and skills on their own
- Think, solve problems, and make decisions, utilizing valid processes and common sense
- Adapt and be flexible to change
- Exhibit a positive attitude and perform duties with a positive work ethic
- Initiate job duties without a direct assignment from a supervisor
- Perform effectively with a variety of work groups
- Assist in building cohesive work groups
- Develop and maintain positive relations with supervisors and other employees
- Use creativity to take advantage of opportunities
- Understand the economics and culture of work
- Pursue personal and career development through self initiative
- Utilize goal setting, planning, and organizing processes to progress in work and personal activities

---

If business educators are to attempt to help youth and adults prepare for the workplace and work force of the 1990s and beyond, they will have to adapt, invent, and collaborate with individuals inside and outside of school settings. The skills listed above have consistently and repeatedly been identified. It is up to business educators to determine effective means to address these needs through curriculum development and instructional practice.

CURRICULUM DEVELOPMENT AND INSTRUCTIONAL PRACTICE

Chaucer said, "Gladly would he learn, and gladly teach." In reviewing the skills needed for the work force and workplace of the future, a variety of educational strategies have been tested in a number of settings. The Carl D. Perkins Vocational and Applied Technology Education Act, Public Law 101-392, has as its basic objective the mandate to assist youth to develop the skills for successful transition from school to work. Two key components of this legislation have a direct impact on the way in which business and vocational education develop these skills. The first component is the integration of academic and vocational education. With this theme, curriculum development and instructional practices are emphasizing basic skills (English, mathematics, and science) instruction in vocational education classes developing more applied, real-life learning activities and materials for academic courses. Grubb and his colleagues (1990) have identified eight basic models of integrating academic with vocational education. These include:

- Incorporating academic competencies in vocational courses;
- Combining academic and vocational teachers to incorporate academic competencies in vocational courses;
- Making the academic curriculum more vocationally relevant;
- Modifying both academic and vocational education via curriculum alignment between courses and programs;
- Developing academies or schools within schools that combine basic academic instruction and technical instruction;
- Developing occupational clusters in high schools instead of departments;
- Organizing single occupational high schools; and
- Creating career paths or occupational majors.

Much of the endeavor to develop these basic skills include the development and use of applied course curricula including Principles of Technology, Applied Communications, Applied Mathematics, and Applied Biology/Chemistry by the Agency for Instructional Technology (AIT) and Center for Occupational Research and Development (CORD) (Haynes, et al, 1990). In addition, several states and private business firms have developed applied science, mathematics, and language courses to assist with specific regional employment needs related to basic skills.

Instructional practices, where academic and vocational teachers collaborate, is a hallmark of the integration movement. Teachers sharing concerns, expertise, ideas and actions have lead to a number of positive outcomes, including revitalization, interest development, and real-life learning activities. This educational collaboration has its roots in mirroring the positive impact cooperative work groups have had in business settings. It calls for the teacher to be a model, expert learner, and then facilitate student learning.

The second major component of this legislation deals with the development of Tech Prep programs to assist students in preparing for technical occupations that will require preparation beyond the high school diploma. These programs forge three major partnerships:

1. between academic and vocational teachers to focus on the integration of rigorous academic content into vocational programs to build basic skills;

2. between secondary and post-secondary educators to build articulated programs that are efficient and effective; and

3. between business and education to build commitment and support for the programs.

Teachers involved with collaborative activities to integrate academic with vocational education and to develop Tech Prep programs are taking a much more empowered position in leading educational program development. But they will need skills to assist them. Not only will they need strong interpersonal skills, but they will also depend upon strong communication skills as well as learning skills. In the classroom, teachers will need to replicate situations that are taking place in the workplace. This suggests that they lead their students in a much more facilitative, coaching mode than in the past and that students should work on "real" work-related problems in groups. This will not only help the teachers build relationships and motivate the students, but it will provide a model for what students will experience in the workplace.

Also of utmost concern to business educators are the keyboarding skills of their students. The impact of computer technology in business settings has highlighted the importance of communication skills. Wentling (1990) found in her study that business professionals cited that an improvement in keyboarding skills would directly lead to productivity gains in the workplace and that keyboarding skills were applicable for almost all business-related occupations. Associated with keyboarding skills are reading and writing skills, including proofreading, grammar, punctuation, formatting, and composition.

Other technology-related issues concern telecommunications, satellite broadcasts, facsimile machines, and a variety of telephone features, such as conference calling. These forms of technology are commonplace in today's business environment and the way in which future business people are able to speak, use nonverbal communications, and utilize technology will be critical for their tenure, as well as their businesses' success.

SUMMARY

Understanding the culture and economics of the workplace becomes a priority in a changing global environment. To understand the big picture is to put into action the mission and goals of the organization. When workers have this perspective, they have a foundation for handling problems, for dealing interpersonally with workers and leaders, and for understanding the skills and attitudes needed to be successful. Students will need to pursue a business education that develops their understanding of the changing nature of the business environment. They need to have the skills that will enable them to learn on their own and to understand why this skill is critical. If business educators will endeavor to understand our past and examine our current position, we will be better prepared to adapt to the changes that the future will bring.

REFERENCES

Bailey, Thomas. *Changes in the Nature and Structure of Work: Duplications for Skill Requirements and Skill Formation.* Berkeley, CA: National Center for Research in Vocational Education, May, 1990.

Bell, Daniel. *The Coming of the Post-Industrial Society.* New York: Basic Books, 1973.

Braverman, Harry. *Labor and Monopoly Capital: The Degradation of Work in the Twentieth Century.* New York: Monthly Review Press, 1974.

Carnevale, Anthony; Gainer, Leila; and Meltzer, Ann. *Work Force Basics: The Skills Employers Want.* Washington, D.C.: U.S. Department of Labor, Employment and Training Department and The American Society for Training and Development, 1988.

Cetron, Marvin and Gayle, Margaret. *Educational Renaissance: Our Schools at the Turn of the Twenty-First Century.* New York: St. Martin's Press, 1991, in press.

Clark, Kim; Chew, Bruce; and Fujimoto, Takahiro. "Product Development in the World Auto Industry." *Brookings Papers on Economic Activity* 3; 1987. pgs. 729-771.

Grubb, Norton; Davis, Gary; Lum, Jeannie; Plihal, Jane; and Morgaine, Carol. *The Cunning Hand, The Cultured Mind: Models for Integrating Vocational and Academic Education.* Berkeley, CA: National Center for Research in Vocational Education, July, 1990.

Haynes, Thomas; Law, Dale; Pepple, Jerry; and Valdez, Costanza. "Integrating Academic Content into Business Education." In the *Delta Pi Epsilon Research Conference Proceedings.* Little Rock, AR: Delta Pi Epsilon, 1990. pp. 77-90.

Johnston, William and Packer, Arnold. *Work Force 2000: Work and Workers for the 21st Century.* Indianapolis, IN: Hudson Institute, 1987.

Kutscher, Ronald. "Overview and Implications of the Projections to 2000." *Monthly Labor Review* 110:9; September, 1987. pgs. 3-9.

Naisbitt, John and Aburdene, Patricia. *Megatrends 2000: Ten New Directions for the 1990's.* New York: William Morrow, 1990.

National Council on Family Relations. Olson and Hanson, Eds., *2001: Preparing Families for the Future.* Minneapolis, MN: Author, 1990.

Office of Technological Assessment (OTA). *Technology and the American Economic Transition: Choices for the Future* (OTA-TET-283). Washington, D.C.: U.S. Government Printing Office, 1988.

Parnell, Dale. *The Neglected Majority.* Washington, D.C.: American Association of Community and Junior Colleges, 1985.

Raizen, Senta. *Reforming Education for Work: A Cognitive Science Perspective.* Berkeley, CA: National Center for Research in Vocational Education, December, 1989.

Rumberger, Russell. "The Job Market for College Graduates, 1960-1990." *Journal of Higher Education* 55: July/August, 1984. pgs. 433-454.

Schwartz, Sherry and Turner, Caroline. "Social and Political Trends Affecting Vocational Education" In Frantz and Miller, Eds., *A Context for Change: Vocational-Technical Education and the Future.* Lexington, KY: University Council for Vocational Education, 1990. pgs. 1-40.

Silvestri, George and Lukasiewicz, John. "Projections of Occupational Employment: 1988-2000." *Monthly Labor Review* 112:11; November, 1989. pgs. 42-65.

Wentling, Rosemary. "Computer Keyboarding Skills Needed by Business Professionals." *Delta Pi Epsilon Journal* 32:1; Winter 1990. pgs 15-25.

CHAPTER 3

The Teacher as Facilitator of the Hidden Curriculum

SHARON LUND O'NEIL
University of Houston, Houston, TX

B. JUNE SCHMIDT
Virginia Polytechnic Institute and State University, Blacksburg, VA

The workplace challenges facing today's entry-level workers include a variety of elements that are natural to every business education program. Some of these natural elements may be referred to as hidden curriculum elements because they may not be taught as a specific subject or content area. While many hidden curriculum elements may be subtle in nature, most are crucial to an employee's success in maintaining occupational survival. A vast majority of these hidden curriculum elements form the basic underpinings and are at the very core of successful businesses.

Most employers can identify the types of skills they want workers to have. However, business owners whose employees have demonstrated dependability, responsibility, and honesty in their work may overlook these skills in hiring potential employees. Yet, most employers rank dependability, responsibility, and honesty at the top of the list of desirable worker traits— traits that frequently fall within the category of hidden curriculum elements. These traits, as well as skills associated with good human relations and communications, must be stressed daily in the classroom. Even with all that is known about the importance of developing these skills, the lack of human relations and communications skills is still the number one reason for employment termination.

The concept of integratedness has contributed to the breadth of a hidden curriculum. As life skills, workplace elements, and personal attributes become an intertwined mesh that is transformed by change, the list of hidden curriculum elements grows. The hidden curriculum must continue to be defined and redefined just as workplace needs must be systematically identified and studied. Thus, teaching the hidden curriculum elements presents many interesting challenges for academic reinforcement within business education classrooms.

ORCHESTRATED LEARNING

Business teachers who stress the hidden curriculum elements in their classrooms are, in fact, facilitators of well-orchestrated learning. The teacher may be likened to a skilled architect who, by following a curriculum blueprint, builds a framework for further developmental growth. A teacher can provide instructional leadership through a variety of instructional strategies. Teaching strategies such as lecture, teacher demonstration, and directed discussion all capitalize on the instructor as a role model.

Modeling can be an excellent strategy for indirectly teaching many of the hidden curriculum elements. For example, students may model the instructor's personal style, sincerity, preciseness, and personal habits. In respect to content students will attach importance to the points that are emphasized in the presentation. Students also will learn important life skills from a presentation that is well planned around a central theme, is presented in an organized manner, and has substantial content. Instructors who use humor appropriately, express a caring attitude, and present a positive image—including personal grooming—are teaching hidden curriculum elements that are considered valuable, if not essential, by the business world.

Students will model a teacher's leadership style insofar as it has direction and meaning for them. A leadership style based on a "do as I do" approach will provide a much more positive atmosphere than a "do as I say" approach. Students can model and develop good leadership skills and can assess their own individual personality differences that may, in fact, dictate the success or lack thereof in mimicking or adopting a style. Just as curriculum must always be re-evaluated, good instructors should continually assess and refine the ways hidden curriculum elements are presented in the classroom. Much of an instructor's success in the realm of the hidden curriculum will depend on a simple premise—the instructor's ability to facilitate the learning process by practicing what is preached.

TEACHING INTEGRATED SKILLS

Learning can be optimum if it takes place in an active environment rather than in a vacuum. There is little doubt that the personal attributes of the teacher play a crucial role in determining whether or not the learning environment is active. Active learning employs teaching strategies that focus on team projects and cooperative learning. At the core of cooperative learning is the facilitation of group processes. The teacher provides initial leadership and enough direction for groups or teams to solve problems by capitalizing on the strengths of the team members. Ideally, individual weaknesses are diminished and rechanneled into strengths. Individuals grow personally and professionally in this team project environment. An integrated team approach to problem solving will foster decision-making skills as well as provide a mechanism for each team member to see the alternatives and broader perspectives of an issue.

The global economy is a good example of why business educators must teach the concepts related to integratedness and interrelatedness—both in life and business. More and more importance is being placed on understanding the global aspects of businesses that employ integrated and interrelated skills and technologies. Information resources and communication access resulting from today's technology have brought the many cultures of the world closer together. The global economy is an integrated system that dictates that collaboration and competition must co-exist. Both collaboration and competition, especially in worldwide markets, present many ethical and moral issues that have, in the past, been taken for granted. It is becoming necessary to understand the cultural mores and ethical norms of other countries as world trade and merchandizing merge with American business practices.

An integrated approach to the world economy is not unlike teaching about a systems approach and the interrelated elements of a business system. Many business systems are extremely complex, and it is important to learn how the various parts of a system work together. Classroom learning that emphasizes the systems concept will integrate good work habits with interrelated concepts. Within such a maze, as frequently is the case with integrated learning, instructors can incorporate such concepts as the components of a work ethic, cooperative work attitudes, adapting to change, and building team spirit.

Teaching and practicing these concepts reinforce the systems approach. One focus of the team project is to be productive while broadening one's perspective on issues. The teacher as a facilitator of learning should be the catalyst who fosters a positive atmosphere for solving problems by the team approach. The need for a multiplicity of skills to function in society is seen in the fact that for the first time in history, a postsecondary education is now needed for most jobs. Postsecondary education cannot have only one focus. It, too, must be an integration of components where the educated person has a cadre of life skills—hidden curriculum elements—that are transferrable from one career to another.

REACHING POTENTIAL THROUGH LEARNING STYLES

Notwithstanding equipment and other tangible resources, there is a vast array of excellent resources that can contribute to teaching hidden curriculum elements. Many of these resources are a result of being creative and capitalizing on learning styles. Providing students with the skills they need to be productive members of society may be as simple as identifying their value systems. Much can be learned by having students do a values profile. A list of values such as self-esteem, confidence, honesty, loyalty, fairness, courtesy, political savvy, life, and money can be developed for rank ordering individually and then in groups. Students learn a great deal about themselves and how others perceive them with this activity. In turn, much can be learned about individual students and their learning styles merely from observing their behavior.

Encouraging students to reach their maximum potential is a concern of every teacher. Capitalizing on the learning styles of students by using a variety of instructional strategies is an excellent way to optimize the learning process. Role playing as a strategy for learning is extremely effective and can be modified to include skits, sociodramas, dramatizations, theatrical acting, and case studies. Brainstorming a problem can be another effective way of getting students to accept the point of view of others, to build team spirit, and to be creative—all important skills that may be considered elements in the hidden curriculum.

While teamwork has been stressed here, it should be pointed out that individual goal setting, frequently a hidden curriculum element, also is important to living and working in a fast-paced society. Goal setting is easily incorporated into daily classroom activities and can be useful in helping to develop other important life skills. Self-motivation, being happy with intrinsic rewards, and developing self-worth are attributes that can be directly proportional to how successful one is at establishing personal goals. Students need to learn how to prioritize and organize their work, set realistic short- and long-term goals, and develop and follow schedules that balance school, work, and leisure activities.

CREATIVITY, DECISION-MAKING, AND CHANGE

At the very root of basic skills development is the vitally important daily survival skill of decision making. Decision making in business is becoming more and more important as organizations become flatter. As levels of management are merging and even disappearing altogether, many organizations are promoting decision making at the lowest possible level. Decision-making skills are directly linked to good thinking skills, and both contribute to leadership ability. Because these skills are such vitally important skills to business and personal success, they cannot be obscure in the curriculum; they should be central to the business education curriculum.

Change in and of itself has become a way of life. Business teachers who can accept and adapt to change as well as teach toward change need to learn to be good risk takers. Facilitators of change must have good risk-taking skills before risk-taking can be taught successfully. As business teachers become adept at these important skills, they will be able to teach students how to accept change, to look for change, and to foster change. In turn, students will sharpen their creative and innovative thinking skills. There is little doubt that future workers will need to be action-oriented change agents merely to be considered as contributing employees who function in an acceptable way.

PRODUCTIVITY CURRICULA

Business teachers are keenly aware that information exchange is becoming easier because of the connectivity of all media. Information exchange is possible because of the increasing number of information processing support tools. Many of these tools are taken for granted—for example, software that converts raw data into graphs, or windowing capabilities that permit easy access to several applications. These support tools are important to accomplishing work tasks as well as an important part of living in a technological society.

In addition to learning the specific technology support tools taught in content courses, students need to learn to use these tools within a conceptual framework that is ever changing. In this context productivity takes on new meaning. The productivity curricula include learning how to be an implementer of ideas and thoughts under critical time factors and how to become a director of information seeking. Students must develop research and inquiry skills, sorting skills (eliminating the nonessential facts from those which are important), and presentation skills (communicating ideas and thought verbally and in writing) for marketing a concept, idea, product, or service.

FRAMEWORK FOR ASSESSING THE HIDDEN CURRICULUM

The business teacher who wants to help students develop skills in the hidden curriculum needs a framework for categorizing the skills. Fortunately, such a framework exists and has been widely published. It is presented in *Workplace Basics: The Skills Employers Want*,[1] a publication sponsored by the American Society for Training and Development and the U.S. Department of Education. The seven skill areas the authors identify are ones that naturally fit the goals of business education—attainment of business competence for the management of personal affairs, including career exploration, and preparation for entering business occupations or for continued education. An examination of the seven skills as they relate to business education instruction follows.

Learning to learn. Observation of instruction provided by vocational teachers, including business teachers and academic teachers, quickly reveals how eager teachers are for students to get the right answers, with very little concern as to how the answers are obtained. Further, most of the answers are at the low levels of learning, the knowledge or comprehension levels, and require mere reiteration of information.

During the 60s, instruction that emphasized right answers made sense, as there seemed to be more right answers, and life was less complex. Today, however, the situation has changed in both students' personal and work lives. As an example, think of how business educators had precise rules for formatting documents and made sure students adhered to them. Now, with the various limitations of word processing software and accompanying printers, many formatting variations have become acceptable. Another example is the acceptance of much more informality in the work setting. Wouldn't it seem out of place to follow the old rule of giving a position of honor to a married woman when making introductions? Yet, these are just the types of things business educators have taught, the types of things for which there were exact answers.

The tendency to emphasize right answers at the expense of learning is very easy because to do so seems to make sense. Yet the student who is not continually able to learn and to confront new and varied work requirements will be short changed. Business students must learn to cope with assignments that do not have one set of correct answers. When teaching spreadsheet or

---

[1]Carnevale, A. P., Gainer, L. J., and Meltzer, A. S. *Workplace Basics: The Skills Employers Want.* Washington, D.C.: The American Society for Training and Development and the U.S. Department of Labor, Employment, and Training, 1989.

database application software, is there any reason for all students to be working on the same application? Wouldn't it be better, once students are introduced to the software, to have them create their own applications, drawing data from a myriad of possible sources? Reports they prepare from this input should be ones useful for making business decisions, with justification from the students themselves as to how the reports can be used to make such decisions. Students taught this way might not learn every feature of a particular type of software, but they will learn to use needed features of the software thoroughly and will learn how to learn.

Reading, writing, computing (3Rs). Business teachers often fret over the lack of competence in reading, writing, and computing that their students exhibit. Teaching these skills at a level acceptable for today's technological workplace will require the concerted effort of all teachers. The current interest in integrating vocational and academic education is growing—a concept that affects academic teachers as much as vocational teachers.

To begin with, school-based use of these three skills is often quite different from workplace use of them. For example, reading in school is for the purpose of reading to learn; while work-related reading, the bulk of adult reading, is for reading to do. Examination of any office document will quickly reveal the difference in the two types of reading. Research outcomes[2] substantiate that the reading level of office documents is much higher than that of most school reading, averaging from the eleventh- to the thirteenth-grade level for different types of businesses. Thus, one logical approach for business teachers would be to emphasize the reading of office documents, documents collected from community businesses. Another approach would be to have students use the technical manuals that accompany software to create selected computer applications—a task frequently confronted in any office setting.

As with reading, computing or mathematics learned in school often has little relevance to mathematics used in work settings. Employers express concern that students cannot do such simple things as use a ruler, Yet they have been taught this skill over and over in school. Unfortunately, the teaching has focused on concepts of measuring rather than on application and transfer of measuring skills to real-world settings. Assuming that once students know concepts they can easily apply them has never been proven, and observation of students' performance once they enter the work world indicates that this transfer cannot be assumed. Numerous opportunities to teach mathematics applications exist in business classes. They exist in accounting, computer software, and basic business courses to name a few. As an example, wouldn't it be better for students to be learning mathematics skills as part of their spreadsheet instruction than to be learning the use of every last feature of the software package, features that will change with the next piece of software introduced?

Writing is a skill that can and should be used for learning, a skill that often

---

[2]Schmidt, B. J. *A Comparison of Technical Reading Skills Development of Business Students in an Experimental and a Control Group.* Paper presentation, American Educational Research Association Meeting, Las Vegas, 1987.

receives minimal attention, particularly at the secondary level. Observations completed in 248 high school classes of vocational and academic teachers revealed that of the 1,758 episodes recorded for the classes,[3] writing occurred in only 254 of them. Even more to the point, only 28 were for purposes of learning to write. Needless to say, writing is one of the most critical skills for office workers—one that every business teacher should stress. The last ten minutes of any class can be used to have students simply describe in writing what they have learned. A teacher who collects and reads these statements is frequently surprised to learn what students thought they were taught. This writing process has proven to be effective in helping students learn.

Every student in keyboarding classes should learn to write at the keyboard as soon as possible—writing at the keyboard is a lifelong skill that few can get along without today. In the beginning, students can give one- or two-word responses to simple questions; then they can respond with full sentences; next they can move to letters to friends; then they can progress to more complex writing, including reports. Business teachers may claim that they are not qualified to help students learn writing skills, yet they cannot ignore the importance of helping their students develop these skills.

Listening and oral communication. Of all skills, listening and oral communication skills may be the most important in adapting to the requirements of a technological workplace. Few jobs exist, especially for business students, that do not require extensive use of these two skills. Further, numerous articles and sections of textbooks have been published that address the teaching of them. Yet, teachers, perhaps not well prepared in the two skills themselves, seem reluctant to give class time to them. For the 248 high school classes observed that were mentioned previously, student speaking occurred in 757 of the 1,758 episodes recorded. Learning to speak, however, was the purpose for speaking in only 28 of the episodes.

Teachers seem so eager to hear the right answer that they allow students to get by with all sorts of mumbled responses. Taking time to ensure that each student responds clearly, distinctly, and in complete sentences would be one of the best possible uses of class time. Business teachers owe it to their students to help them develop effective speech patterns, ones that others can easily understand and that are free of grammatical errors—errors that can label a person as poorly educated.

Creative thinking/problem solving. Life is a series of challenges requiring the ability to solve problems. The more creative a student can be in finding solutions, the more rewarding that student will find life to be. In the past the ability to solve problems creatively was generally considered to be an innate ability granted to a select few at birth. Nothing could be further from the truth as Thomas Alva Edison noted in his renowned statement that

---

[3]Schmidt, B. J., Isom, M., and Evers, M. J. *Two-Year Comparison of Instruction Students in High School Business and Vocational Programs Receive in Academic Competencies.* Paper presentation, National Association for Business Teacher Education Research Conference, Nashville, 1991.

"Invention is 10 percent innovation and 90 percent perspiration." Developing the ability to accept problems as challenges to be solved is a major step in achieving the maturity needed to hold a job and to advance in any career. Here again, teachers must relinquish their ties to having students complete only assignments that have one correct answer. An easy-to-prepare exercise for developing this skill is one where limited resources must meet expanded needs—the reality of most individuals' and organizations' existence. The limited resources can be time, money, supplies, equipment, labor, or any other variable. Students can form groups to brainstorm ways to make do with the resources available. The brainstorming process is only the beginning, however. Once an idea is selected, the students must then find facts and figures to back it up and present them formally in both written and oral form to other members of the class.

Self-esteem/goal setting/motivation/personal and career development. Helping students build self-esteem, set long-range goals, and keep motivated are among the most difficult tasks any teacher can face. To do so, the teacher must begin, as noted previously in this chapter, by serving as an example. In addition, the teacher must develop a personal interest in each student. Only through understanding a student's reasons for low self-esteem and poor motivation can a teacher help the student overcome them. This type of help is not something easily provided by one teacher alone. A critical need exists for teachers to work together to help students with these skills. Further, some students may need help beyond what the classroom teacher can provide. The classroom teacher should, however, be among the first to realize when a particular student needs help.

Helping students establish personal and career goals is an on-going part of the instruction in every business class. Regardless of the business subject taught, numerous opportunities exist for helping students to learn about related career opportunities and to examine their personal qualifications in relation to those required for the careers. Business teachers do not need to wait for specific units on career development to help students learn about business-related careers—particularly those that include jobs with extensive employment growth or with large numbers of individuals employed in them.

Interpersonal relations/negotiation/teamwork. Most school assignments are geared to students' competing on an individual basis. In the work world, the opposite situation exists. There workers must cooperate to achieve the goals of their organization, regardless of whether the organization is large or small. For many small businesses, owners rely on cooperative efforts between themselves and those who work for them to serve customers' needs and to make a profit. In the work world individuals do not have the luxury of working alone; they must work as teams, employing to the fullest extent their interpersonal and negotiation skills.

As a first step in developing these skills, teachers must be willing to give group assignments, with grades awarded on the basis of group performance. Employers note that when workers are asked to work as teams, they are suspicious of one another, unwilling to share, and ineffective in communicating their ideas. Examination of the school preparation students receive quickly reveals why these attitudes exist. Students have few opportunities in school settings to develop the skills needed for teamwork situations. Expecting students to convert automatically to a different way of viewing those around them once they enter the work world is not realistic. They need the opportunity to develop teamwork skills throughout their years in school.

Organizational effectiveness/leadership. Student organizations provide an ideal forum for helping students develop organizational effectiveness and leadership skills. These skills emerge as students practice them through student-organization participation. The key to helping students develop the skills is for teachers to let students develop—that is, not to be so determined that everything be done perfectly that students have no chance to develop. The individual who, once employed, displays leadership qualities is usually the one who receives first consideration for promotion. Leadership skills encompass all of the skills addressed in the other six skill areas. Those who have leadership skills have the advantage of being able to get others to do what is needed to complete a task or to achieve the goals of an organization.

GIVING THE HIDDEN CURRICULUM THE PRIORITY IT DESERVES

The effective teacher is one who displays a positive attitude, a knowledge of content, and management skills. Delivery of instruction for the hidden curriculum relies on teacher commitment in all three areas. The first step in that commitment is for the teacher to give the hidden curriculum the priority it deserves.

A teacher's attitude quickly reveals what the teacher believes is important. If the teacher is overly focused on teaching the topical content of the subject at the expense of the skills of the hidden curriculum, the students quickly perceive and follow the teacher's lead. They, too, will emphasize knowledge of the trivial at the expense of developing the important lifelong skills of the hidden curriculum.

An analogy can be made to managerial models that characterize the ideal management style as one that demonstrates high concern for task completion along with high concern for people rather than accepting high concern for one and low concern for the other. Teachers who stress the hidden curriculum confront the same challenge. They must emphasize simultaneously both the subject matter they are teaching and the skills of the hidden curriculum. One must not be ignored at the expense of the other.

Fortunately, teaching the skills of the hidden curriculum actually strengthens the teaching of subject matter. Hidden curriculum skills can provide a meaningful context for the subject-specific content. The hidden curriculum allows the teacher to focus on the application and transfer of learning. It provides the vehicle for relating the subject matter being learned to real-world uses of it. For example, students enter most business classes with a knowledge of how telephones work and how to carry on informal telephone conversations. Yet, few know the important aspects of business telephone use that are part of the hidden curriculum—how the tone of their voice, the adequacy of their grammar, their pronunciation of words, their abilities to listen, their approaches to helping others with problems, and their abilities to negotiate an acceptable solution impact the message they send. The hidden curriculum requires the business teacher to address these skills as well as the technical skills of placing and receiving calls.

For the agriculture society of the past, the most strategic resource was land; for the industrial society, it was capital. For today's information society the most strategic resource is the knowledge base of the workforce. To sustain and improve the quality of life, the United States must now direct its resources toward improving the quality of its people. Development of a world-class workforce, one that can compete in a highly competitive global market, depends on having the best "mindware" possible. Jim Frasier,[4] a training executive for Motorola, Inc., an organization that invests heavily in human resource development, notes that his organization needs employees with high-school level literacy, the ability to learn, and interpersonal skills—all part of the hidden curriculum.

Executives at Motorola, Inc., winner of the first Malcolm Baldrige award for quality of production in the United States, consider isolated knowledge a detriment to their organization and shared knowledge an asset—an asset that may soon appear as a line item on the balance sheet of many organizations. By giving the hidden curriculum the priority it deserves, business educators can contribute significantly to the development of this asset.

Evidence thus exists that establishes the need for business educators to give more emphasis to the hidden curriculum. To effectively teach it, the business teacher must serve as a role model, must seize every opportunity to integrate the skills of it into on-going instruction, and must mediate the learning styles of students with the work styles required in business settings. Fortunately, cognitive psychologists have determined that students learn best when they apply what they learn. Therefore, teaching the skills of the hidden curriculum—including learning to learn; job-related use of reading, writing, and computation; listening and oral communication; creative thinking; problem solving; goal setting; self motivation; negotiation and teamwork; and organizational effectiveness—requires teaching them through application and transfer, just as the technical skills of business education have always been taught. In determining whether or not to emphasize the skills of the hidden curriculum, business educators need only ponder the simple truth of this statement: *We don't have to change, survival is not mandatory!*

---

[4]Frasier, J. *Motorola's Basic Skills Evaluation Process*, Paper presentation, American Educational Research Association Meeting, Chicago, 1991.

Part II
THE HIDDEN CURRICULUM: CHALLENGES FOR ACADEMIC REINFORCEMENT

CHAPTER 4

Hidden Agendas for Reading Skills

RITA B. OLSEN
Green Bay, Wisconsin

During the last decade educators have been teaching to a new standard of literacy, the application standard, that addresses the deficiencies in students' problem-solving or critical-thinking skills. Today's students must be able to make judgments and inferences from ideas that are not explicit in the materials they read, and educators need to teach the qualitative skills of synthesis, analysis, and representation that students will use in the workplace.

The application standard of literacy should be relatively easy for business educators to address because vocational courses are application courses for the workplace. The business educator teaches courses for and about business, stressing not only being prepared to work in a business-related career but also to live in a society composed of businesses. Business teachers have a natural groundwork for successfully teaching to the application standard of literacy, and students can develop problem-solving and critical-thinking skills if they are shown how.

This hidden agenda of literacy or reading in the business curriculum can be a challenge for business educators because it takes time to prepare and to implement. However, there are major justifications for taking the time to teach reading skills to business students. Business educators need to train students for independence and to teach for transfer. By teaching students to be independent in the classroom, teachers will also be preparing their students to work independently in the workplace. In today's information society workers need to be able to read and comprehend highly technical material. A person may be able to read and comprehend a textbook, but that same person must also be able to transfer that ability to a technical manual. This takes training by professionals in the classroom. By taking the time to teach reading skills in the business classroom, teachers will increase student efficiency in learning business skills and concepts.

Educators can teach reading for independence and transfer in several different ways. Two of those are teaching reading skills that help students comprehend and teaching reading skills that help students follow directions.

READING TO COMPREHEND

Reading skills that help students comprehend will also help build problem-solving and critical-thinking skills. Reading techniques that are best suited for this purpose and to the business curriculum are those that teach vocabulary and concepts. One of the most important resources a teacher has in teaching vocabulary and concepts to students is the background knowledge of the learner. Because students come to the business classroom with varying degrees of background knowledge, teachers must assess that knowledge and then use it as a frame of reference.

Vocabulary words can be introduced through word puzzles and matching exercises. These should not be used often, but they can be helpful. Teachers should not introduce more than five or six new terms at a time. Most textbooks contain glossaries. However, many definitions in the glossaries use words that are too difficult for students to understand. Teachers should be aware of this and make available definitions that students can understand. Vocabulary is not spelling, and memorizing meanings does not guarantee conceptual understanding. Technical and specialized terms that are often part of business courses are prime candidates for vocabulary instruction. Common words that have specialized meanings such as *yields* and *menu* can be taught by activating the background knowledge of the students and linking what students know with what they are about to learn. A matching activity will help students associate the technical terms in the text with familiar synonyms. This linkage is crucial to concept attainment.

Vocabulary should be reinforced before, during, and after reading. Before students read text assignments, it is helpful to demonstrate vocabulary inquiry skills. A useful tool in vocabulary inquiry is context analysis. Some students may do this automatically; others need instruction.

First, point out formatting aids in the text such as bold or italic print, footnotes, parenthesized definitions, and figures and graphs. Next, point out semantic aids. These are more subtle than formatting aids, but are very useful. Forms of the verb *to be, is* and *are* signal a definition. For example, a mortgage is a loan. Textbook authors often link familiar synonyms with unfamiliar words or provide further information through appositives, examples, or restatements. Students should be taught to look for these kinds of aids in their reading assignments.

Teachers can demonstrate or model context analysis using the chalkboard or overhead transparency. First, write the unknown word on the board. Second, ask students for definitions of the word and write these on the board. Third, write a sentence on the board from the textbook that uses the unknown word and ask students which of the definitions best fits the sentence. Continue the inquiry by asking students what other words or phrases in the sentence help in understanding the meaning. Conclude the demonstration by writing several other new words on the board and telling students to watch for these words in their reading and to use this technique to find the meanings. If this vocabulary inquiry is modeled for the students several times each week, students will begin to do it on their own and thus become more independent learners.

Vocabulary and concepts should be developed further during reading. There is a close relationship between word meanings and concept development. Words are labels for a concept. Students learn concepts best through direct personal experiences. Some business courses can provide these experiences such as cooperative education. However, direct personal experiences cannot be provided for all aspects of the business curriculum. Therefore, concepts must be developed and learned through various levels of vicarious experience such as simulations, demonstrations, field trips, movies, role playing, and oral and written language.

Techniques that are used to reinforce vocabulary and to develop concepts through oral and written language include prototype analogies, word sorts, categorizing activities, and questioning strategies. These techniques can be used before, during, or after reading.

Prototype analogies can help solve many vocabulary problems. Students will not only learn the meaning of specialized vocabularies through these analogies but also gain a conceptual base to which problem-solving skills can be applied. For instance, when teaching accounting students about assets, a useful prototype analogy would be to have students think about the items they own such as bicycles, stereos, clothes, and watches. They can then attach dollar amounts to these items. As students learn about liabilities, capital, and depreciation, the same prototype can be used and expanded. In a beginning computer or word processing course, students can learn formatting, storing, and retrieving concepts by likening the operations of a computer to the mail system, which organizes our mail boxes in order to deliver the mail to the appropriate places. All the mail boxes have addresses and when any mail or information needs to go to a certain mailbox, the mail carrier finds the mailbox from the address. These analogies can be used and activated when students are faced with problems to solve. The key to prototype analogies is to relate the concepts or vocabulary to something with which the students are familiar, thus activating their background knowledge.

Word sorts can be done individually or in groups. Technical terms can be written on cards and then sorted into categories by using shared meanings. Teachers can make this activity inductive by having students search for relationships and develop the different categories themselves. For instance, an accounting teacher could write the following words on cards: assets, liabilities, income, expenses, net worth, and capital. The students would then decide into what main categories these words could be sorted. This causes students to discuss concepts and ideas with each other, to think critically, and to understand relationships.

A categorizing activity is very similar to word sorting and is very powerful. The difference is that the teacher provides the structure. For example, give students sets of words and have them cross out the words that do not belong in the sets, or have them list the words that are coordinate, subordinate, or superordinate with other words.

Concepts can be further enhanced or developed through questioning strategies such as reciprocal questioning and directed reading-thinking activities. These strategies can be put to good use in the business curriculum.

Reciprocal questioning is known as ReQuest. It encourages students to ask questions and provides the teacher with an opportunity to model good questioning and answering techniques. First, a short passage of one or two paragraphs is selected for the class to read and is read silently together. Second, the teacher closes the book and the students are allowed to ask questions about what was read. The teacher should model good answers using connections to prior knowledge. Third, the roles are reversed and the teacher asks questions of the students about the content or the structure of the passage. The teacher can use this time to shape reading behavior by asking students to make connections or relationships to what they have read. The teacher should repeat the steps until the students have sufficient knowledge or until they have a sense of what they should be looking for when they read the rest of the selection.

A directed reading-thinking activity (DR-TA) is one in which the students do most of the work and the teacher guides the activity. It is a process involving prediction, verification, judgment, and extension of thought. The first general step in the DR-TA is to have students look at a section or chapter in the textbook noting the title, subheadings, and illustrations. Ask the students what they think the section will be about. Encourage students to make predictions about the material. Second, have the students read silently a predetermined portion of the text. Third, ask the students once again what the material is about. Their predictions will be refined and they may formulate new predictions. Teachers can encourage verification of these predictions by asking, "How do you know?" Finally, steps two and three are repeated to the end of the material. Teachers could use the board to record student responses. Teachers should also promote discussion throughout the process to encourage judgments and extensions of thought. Small group discussions are valuable in this activity as are open-ended questioning techniques. Follow-up activities to the DR-TA could be further reading, more discussion, or a writing activity.

Any of the previous activities can be used with printed material other than textbooks. When students enter the world of work, they will be required to read professional journals, technical manuals, and business reports. In fact, business and professional people spend about 16 percent of their time reading. Teachers should have students read these other types of printed materials to bridge knowledge gaps in the text, to refine and expand a concept or idea presented in the text, and to expose students to different styles of printed materials.

If business educators implement these reading skills to help students comprehend text material, they will be promoting independent learning and thinking skills for the workplace as well as the classroom. Educators will also be providing valuable skills for students to transfer their reading abilities from expository text material to technical manuals they will be required to read and comprehend at the workplace.

READING TO FOLLOW DIRECTIONS

The inability to follow directions is a weakness not only in the classroom but also in the workplace. Teachers sometimes encourage this weakness by giving students printed directions and then explaining the directions orally. Reading to follow directions involves the ability to visualize, to pay attention to detail, and to detect sequence. It also requires memory. Because of these requirements, reading to follow directions is tedious and involves considerable rereading. The following procedure will help teachers of the skilled business courses, such as word processing, office procedures, or data base management, to teach reading to follow directions.

1. Select a passage in the text or manual that contains three to five steps in the procedure.
2. Have the students read the entire passage with the purpose of gaining an overview of the task.
3. Make students aware of any pictorial aids that will help them understand any of the steps in the procedure.
4. Have students make a list of modifiers or words that signal quality, amounts, and comparisons such as *must always, two times, in, at, above.* The students could highlight these words in their books or the list could be put on the board in a whole-class activity.
5. Make a second list of words that show sequence such as *first, next,* and *finally.* These words can be noted in the same manner as in Step 4.
6. Have the students reread the passage while visualizing the procedure in their minds.

As students learn to read carefully, to recognize signal words, and to visualize the end result, they will become better at reading to follow directions.

Teachers should make it a practice to refer students to printed directions rather than telling them the steps in a procedure. Encourage students to read the directions then tell the directions in their own words. Teachers can also help students understand the meanings of common terms they will encounter in written directions such as *affix, estimate, horizonal,* and *vertical.*

The business courses normally referred to as skills courses are excellent content areas in which to present technical manuals to students. Teachers should allow students to become familiar with software documentation manuals and other technical manuals they are sure to encounter in the workplace. Teachers can use the same reading approaches as they use with textbooks to help students understand these kinds of printed materials. In this manner, teachers will not only be teaching students to read to follow directions but also to transfer these skills to other kinds of printed materials.

Students come to the business classroom with metacognitive abilities and background knowledge that can be used and activated to help them read to comprehend and read to follow directions. By using some of the reading strategies and techniques presented here and in other literature, business teachers will be preparing their students to become independent learners and workers and to be able to transfer literacy skills from the classroom to the workplace and from a textbook to a technical manual or business report. In this manner, the hidden agendas for readings skills will become open agendas for problem-solving and critical-thinking skills.

CHAPTER 5

Hidden Agendas for Proofreading Skills

RANDY L. JOYNER

East Carolina University, Greenville, North Carolina

The United States is an information-oriented society. Management needs information that is accurate and timely when making decisions. Relevant and accurate information depends upon office employees being able to detect and correct errors in hard copy as well as soft copy formats. A major component of the error-detection process is the use of correct spelling, punctuation, and grammar.

COMPUTERS AND PROOFREADING

Technology has apparently given keyboardists a false sense of security (Camp, 1983) since users of today's electronic equipment depend upon its features to locate and indicate errors to be corrected. Microcomputers and related software are often used by office employees to proofread and revise all types of keyboarding errors. Reading keyboarded text from a computer screen or paper to locate errors is no longer perceived as an important task by office workers. Even good keyboardists often become careless and make more errors when they use word-processing software, because they believe the new technology makes error correction easier.

Word processing software packages contain a component to assist in detecting and correcting errors, but it only checks or verifies spelling. Typographical errors that spell a word (omitting the "k" from "know" spells "now") will not be detected by a spelling checker, nor does the spelling checker analyze correct word usage. Therefore, homonyms and certain typographical errors create a problem if office employees using word-processing software depend totally upon microcomputer software to proofread keyboarded text. Artificial intelligence or artificial knowledge eventually may alleviate these problems, but a time delay is likely before its use is widespread.

Therefore, the proofreading or error-detecting ability of a keyboardist must be combined with the error-correction capability of the equipment. Proofreading is still a vital skill for office employees. Spelling, punctuation, composition, and grammar skills required for effective proofreading will be needed even more with the increased usage of different types of electronic equipment by office employees. In the future when voice-activated computer terminals replace typewriters, electronic typewriters, and word processors, proofreading will become a major task.

Hard copy vs. screen. Both time and paper can be saved when proofreading from a video display terminal. By using the cursor—a pointer that moves—an office employee's eyes never stray from the computer screen. Also, revisions are made only once—as the office employee reads from the computer screen before printing a final copy.

But accuracy in detecting errors is thought to be lower when proofreading from a computer screen than from paper (Schell, 1986). Schell concluded that the time necessary to read keyboarded copy from a computer screen was longer than the time necessary for reading the same copy from paper. According to Fluegelman and Hewers (1983), typographical errors and awkward phrases are easier to locate when proofreading from paper. In the future the quality, readability, and resolution of the computer screen may alter this belief.

Two other disadvantages are cited by Fluegelman and Hewes pertaining to proofreading from a computer screen: (1) the portion of the document displayed on the computer screen is limited, thereby affecting an office employee's ability to sense the flow of the writing, and (2) the chance of creating additional errors when correcting mistakes is increased.

Vision problems associated with extensive computer screen use may reduce the quality and production of office documents. The most common video-display-terminal complaints include headaches, blurring of both far and near vision, itching and burning eyes, eye fatigue, flickering sensations, and double vision. Verifying a displayed copy from a screen is so unpleasant for many people that they insist upon printing one or more copies of a document for proofreading before making corrections and printing a final copy.

Mourant, Lakshmanan, and Herman (1979) concluded (1) visual fatigue is greater when the time required to perform visual tasks on computer screens increases; (2) the time to focus the eyes from a near point to a far point increases when extended visual tasks are undertaken with computer screens; and (3) the amount of information to be processed has an effect on visual fatigue. Their major premise was that the images of hard copy material and computer screens are different. Computer screen characters appear relatively blurred and flicker on the screen. The blurred computer screen characters cause the eye lens to refocus continuously to maintain the proper focus to see the computer screen images—resulting in visual discomfort and fatigue.

Proofreading from a computer screen and a hard copy document requires an office employee to use two completely different media. Both media—hard copy and soft copy—require different lighting, contrasts, and visual angles while presenting material in different type fonts, pitches, line spacing, and viewing distances. Consequently, a headache and eyestrain may result when using both computer screens and hard copy materials.

Fitschen (1976) lists three advantages of proofreading hard copy material: (1) computer and writing anxiety are reduced since the proofreader can verify keyboarded material using a hard copy document; (2) viewing the text on paper provides a different perspective—the author or proofreader can perceive or sense the flow of the text; and (3) it is more familiar to proofread from a hard copy document. More spelling and grammatical errors are detected when proofreading from hard copy material. Proofreading from a computer screen may create unneeded operator anxiety—cyberphobia or computer phobia.

Importance of proofreading. Two recurring themes concerning proofreading instruction and its relationship to increased productivity are (1) management perceives proofreading as a vital office skill and (2) business educators believe proofreading instruction should be incorporated into all business courses offered. The most rapid keyboardist, using the latest equipment, will have a low productivity level if he or she is unable to locate and correct errors. Within the keyboarding course, a major thrust should be to develop effective proofreading skills in the students.

Taylor and Stout (1985) support the belief that proofreading is an important office skill. Clerical and professional personnel from the *Fortune 500* companies, as well as business teacher educators from 163 National Association for Business Teacher Education (NABTE) institutions, participated in a study to identify important office skills. A five-item Likert scale was used to assess the skills needed for information processing technology. A skill receiving a mean score of 4.0 or greater was interpreted as an important skill for information processing. Three skills associated with preparing error-free office documents—proofreading, typewriting with accuracy, and spelling correctly—received mean scores of 4.5 or greater by both the *Fortune 500* clerical personnel and the NABTE educators. However, only one of the three identified office skills—proofreading—received a mean score greater than 4.0 from the professional personnel responding to the instrument. Therefore, clerical and professional employees as well as business teacher educators concur—proofreading is a vital office skill.

Further, a survey of 35 firms employing over 700,000 people in 13 states indicated proofreading skills are essential for the success of new employees (Kaisershot, 1987). The ability to proofread received a 3.68 importance rating from a possible 5.0 rating by the communication supervisors who apparently consider proofreading an important skill.

Keyboarding studies revealed the ability to proofread was one of the five specific keyboarding skills used frequently by managers. The percentage of managers indicating that proofreading was a frequently used skill decreased from 62 in 1984 to 59 in 1986—a minute change in the number of managers who indicated proofreading skills were vital to the office.

Employers seek future office employees who have developed good verbal and written communication skills and who are capable of composing written correspondence and reports. Consequently, business educators possess a responsibility to develop language arts skills—punctuation, spelling, grammar, business vocabulary, and proofreading—as essential components of the office-technology curriculum.

Proofreading skill ignored. Business educators have been inclined to only teach the features of automated typewriting equipment and eliminate certain fundamental elements of traditional typewriting instruction. Walter (1980) reported that some business educators ignore their responsibility to teach basic skills normally covered in typewriting instruction when using electronic equipment. These neglected skills include grammar, spelling, punctuation, sentence structure, and typewriting accuracy—all components of proofreading. Yet, most businesses require good spelling and proofreading skills for entry-level employment. Today's office employees must possess the ability to correctly use the English language, to spell, to punctuate, to correct, and to edit text. Keyboardists have the responsibility of locating and correcting errors before a final copy is prepared for distribution.

Efficient and effective use of a word-processing system depends upon the skills of the individuals who use a word processor to generate usable business correspondence. Keyboardists, using word processors with computer screens, should possess certain skills relating to proofreading or locating errors. Excellent keyboarding skills, polished grammatical skills, capable proofreading or error-detection techniques, and consistent spelling ability are imperative for an individual to succeed in the office of the future. Proofreading, grammar, spelling, and formatting skills are the core of the traditional and the electronically-automated office; therefore, these skills cannot be overemphasized.

Certain errors, i.e., "ths" for "this" or "gok" for "go", are the result of poor keyboarding proficiency instead of poor spelling or proofreading ability. Haggblade's findings (1988) differ from the majority of opinions of business educators. Eighty-one reports containing 1,000 to 1,500 typewritten words were analyzed by Haggblade to determine what percentage of errors could be located by microcomputer spell-check programs. Seventy-six percent of the errors keyboarded would have been located before printing if a spell check program had been used; 24 percent would not have been located by a spell-check program. Therefore, not all incorrect words appearing in keyboarded copy are attributable to the keyboardist's spelling ability.

The ability to input data accurately and to detect errors consistently are essential skills on the job. Potential office employees must be taught how to locate errors and correct them. Consequently, the development of proofreading skills requires knowledge of acceptable keyboarding formats as well as basic communication skills—grammar, punctuation, etc. Technological advances can multiply the effect of undetected errors. As a result of the ease in reproducing additional copies of a document, paperwork proliferates; and if a document contains an error, the number of reproductions of a document containing an error multiplies the effect of that error.

Programs are available to assist in improving the mechanics of writing by helping authors to detect selected types of errors. The most popular type of word-processor accessory is the dictionary or spell checker; however, many software packages now include a thesaurus. The dictionary or spell-check program compares word misspellings and other typographical errors to the words stored within the dictionary of the program. Another feature or accessory is the grammar or style-checker program that analyzes keyboarded text to a set of rules stored within the software and displays errors on the computer screen. Punctuation and grammar are checked by the user as the text is keyboarded or revised. Advanced style-check programs indicate awkward expressions, incorrect word usage, cliches, and wordiness (Solomon, 1986).

One advanced style-check program, *Writer's Workbench*, contains a series of 30 computer programs designed to edit and analyze the quality of written material. In essense, it operates by performing many of the same functions as a human editor. However, it does not make changes in the text—it only identifies areas needing improvement (Sterkel, Johnson, & Sjogren, 1986). The programs are capable of reviewing a document to identify misspellings and simple punctuation errors according to punctuation rules and a dictionary contained within the software. The proofreading program invokes five separate subprograms to verify spelling and punctuation, to check for consecutive occurrences of the same word or faulty phrasing, and to examine sentence construction for split infinitives. The five subprograms are designed to be executed simultaneously; yet, they can function individually. The five subprograms identify as possible misspellings all words not listed in the computer's built-in corpus of words. Subsequently, the user must decide if the words are misspelled. Likewise, the programs do *not* identify *all* errors in mechanics, tone, and style. Incorrectly used commas, noun/verb disagreements, faulty logic, incorrect data, or missing data are examples of errors that would not be flagged as an error by this series of computer programs.

Writing-analysis programs should be used by individuals composing and generating written correspondence, but individuals using writing-analysis programs must understand what the programs can and cannot do. Dauwalder (1988) believed writing-analysis programs can identify decision points; potential problems; and emphasize the use of a proper readability level, precise wording, active voice, concrete wording, and shorter sentences. Writing analysis programs cannot decide how something must be changed, locate all types of errors, nor comprehend what is written—they can only locate selected, preprogrammed types of errors.

Programmers or authors of future text editing or writing analysis software must consider how the programs will affect the people that use the programs. Their expanded use will depend upon the adaptability of the program to individuals with various aptitudes, backgrounds, and experiences. Computer programs designed to determine grammar-rule violations or pompous writing styles could play an important role in the office of the future and the business education classroom.

VISION AND PROOFREADING

Proofreading errors occur because proofreaders do not see the errors rather than because proofreaders do not know the correct spelling of words or correct grammar rules (West, 1983). Consequently, the visual perception of the word or words when reading or proofreading affects the error-detection process. Smith (1986) defines the visual-perception process as condensing sensory visual stimuli into specific segregated units, which does not involve merely a mechanical recording of the stimuli.

Smith (1986) reviewed business education research and psychological research to describe visual perception and its relationship to locating errors. Reported within his study were two major themes: (1) specific language-arts or spelling instruction had no effect on increasing an individual's ability to detect and correct errors and (2) the way a proofreader perceives words may affect the ability to detect errors. Smith reaffirmed West's conclusion that explicit instruction in language mechanics can be found to produce improvement in those mechanics. The improvement in those mechanics was *not* transferable to increasing proofreading proficiency because the reader's eyes move forward when comprehension occurs. Therefore, the composition of the word is not perceived (West, 1983).

Wong (1975) suggests errors are not found when proofreading because of the perceptual factor in reading and proofreading. Her definition of the visual perception process follows:

> Eyes are the receptors and the channel by which the brain receives information. Through years of practice, beginning at the elementary grades, our eyes have been trained to follow continuing cycles of fixation, saccade, fixation, and saccade along a line of print. During a fixation, our eyes focus on a small area of space; groups of abstract symbols (letters) are transferred to the brain, where they are absorbed and reconstituted into meaningful experience. The direction of a fixation may also be backward, allowing the reader to refocus on previously read material as the need arises. At the completion of a fixation, the eyes advance to the next group of words through the move called a saccade. At the end of a line, the eyes make a special type of saccade—the return sweep—to advance to the next line. Throughout this process, the reader is unconscious of, and cannot control, the movements of the muscles of the visual system. One is typically unaware of the number of words perceived during a fixation and of the speed advance during a saccade. For example, in reading the sentence, "The brawn fox jumped over the lazy dog," the reader cannot count the total number of fixations or saccades. Nor can one remember the number of words perceived during any fixation. . . .
>
> The complexity of proofreading lies in what occurs during the fixation phase when the symbols are being processed by the brain. As the eyes focus on the words, the brain is testing alternative hypotheses about the meaning of the symbols. Once the need for comprehension is satisfied by an acceptable solution, a saccade begins and the reader proceeds to the next fixation even though errors may be present. Returning to our sentence, for example, how many of you read the "brawn fox" as "brown fox"? (pp. 16-17)

It is difficult for a reader or proofreader to alter this pattern of reading text when proofreading. If the proofreading instruction to read letter-by-letter is accepted and followed, the reader usually reverts unconsciously to word-group reading by force of habit (Lasky, 1960). Lasky believes proofreading requires a larger number of fixations than any other type of vision; but even if a proofreader desired to advance or impede his rate and number of fixations and saccades, he or she cannot control the eye muscles. Altering proofreading patterns to generate accurate correspondence is a major problem; and with the continued increased usage of electronic data processing, the number of errors and their effect will multiply.

JOB STRESS

The burgeoning applications of computer technology and the accompanying use of computer screens are revolutionizing the office work place in the United States; and in all likelihood, their use will continue to grow at a rapid rate in the coming years. The increased usage of computer screens means important benefits for business and industry in the United States, but computer-screen usage is not without its problems. Health-related complaints concerning the use of computer screens proliferate. Due to prolonged periods of computer-screen use, health problems associated with eyestrain and vision are common; but job stress is also emerging as a health problem related to computer screens. Either of these problems may affect the accuracy of documents produced by office employees.

Job stress among office employees using computer screens is higher than for any other congregational group—including air traffic controllers—according to a study by the National Institute for Occupational Safety and Health (NIOSH). However, job stress in today's office is usually not the result of advanced technology, nor is job stress unique to the office because numerous employees enjoy using microcomputers to reduce the volume of routine, repetitive chores. Many of the stress-related complaints pertain to nonequipment problems. Areas identified as contributing to stress are less than adequate planning by management, lack of training for the electronic office, or poor scheduling of office tasks using computer screens (O'Conner & Regan, 1986).

Job stress that produces physical symptoms is often attributed to computer screens. Computer-screen use demands intense concentration on a task close at hand, usually at a distance of about two feet, which is contrary to the structure of the human eye. The physical symptoms associated with computer screens and the related stress may affect the quality and quantity of work produced in an office.

LIGHTING

Traditional office lighting is fluorescent. The computer screen itself is a light source. Consequently, any light reflecting on the screen directly, whether from an overhead light or a window, can create glare on the computer screen that results in eyestrain. The volume of light needed varies with individuals; but, generally, overall illumination for computer-screen operation should be 30 to 40 foot candles, which is less than customary office-lighting levels. A lower level of general room lighting can be achieved by using fewer bulbs and fluorescent tubes or by replacing cool-white tubes with cool-white deluxe tubes that provide less light, creating a more comfortable and pleasant working environment and atmosphere. Computer-screen characters should be in a comfortable contrast to the screen background color and should not be affected by an external light source. Reflected glare on a computer screen can be reduced by positioning computer screens so that windows and other sources of bright light are not behind the operator.

COMPUTER SCREENS

With the increased usage of computer-screen technology, questions have been raised regarding the health and safety hazards associated with computer-screen usage. Computer-screen usage has not been proven to cause permanent visual or musculoskeletal damage. Many users report temporary visual discomfort and musculoskeletal symptoms such as shoulder, back, and neck pain. These problems can be created or aggravated by poor computer-screen design, inadequate computer-screen maintenance, poor workstation design, inappropriate illumination, glare, excessively long periods of uninterrupted computer screen work, poorly corrected vision, or the wearing of corrective lenses that are not appropriate for computer-screen work (Meister, 1985).

Features related to the work environment such as furniture and light levels may be the key to reducing health problems associated with computer screens. Conventional offices were designed and constructed prior to the implementation of computer screen and microcomputer technology. Consequently, offices designed for conventional office work may not be suitable for extensive computer-screen use. Changes in the manner in which office tasks are performed result from the implementation of computer-screen technology, which may cause employee job dissatisfaction that leads to job stress (Meister, 1985). Problems such as visual discomfort and backache may be experienced and verbalized by computer-screen users if proper planning does not occur prior to the installation of computer screens in the office.

Diamond (1985) and Waters (1983) both advocate that people are the key element in any past, present, or future office. If people are not considered, new technology will never succeed in the office. The reason for adopting word-processing equipment is to increase office productivity, but productivity may not increase—office employees may perceive themselves as manual laborers since their tasks are primarily data entry. Office employees believe the only needed skill for employment in today's office is the ability to keyboard since the equipment will perform the required revision tasks by depressing a key or a series of keys.

Waters (1983) also believes lights, chairs, desks, heating and air conditioning systems—all generally designed for the "paper office"—may counteract the advantages of an electronic office. An 8 percent to 20 percent reduction in operator speed, accuracy, and comprehension was reported by Waters when operators at Ryberg of FMI (part of Herman Miller, Inc.) spent more than 20 percent to 30 percent of their work day using computer screens. Computer screens directly affect the human body because computer screens impact users' physical and mental health as well as their productivity.

COMPUTER SCREEN COLOR CONFIGURATIONS

Much debate exists regarding the color configurations of computer screens. No concrete recommendation regarding the optimum computer screen-color configuration for character and screen color has been developed. Dolecheck (1984) concurs with the majority of reported findings whereby most authorities consider light characters on a dark background better than dark characters on a light background. Yet, Isensee and Bennett (1983) conclude reverse video (dark characters on a light background) is slightly preferable to normal or positive video (light characters on a dark background). However, when an individual works with both hard copy and soft copy materials, reverse video may be preferable. Less adaptation is required by the user when moving from white paper with black characters to a monitor with light background and dark characters than when moving from white paper with black characters to a display with a dark background and light characters.

Most computer-screen research associated with color foreground and background color contrasts concludes amber text on a green/brown background is the easiest to see. An amber foreground brightens the viewing area, increases the amount of contrast, and reduces glare. Problems with other light sources affecting the readability of an amber foreground decrease because amber is in the middle of the visual spectrum. O'Conner (1986) further recommends users keyboarding primarily business correspondence or text should consider opting for the high resolution monochrome computer screen.

The user's ability to view images projected by a computer screen is dependent upon the contrast and stability of the computer screen. Schnure (1986) states that a positive contrast (light characters on a dark background) reduces the flicker sensitivity of the eye. Consequently, the eye of the user is allowed to view and interpret a stable character. A negative contrast (dark letters on a light background) only reduces problems associated with adapting quickly to variable brightness levels on a computer screen. Further, a negative contrast does not affect the flicker sensitivity of the eye when reading from a computer screen.

Edstrom (1987) and Schnure (1986) agree that eye problems associated with the use of a computer screen can be alleviated by using high resolution and no-flicker monitors. Dark text on a light background creates a negative contrast. Thus, the eyes can adjust to the change from screen to hard copy easier. Consequently, the switch from hard copy to soft copy documents is not as fatiguing, and the negative contrast does not require any special lighting. A positive contrast—light text on a dark background—on a computer screen creates less flicker and is recommended favorably by Gruning (1985). However, a negative contrast results in greater legibility.

The relationship between the color or contrast of a computer screen and a user's ability to locate and correct errors was not definitively defined. Prolonged periods of computer-screen use during a work day may affect a user's vision, thereby decreasing the quality of work produced. An additional factor impacting a user's ability to locate and correct errors is the resolution quality of the computer screen.

Computer screens may generate visual problems of a different magnitude and type than are generally found with traditional equipment producing hard copy material (Dainoff, Happ, & Crane, 1981). Computer screens present dot-matrix images or characters on a screen that may appear blurred to a user. The automatic focusing mechanisms of the user's eyes continually operate in a futile attempt to produce a clear image. The continual operation of the internal and external eye muscles may cause visual fatigue—resulting in a user's inability to accurately locate and correct errors.

COMPUTER SCREENS AND WORK ENVIRONMENT

The pain and discomfort experienced by computer-screen users during an extended use may not be the result of the equipment. Computer screens are placed in work environments created for paperwork on horizontal surfaces instead of computer-screen work on a vertical surface. Created by a poorly designed work environment, the resulting problems of headaches; sore, tired, red, or burning eyes; or any other visual complaints may affect the quality of work produced in an office. The National Institute of Occupational Safety and Health reports that productivity could be enhanced by 25 percent by solving visual problems associated with computer screens and related furniture. Prolonged viewing of computer screens at close distances is suspect as the cause of undue visual fatigue of the eye accommodation and vergence systems (Smith, 1979). Vergence is a movement of both eyes where the visual axes intercept at the same point (Smith, 1979). Eye accommodation and vergence are affected when viewing information from hard copy material and a computer screen simultaneously; unneeded stress may be placed on the eye's pupillary system due to differences in media brightness (Smith, 1979). The stress resulting from the difference in media brightness may affect the vision and accuracy of the user.

The *Harvard Medical School Health Letter* reports more than half of computer-screen users suffer from some type of eye disorder (McQuade, 1984). The source of the eye disorder is related to the distance between the eye and the printed word. Ordinary desk work normally requires 14 to 16 inches between the eye and the hard copy document; however, the normal viewing distance between the eye and the computer screen is 25 inches. Repetitious focal adjustments are necessary as the keyboarded data is displayed on the computer screen. Consequently, the recurring focal adjustment may result in the likelihood of increased undetected errors.

The majority of computer screens, as reported by Harvard Medical School, display data using green characters upon a black background. The green or black color configuration provides excellent color contrast for a time, but the user may see a pink halo after several hours of use (McQuade, 1984). The pink halo may affect a user's vision, thereby reducing the ability to locate and correct errors.

CURRICULUM IMPLICATIONS

With the continued demand for excellence in education, all educators must respond with teaching skills that are vital for success in the 90s. One of those skills is generating accurate, understandable, and usable information. Proofreading should be incorporated early into the curriculum and reinforced throughout the curriculum; subsequently, office employees will be aware of the importance of generating accurate and reliable information. Business educators need assistance from other faculty members in their own discipline and other disciplines to develop students' error detection skills.

Error detection or proofreading is a skill that must be taught in all phases of education. When teaching the skill of proofreading or detecting errors, the following should be considered in developing the error detection or proofreading program.

1. Error detection or proofreading is as accurate when reading from soft copy as hard copy (Seibel, 1988).

2. Consider the following when teaching error detection or proofreading:

   Errors made by keyboardists
   Placement of errors
   Spelling verifier capability
   Students' abilities.

3. When detecting errors or proofreading, read twice:

   Once for content
   Once for mechanical errors.

4. Error detection/proofreading should be taught early in the instructional program and reinforced throughout.

SUMMARY

With modern technology, error correction is easy; but the error-correction process is time-consuming and very costly. Too many office employees believe that it is not important to be accurate today—errors can be located and corrected later. Consequently, more errors go undetected and appear in final copies of a document. Keyboardists must accept full responsibility for keyboarding accurately and proofreading carefully.

Today's office environment has been revolutionized by electronic data processing. Microcomputers or computers systems equipped with computer screens or monitors are the focal point of electronic information processing. Computer screens and data processing systems are designed to improve office efficiency and productivity, but recent research does not totally support the premise of improved office productivity. The prolonged usage of computer screens by office employees is linked to health and safety hazards that impact the quality and quantities of work produced.

One component of office productivity, proofreading, may be affected by the use of computer screens. A user's ability to proofread or locate errors in keyboarded text may be impaired by computer-screen resolution quality, color, and contrast configurations. A perceptual process, proofreading or locating errors, may be affected by the way a user sees words. Conflicting information has been reported concerning the relationship between computer screen color and contrast configurations and their effects on a user's vision and the ability to locate errors. Yet, the inability to see an error due to poor computer screen resolution or color configuration may explain why office productivity is not increasing as anticipated.

The transfer of language-arts instruction—appropriate grammar usage— is unlikely during the proofreading process (West, 1983). However, professional personnel believe language-arts instruction will improve the ability to locate and correct errors. Therefore, research does not present conclusive evidence concerning the relationship between language-arts instruction and the proofreading process.

Modern office technology can improve office productivity, but word-processing equipment and related software are only as good as the individual using the electronic equipment. If the user cannot keyboard accurately, no amount of expensive equipment will make a difference as keyboarding errors have become too costly to tolerate (Camp, 1983). The ability to proofread and locate errors without computerized assistance or analyses is a vital office skill for the office of today as well as the office of the future.

America is dependent upon accurate and timely information from office personnel. As the ability to locate and correct errors is a major component of office tasks, business educators face a tremendous challenge to prepare future office employees with proper and efficient error detection skills. Business educators teaching error detecting need assistance from other faculty members in their own discipline and other disciplines to develop students' error detection skills. Therefore, error detection instruction should be emphasized in all educational programs.

REFERENCES

Anderson, R. I. (1976). "Proofreading: A Must in Word Processing." *Journal of Business Education, 52*(2), 60-63.

Camp, S. C. (1983). "Accuracy and Proofreading: Skills in Demand." *Business Education World, 63*(4), 16.

Cherry, L. L., Fox, M. L., Frase, L. T., Gingrich, P. S., Keenan, S. A., & MacDonald, N. H. (1983, May-June). "Computer Aids for Text Analysis." *Bell Laboratories Record, 61*, 10-16.

Chol, W. F. (1985). "The Role of Ergonomics in Aiding Productivity." *The Office, 101*(3), 17, 20.

Dainoff, M. J., Happ, A., & Crane, P. (1981). "Visual Fatigue and Occupational Stress in VDT Operators." *Human Factors, 23*(4), 421-437.

Dauwalder, D. P. (1988). "An Evaluation of the Use of the Microcomputer Software for Completing Assignments, Reviewing Grammar, and Evaluating Writing Style." *Business Education Forum, 42*(5), 26-29.

Diamond, M. L. (1985). "People Considerations in Word Processing." *Business Education Forum, 40*(4), 3-7.

Dolecheck, C. C. (1984). "Ergonomic Design and VDT Equipment: What Educators Should Be Teaching." *The Balance Sheet, 66*(2), 33-37.

Dyson, E. (Speaker). (1987). *People, Computers, and You: Artificial Knowledge.* (Cassette Recording). Powersharing Series.

Edstrom, M. (1987). "Screens and Displays." *Online Review, 11*(4), 207-216.

Fitschen, K. (1976, May). "Effective Advice to Beginning Writers: Revise on Hard Copy." *TETYC, 13,* 104-108.

Fluegelman, A. & Hewes, J. J. (1983). *Writing in the Computer Age: Word Processing Skills and Style for Every Writer.* Garden City, NJ: Anchor Press/Doubleday.

Gigliotti, C. C. (1986). "Success or Failure in the Nineties: It's Our Choice." *Business Education Forum, 41*(3), 3-4, 6.

Gruning, C. R. (1985). "VDTs and Vision—New Problems for the '80s." *The Office, 101*(2), 19, 22, 34.

Haggblade, B. (1988). "Has Technology Solved the Spelling Problem?" *The Bulletin of the Association for Business Communication,* LI(1), 23-25.

Hulbert, J. E. (1977). "Preparing Students for Word Processing Careers." *Journal of Business Education, 52*(4).

Isensee, S. H. & Bennett, C. A. (1983). "The Perception of Flicker and Glare on Computer CRT Displays." *Human Factors, 25*(2), 177-184.

Joyner, R. L. (1989). *A Comparison of Errors Detected: Video Display Terminals vs. Hard Copy.* Unpublished doctoral dissertation, Virginia Polytechnic Institute and State University, Blacksburg.

Kaisershot, A. L. (1987). "Communication Skills Rated by Office Supervisors." *Business Education Forum, 42*(1), 15-16.

Krey, I. A., D. C. Henry, & D. M. Donin. (1985, November-December). "Computers Essential for Secretarial/Office Practice and Procedures." *The Balance Sheet, 67,* 19-23.

Lasky, B. (1960). "Proofreaders Need Periodic Reviews." *Inland and American Printer and Lithographer, 146*(3), 73.

McQuade, W. (1984, March 19). "Easing Tensions Between Man and Machine." *Fortune, 109,* 58-66.

Meister, K. A. (1985). *Health and Safety Aspects of Video Display Terminals* (2nd ed.)., New Jersey, American Council on Science and Health.

Moody, P. G. & Matthews, A. L. (1980, October). "Word Processing Without Equipment—It Can Be Done!" *The Balance Sheet, 62,* 63-65, 96.

Mourant, R. R., Lakshmanan, R., & Herman, M. (1979). "Hard Copy and Cathode Ray Tube Visual Performance—Are There Differences?" *Proceedings of the Human Factors Society, 23rd Annual Meeting,* 367-368.

Ober, S. & Kocar, M. J. (1986). "The Effect of Student Use of a Computerized Writing-Analysis Program on Writing Achievement." *The Delta Pi Epsilon Journal, XXVIII*(2), 99-106.

O'Conner, B. N. & Regan, E. A. (1986). "Reducing Stress in the Automated Office." *Business Education Forum, 41*(1), 22-24.

Schell, D. A. (1986, February). Research notes. *Simply Stated, 63,* 2.

Schnure, A. (1986, May-June). "Computer Corner." *Journal of Property Management, 51,* 61-62.

Seibel, K. K. (1988). *Analysis of Errors Located by Business Students in Hard Copy versus Soft Copy Documents.* Unpublished master's thesis, Virginia Polytechnic Institute and State University, Blacksburg.

Smith, D. C. (1986). *Error Detection in Keyboarded Text: a Perceptual Approach.* Unpublished doctoral dissertation, Arizona State University at Tempe.

Smith, W. J. (1979). *A Review of Literature Relating to Visual Fatigue,* Paper presented at the 23rd Annual Meeting, Human Factors Society at Boston.

Solomon, G. (1986). *Teaching Writing with Computers: The Power Process.* Englewood Cliffs: Prentice Hall, Inc., pp. 35-37.

Sox, C. W. (1988). "Identifying Keyboarding Skills Needed by Managers." *Business Education Forum, 42*(6), 29-31.

Sterkel, K. S., Johnson, M. I., & Sjogren, D. D. (1986). "Textual Analysis with Computers To Improve the Writing Skills of Business Communication Students." *Journal of Business Communication, 23*(1), 43-61.

Taylor, H. W. & Stout, V. J. (1985). "Validation of Skills Necessary for Information Technology." *NABTE Review: A Journal of the National Association for Business Teacher Education, 12,* 18-20.

Vision and the VDT Operator. (1983). American Optometric Association.

Walter, M. J. O. (1980). "Word Processing: Implications for the Typewriting Teacher," in Van Nassy (ed.) *Readings in the Teaching of Business Subjects.* Belmont, CA: Fearon Putman Publishers, Inc., 293-295.

Waters, C. R. (1983). "Just When You Thought It Was Safe To Go Back in the Office." *Inc., 5*(1), 69-74.

West, L. J. (1983). "Review of Research on Proofreading with Recommendations for Improving Proofreading Proficiency." *Journal of Business Education, 58*(8), 284-288.

Wong, S. M. (1975). "Proofreading Pitfalls." *Business Education Forum, 29*(8), 16-17.

CHAPTER 6

Hidden Agendas for the Basic Business Subjects

LONNIE ECHTERNACHT

University of Missouri-Columbia, Columbia, Missouri

Basic business subjects focus on business and economic understanding and contribute to the general education of all students. Subjects typically classified as basic business include: basic business, business law, economics, consumer economics, business principles and management, and private enterprise/ entrepreneurship.

Basic business courses are typically designed to help students learn about business and attain the basic knowledge, skills, and attitudes that will enable them to become more productive members of society. However, there are also many important intellectual and personal skills that should be enhanced as students study about the exciting world of business and prepare for their roles as consumers, workers, and citizens. When teaching-learning activities are planned for basic business classes, attention should be given not only to the content but to improving the following fundamental skills: critical thinking, goal setting, problem solving, conflict resolution, assertiveness, small group processes, and leadership. Students need these skills to function efficiently and effectively as consumers, as workers, and as citizens. Employers continue to stress that these skills are necessary if individuals are to succeed and progress on the job. As our society becomes more diversified, as our world becomes more global, as our government's role changes, and as businesses become more complex, students need to be able to think critically, set goals, solve problems, resolve conflicts, be assertive, function in small groups, and assume leadership.

CRITICAL THINKING

The development of the ability to think has long been an important goal of education. Good thinking skills are considered crucial for success in school and in life. Schools must produce educational environments where the cognitive, psychomotor, and affective domains of learning become objects of inquiry and instruments for reasoning. Thus, as students achieve desired performance goals they also acquire abilities to think, reason, and continue learning.

With today's world facing population growth, nuclear weapons, value shifts, rapid communications, life-style changes, and technological advances, thinking becomes a key for future adaptation and survival. Individuals must be equipped with critical thinking skills—constructive tools needed for the future to help them adapt to a rapidly changing environment.

Levels of thinking. Levels of thinking may parallel Bloom's taxonomic levels of the cognitive domain. Learning tasks that focus on a basic business topic, endorsement of checks, are used to illustrate the various levels of the cognitive domain:[1]

KNOWLEDGE, the lowest level of thinking, includes the recall or recognition of information learned previously. Example: List the three types of check endorsements.

COMPREHENSION includes translating information from one form to another, interpreting relationships between two or more information forms, and estimating future trends implied in information. Example: Explain when a restrictive check endorsement should be used.

APPLICATION includes using information that has been learned in one setting and applying it to other situations. Example: Use the appropriate types of check endorsements in different situations.

ANALYSIS includes determining how information is organized, perceiving similarities and differences, and classifying information. Example: Differentiate between the three types of check endorsements.

SYNTHESIS includes putting information together to create a new pattern, plan, or structure. Example: Formulate a procedure for endorsing checks received by a business.

EVALUATION, the highest level of thinking, includes the ability to judge the value of information for a given purpose using definite criteria. Example: Evaluate the cash control procedures of a business as they relate to the processing of checks received.

Teaching critical thinking skills. The following guidelines are suggested for teaching critical thinking skills in basic business classes:

- Adopt a perspective toward the teaching of thinking that anticipates that failtures will occur, and when they do, will be viewed as problems to be solved.

- Formulate a clear set of performance objectives that require higher levels of thinking skills, and plan a sequence of learning activities to develop those skills.

- Analyze the thinking skills that are being taught.

- Provide opportunities systematically to practice and refine thinking skills.

- Ensure that *all* students are actively involved and practicing the skills.

- Ask broad, stimulating questions that cause students to process rather than simply repeat information.

- Use covert and overt student participation techniques with appropriate wait time to develop answers.

- Follow up student responses by asking for refinement, elaboration, and support.

- Encourage students to be aware of their own thinking processes—small groups increase students' opportunities to verbalize their thoughts.

---

[1]Bloom, Benjamin S., ed. *Taxonomy of Educational Objectives: The Classification of Educational Goals, Handbook I, Cognitive Domain.* New York: David McKay Company, Inc., 1956, p. 18.

- Model in-depth thinking processes and analyze the thinking processes of famous business persons.
- Motivate students to ask questions of their own.
- Reinforce positive attempts and small steps in the right direction by students who are striving to improve their thinking skills.
- Recognize that generalizations of learned skills (transfer of learning) will not just occur; a high level of skill must be developed to enable generalizations.

The thinking processes in which basic business students engage can be enhanced by varying teaching-learning activities. Asking different types of in-depth questions that require students to determine comparisons, relationships, classifications, examples, applications, inferences, explanations, observations, summaries, decisions for or against, and cause and effect help students focus their thinking. Other typical student activities that facilitate the development of thinking skills are interpreting graphs and charts, establishing priorities among alternatives, simulating complex situations, listening and summarizing, proceduralizing a process into steps, collecting pertinent data for making a decision of support or nonsupport, outlining relevant information, and critically evaluating ideas and materials. Basic business teachers should encourage students to think critically and to refine, clarify, and support their statements.

GOAL SETTING

Goal setting, when properly used, can be a strong motivation for individuals. Long-range goals give purpose and direction to an individual's life, while intermediate or short-range goals become the means whereby those goals are achieved. With a future that is characterized by change and lifelong learning, the need for self-directed individuals is apparent. Self-directed individuals are characterized by positive self-concepts, initiative, independence, responsibility, future orientation, and well-established goals.

Once individuals are employed, they need to become familiar with the goals of the work organization. Most successful companies will have a planning structure that incorporates the establishment and periodic review of short-range goals as a method of systematically moving toward the long-range goals of the organization. Management by objectives (MBO), a popular approach to management, focuses on directing and coordinating individual employee efforts toward organizational goals. Thus, management and employees work jointly to identify common goals and define areas of responsibility to achieve both the employees' personal goals and the organization's goals.

Techniques for establishing goals. Personal goals should include both long-range and short-range goals, be carefully planned, and reflect what individuals want to do with their lives. When establishing personal goals, consideration should be given to the following criteria to ensure meaningful and achievable goals: reasonable but ambitious, specific, measurable, realistic (personality and aptitude), challenging, reflecting a variety of interests (lateral thinking), amendable, mirroring the real you (needs, values, and abilities), prioritized, and a pleasure to pursue. Careful planning will be required to overcome the following obstacles that may prevent achievement of goals: criticism or negativism of others, procrastination, fear of failure, excessive time required, and inadequate financial resources.

Goal achievement requires self-discipline—hard work, determination, perseverance, and patience. Long-range goals may need to be adjusted or modified periodically because as life changes, needs may change. Some goals may require a thorough study of what is currently involved to reach the goal. When long-range goals are finally achieved, an individual may experience a degree of disappointment or emotional letdown. To alleviate such problems, new goals need to be established and other goals need to be addressed.

Teaching goal-setting skills. Basic business students must understand that the purpose of goal setting is to motivate and facilitate the achievement of the goals. Students need to set goals for the day, the next month, the next year, and the next five years. Since long-range and short-range goals should be correlated, students must realize that long-range goals are seldom achieved without some short-range goals being achieved first. Goals should be written down on paper and reviewed often; formalizing the goals tends to increase commitment to the goals. The following guidelines for setting and achieving personal goals should be explained to basic business students:

- Invest energy and time in activities that match goals.
- Study the unfamiliar—people, products, and procedures.
- Get exposure to new ideas and new sensations.
- Have friends and belong to groups who are supportive.
- Associate with others in your field (professional organizations).
- Cultivate a presence that denotes success (a leader and a worker).
- Avoid potential plateaus of contentment when a short-range goal is achieved.
- Utilize time management techniques.
- Formulate a personal/professional growth strategy.

Students must be encouraged to formulate written goals based on their own priorities and to set realistic deadlines for their completion. They must have commitment to the goals, believe they can be achieved, and work hard. Students will need encouragement, reassurance, direction, and empathy as they deal with obstacles that hinder their accomplishment of goals. Teachers, classmates, and friends can serve as a support system for students as they strive to accomplish their goals. Support groups help students realize the importance of teamwork and the dynamics of small groups.

Typical discussion items focusing on goal setting that can be used in basic business classes are—

- Describe some business persons you consider successful. Do they set goals? Are they inner directed or outer directed?
- Name some obstacles that may hinder goal achievement. What are some ways around these obstacles?
- List some of your long-range goals. How have your classmates influenced your goals? Your family? Your teachers? Others?

- Explain how a mentor may assist an employee to gain or advance on the job. How do you select a mentor? How can a mentor help you reach your goals?

- Being loyal to your employer and conforming to the ground rules of the organization are important traits for employees. Can your personal and professional goals differ? If so, how do you resolve the differences?

- Identify relationships between goal setting and time management. How does your behavior match your goals?

PROBLEM SOLVING

Basic business courses provide many opportunities for students to develop problem-solving competencies. Students need to practice analyzing problems, breaking them down into meaningful interrelations, and reaching their own conclusions. Problem solving involves examining and manipulating the elements of a problem, searching for meaningful relationships and principles that will lead to a solution, and adapting available resources in new and different ways. Teachers must use meaningful everyday problem situations, provide appropriate guidance, and permit students to seek out and discover their own answers by working individually and cooperatively in small and large groups.

A logical, systematic approach to problem solving causes students to interpret business data, make a decision, and defend their decision. Often the applications of data are more important than just the knowledge of the data. To qualify as a problem, however, there must be several viable alternative solutions. Students must be provided appropriate feedback so they recognize that their competency in finding solutions to problems is improving. Once the problem-solving method is learned, students should be encouraged to use it in new situations. Thus, learning is approached as a task of discovering something rather than just reading about it and memorizing facts.

Problem-solving process. The problem-solving process is based on the premise that a problem exists and that there is a desire to find its solution. The formal steps of problem solving may be stated as follows:

1. State the problem clearly and analyze it into various aspects and subproblems.

2. Determine what you already know about the problem.

3. Decide what new knowledge is needed and gather new facts.

4. Sort through the facts and assimilate them to find their interrelations.

5. Interpret and reflect upon relationships and seek plausible solutions.

6. Test conclusions and solutions, choosing the one or ones that seem best under the circumstances.[2]

Problem solving implies reaching a decision. Decisions involve making choices among alternatives. Many decisions that must be made are directly affected or influenced by other individuals, especially decisions made in the

---

[2]Musselman, Vernon A.; Musselman, Donald L.; and Simpson, Kawanna J. *Methods in Teaching Basic Business Subjects.* Fourth edition. Danville: The Interstate Printers & Publishers, Inc., 1980, pp. 93-95.

business world. Objectivity is crucial when solving problems and making decisions that affect other individuals. When decisions involve other people, communicating those decisions, explaining the rationale used, and receiving acceptance are also critical in determining how problem-solving effectiveness is perceived by everyone involved.

Teaching problem-solving skills. Basic business courses have many topics that lend themselves to problem-solving activities. The following guidelines for effective problem-solving should be introduced to basic business students:

- Follow a systematic step-by-step process for arriving at the best solution to a problem.

- Use the advice, opinions, research, and analyses of others to formulate your own decisions.

- Avoid crisis decisions by practicing anticipatory thinking and intelligent planning.

- Postpone making decisions that are of an extremely personal nature until a time when you are less emotionally and personally involved.

- Minimize the emotional pollution (obstacles) for problem-solving by recognizing that no one is perfectly objective.

- Acknowledge that time is required to move systematically through the deliberations required in the problem-solving process.

- Establish criteria that will serve as a basis for judging the proposed solutions.

- State the problem in question format—questions may relate to facts, values, and policies.

- Recognize that no one can expect to be right all of the time—give it your best shot.

Basic business teachers may utilize problem solving in any phase of a daily lesson—stating objectives, providing instructional input, modeling ideal behavior, checking for comprehension, providing guided practice, providing independent practice, and achieving closure.[3] Teachers are encouraged to use real business-problem situations whenever possible and pseudo-problem situations that require students to reach and defend decisions. To obtain maximum benefit from problem-solving activities, the local community should be utilized as a laboratory and source of information. Integrate into problem-solving activities information obtained from the local telephone directory yellow pages, newspapers and magazines, publications available from business and government organizations, and interviews with business professionals. This helps to establish a realistic relationship among the classroom activities, the business world, and the needs of students.

CONFLICT RESOLUTION

When students are in class together, just like when people work together, there will be conflict. Conflict is the emotional state an individual experiences

---

[3]Hunter, Madeline. "Knowing, Teaching, and Supervising." *Using What We Know About Teaching.* Alexandria: Association for Supervision and Curriculum Development, 1984.

when the behavior of another person interferes with his/her own behavior. Students must understand that there will be conflicts in businesses due to changes in procedures, working conditions, salary rights and responsibilities, and philosophies of operation. While in school, students must develop an awareness of potential conflicts by analyzing the source of conflicts, formulating individual/group priorities, and assessing conflict-resolution options.

Sources of conflicts. Specific sources of conflicts in a business environment can be related to and found in many schools and classrooms.

ROLE OF POWER. People who are powerful or powerless tend to act in a certain way. The powerful person may demand, control, or threaten while the powerless person may feel put upon, insecure, and unappreciated.

ORGANIZATIONAL STRUCTURE. Organizations should not align people against each other. Rather, individuals in an organization should work together in a cooperative structure.

FEAR. The constant threat of disciplinary action, temporary layoffs, demotion, or even firing can create a conflict environment in a business. Individuals may feel stressed and act in conflicting ways when they feel watched and not trusted, disciplined and never praised.

PERSONALITY DIFFERENCES. The work environment may place people together who have strong philosophical and ethical differences—seeds from which conflict may grow.

HIDDEN AGENDA. The real motivating but unstated reason some individuals will act a certain way is due to a hidden agenda. Self interests and unconscious needs and drives may create unexpected conflicts.

CHANGE. The possibility for change increases the likelihood of resistance, thus conflict. The acceptance of change takes time and depends on an individual's desire to change.

Individual/group priorities. Conflict resolution attempts to reconcile differences so the conflict can be eliminated, reduced, or accepted. An awareness of the following basic principles of conflict helps one better understand conflict resolution. (1) Conflict does not have to be disposed of or hidden. Reasonable people do not have to be either right or wrong; they can simply disagree and continue to work together. Individuals should recognize that, due to the nature of the conflict, they may be powerless to bring about change. (2) Unless the individuals involved are really interested in solving the conflict, the dilemma cannot be dealt with as an intellectual issue. Explaining something logically to another person will do little good unless that person is willing to listen and accepts the concept of peacemaking. (3) Peacemaking focuses on the principle that behaviors and issues, not personalities and people, should be addressed when resolving conflicts.

Conflict resolution options. The three basic options for conflict resolution are—win-lose, lose-lose, or win-win. Win-lose takes place when one individual or organization wins and another loses. For example, assume that the business student organization is selecting a universal style of jacket for all members to wear. If one student proposes one type of jacket and another student proposes a different one, then a natural competition emerges because only one jacket can be selected. Since no other alternatives are possible, there will be a winner and there will be a loser.

A lose-lose approach occurs when an individual feels so strongly about the issue and oftentimes about the other individual that she/he is willing to lose in order to defeat the other individual. Using the above jacket example, there may be three students who suggest jackets for the business student organization. If student A dislikes one of the other individuals, student B, and there is a chance that student A's suggestion won't be chosen and student B's will, student A may side with student C to make sure that student B doesn't win. Thus student A loses and student B also loses.

A win-win results when individuals are willing to work together through negotiation in order for both to perceive that they have accomplished their goals. Continuing with our example concerning the selection of a jacket, the students may decide to work together and select a jacket that all can take credit for and of which all can be proud.

Styles of managing conflict resolution. While individuals may have unique styles for handling most conflicts, they need to recognize that there are alternatives that will result in win-win situations. Basic business teachers must integrate conflict management styles into their teaching-learning activities so students are prepared to work and live in our society more effectively. Typical conflict management styles include avoidance, accommodation, smoothing over, compromising, competition, and confrontation.[4]

AVOIDANCE. Some individuals will avoid dealing with a problem and choose to accept the status quo. This technique usually takes the form of attempting to withdraw from contact with another person or ignoring the issue of conflict. Avoidance may be considered a lose-leave approach and can be effective only if the conflict is minor in nature or is a temporary, short-lived situation.

ACCOMMODATION. Individuals may put others' needs above their own during a conflict. This conflict management style may be known as a yield-lose approach and rarely solves the problem; one individual gives in and lets the other person have his/her way. The winner feels great while the loser may often feel used. However, the accommodator does have peace and quiet even if it is at all costs. If that is the most important thing, then accommodation can be a positive method.

SMOOTHING OVER. The end result of smoothing over is to give the impression that everything is all right. Oftentimes, the major purpose is to maintain the relationship. The individual who smooths over conflict usually lets the other individual know what they want, but not in a forceful enough way to get the other individual to take the required action. Smoothing over may be appropriate when the relationship is important and the other individual appears willing to end it if his/her request is not met.

COMPROMISING. In its best form, concerns are identified, addressed, and resolved. Compromise should allow each individual to understand the views and needs of the other, propose solutions to the problem, and trade back

---

[4]Adler, Ron; Rosenfeld, Lawrence; and Tonne, Neil. *Interplay.* New York: Holt, Rinehart, and Winston, 1983, pp. 277-301.

and forth until an agreeable settlement is reached. This conflict management style may be considered a lose-lose approach because it often results in both individuals being dissatisfied; neither gets exactly what he/she wants.

COMPETITION. The objective of competition is to win. Power is at the center of competition—someone wins and someone loses. Whoever is stronger, more powerful, and more cunning is going to be the winner. The winner will probably feel good about the victory. However, competitive conflict resolution is a win-lose approach and usually results in hurt feelings, frustrations, and even destructive working relationships and friendships. Even though there are negative aspects to competition, some business people regularly use this aggressive method.

CONFRONTATION. Individuals may choose to confront the problem directly and work toward a solution that all individuals can agree upon. Confrontation, sometimes known as integration, is a win-win approach that is more likely to be effective when the individuals involved have a peer relationship. Confrontation takes time and a commitment that focuses on resolving the problem, achieving a workable solution, and preserving the relationship as well as the dignity of all individuals involved.

Teaching conflict-resolution skills. Basic business students should realize that the six conflict-resolution management styles can be used to resolve or suppress conflicts. However, individuals must consider each situation and select a style that will maintain and strengthen relationships and also result in a more productive environment. The following guidelines for achieving effective conflict resolutions should be discussed by basic business students:

- View conflicts as joint problems—issues causing conflicts may be real or perceived.
- Strive to resolve conflicts, not suppress them.
- Acknowledge that not all conflicts can be resolved.
- Adopt the perspective that each person has a unique style of handling conflicts.
- Encourage at least one of the parties to verbalize the need to preserve the relationship.
- Consider using direct confrontation when the parties have a peer relationship and are willing and able to handle the confrontation.
- Employ resolution as a way to "clear the air" and get on with business.
- Delay confrontation until tempers have cooled and the conflict can be put into its proper perspective (defusion).
- Recognize that the self esteem of the parties involved is often the most critical issue at stake.
- Give evidence that the other party's feelings are understood.
- Refrain from blaming the other party and critiquing the other person's behavior.
- Allow for an honest exchange of ideas—avoid interrupting each other.
- Follow up conflict resolution or suppression to determine if a more productive environment exists.

Basic business students should analyze cases and role-play situations that depict realistic conflicts. The following discussion items illustrate possibilities for involving students in meaningful teacher-learning activities:

- Discuss win-lose, lose-lose, and win-win strategies and give examples of each from your personal/work experiences.
- Explain the role communication plays in resolving conflicts.
- Elaborate on the constant conflict sources/situations that exist in most organizations.
- Describe your own personal conflict-resolution style.
- Think back to a time when you were involved in a conflict. Were issues or personalities discussed? Was the conflict resolved? If so, how? If not, why not?

ASSERTIVENESS

Students must learn to be assertive communicators so they can resolve conflicts more effectively. Assertive individuals, who are neither aggressive nor retiring, usually accomplish their objectives within the group. Assertive individuals consider their needs and decide if the consequences of asserting will be greater than those of not asserting. In most cases the answer will be to take a stand, get at the problem, and solve it.

When being assertive, it is important to describe the perspective. Assertive statements commonly used include "I feel . . . ," and "It makes me feel . . . ." Such statements will get more positive results than "You are . . . ," and "You make me . . . ." Assertive people are polite but firm, open to suggestions but knowledgeable of the pertinent facts, cooperative but willing to take a stand, listen to, and understand other viewpoints but express how they feel, and state precisely what they want but focus on the issues.

Levels of assertiveness. When dealing with a conflict, an individual may choose to be nonassertive, aggressive, or assertive. Nonassertive methods of conflict resolution—avoidance, accommodation, and smoothing over—do not directly attempt to resolve the problem. Aggressive actions do not take into consideration other people. Competition is an aggressive method of handling conflict. When individuals accomplish a task while taking into consideration the feelings and needs of others, an assertive method of conflict resolution is being used. Confrontation is always assertive; compromise when well used is also assertive. Being assertively productive without alienating others is the goal.

Types of assertive messages. Three types of assertive messages that are commonly used are: simple assertive statements, empathetic statements or responses, and confronting responses. A simple assertive statement is said directly to the individual and is usually just an expression of the facts. An empathetic statement or response recognizes the other individual's situation but clearly relates your own needs. It may be the first step in the assertive response or follow a simple assertive statement. A confronting response usually follows a simple assertive statement or an empathetic statement/response and describes the individual's behavior and then states your position.

The type of assertiveness to be used is determined by the situation and the message that needs to be communicated. Examples of each type of assertive message could be developed and discussed by basic business students using numerous school and work situations. For example, assume an individual is waiting to use an automatic teller machine at a bank and someone steps in front of the line to use the machine. "I was here first." said in a matter-of-fact way would be an example of a simple assertive statement. The expectation is that the person will move or wait until you are done, thus solving the problem, "I know you're in a hurry, but I was here first." characterizes an empathetic statement response. You recognize that the individual may have had a reason for doing what was done, but you don't intend to allow it to happen. "I was here first, and you cut in front of me. I would like you to move." These statements are an example of a confronting response; you state what is wrong and how the individual can correct it.

Teaching assertive skills. Learning assertive behavior is an important interpersonal skill for students to develop. Effective assertion requires careful thought and the skill to make statements relative to the situation, problem, and desired change. Sometimes an in-depth message must be developed in order to communicate adequately with the individual to resolve the conflict. Depending on the situation, time frame, and type of message, it may be wise to plan and rehearse the message before presenting it.

Some simple guidelines for enhancing an individual's assertiveness that may be presented to basic business students are—

- Stand up for your beliefs and rights.
- Acknowledge your special talents and share them with others.
- Be firm and direct in conversation.
- Make eye contact when speaking to others.
- Model success through your posture and body language.
- Admit your mistakes and assume responsibility for them.
- Strive to be quietly effective.
- Refuse to let others coerce or manipulate you.
- Keep your composure when you say no.

The following three situations exemplify the many different types of conflicts that can be used by basic business teachers to improve students' assertive behaviors:

- Assume an individual understood from an immediate boss that a 50-cents-an-hour increase would be reflected in next week's paycheck. When the next paycheck was received, however, a 25-cents increase in the hourly rate had occurred. Discuss some assertive techniques that could be used to deal with this situation.

- Assume an individual is checking into a hotel with a confirmed reservation. However, the hotel clerk cannot find any record of the reservation and implies that no rooms are available. Give examples of appropriate statements that would depict the three different types of assertive behavior and explain the intent of each.

- Assume your new coworkers want you to go to lunch with them but you have work to do. Since a blunt no seems too abrupt for this situation, use the "no" sandwich technique (the "no" is placed between two positive statements). Be prepared to discuss these statements.

SMALL GROUP PROCESSES

Businesses, as well as other organizations, are usually structured to divide people into groups. These groups may be called divisions, departments, units, work groups, quality circles, task forces, or committees. Whatever title is used, small groups usually consist of from three to 20 or more individuals who interact with one another and perceive themselves to be a group.

Many decisions made within businesses and organizations are the product of small groups. Small group activity affects almost every aspect of an individual's life and has a significant impact on behavior. There are many advantages to using small groups. Small groups provide opportunities for a number of individuals to participate in the decision-making process. Various points of view as well as feedback can be expressed. Expanded analysis and discussion by the group are permitted. The likelihood increases that decisions once made will be put into action. Individuals are able to get acquainted and better appreciate the capabilities of those in the group. In addition, small groups tend to develop a sense of responsibility and loyalty to the organization.

While small groups may certainly offer advantages to the decision-making process, there are limitations that must be recognized. Group decisions are time consuming; the process can be effective only if time is available. Once made, group decisions must be considered and feedback provided. Communication concerning the disposition of group decisions must be provided to the group if the benefits of participation and commitment are to be realized.

Components of effective small groups. Small groups will be more effective if people understand and have realistic expectations about the purpose of the group, the factors affecting group dynamics and cohesion, and the contributions each participant can make.

GROUP PURPOSE. Business groups usually have a job or task to accomplish, and work is achieved through people interacting and working together as a team. Groups may be utilized to accomplish the following functions:

- a social function that provides members opportunities to interact and get to know each other
- a sharing-of-information function that permits members to ask questions and further refine their understanding
- a value-analysis function that allows members to determine the worth or value of something
- a problem-solving function that enables members to identify issues, arrive at solutions, and establish policies
- a therapeutic function whereby members are able to express their feelings, frustrations, and problems.

GROUP DYNAMICS. Group dynamics refers to those factors, external and internal, that affect the way the group operates. Some of the external factors that affect group dynamics are group size and time and place of meetings. While groups are usually considered to be three or more people, there seems to be consensus among the proponents of small groups that five to seven members is an optimum size. This size enables face-to-face interaction, participation, and majority decision making as well as enough members among which to distribute the work load. However, the best group size depends on the nature of the task and the skills available among the members. In addition, time of day, time allotted, location, seating arrangement, and space available affect the working relationships of small groups. One other factor that may affect the interaction and work of a small group is the presence of individuals (teacher, observer, or resource person) who are not members of the group.

The major internal factors within a group that affect group dynamics are the participants, hidden agendas, cohesiveness, and climate. The group members themselves are the greatest force affecting the dynamics of a small group. While people are creatures of logic, they are also emotional, sensitive, subjective, and capricious. The person who serves as the leader of the group may have been elected, been appointed, or emerged from the group itself. The leader of the group usually performs the roles of coordinator, facilitator, clarifier, tester, gap filler, and summarizer. Certain members of the group may be motivated by hidden agendas—self-interests and unconscious needs or drives. They may even be willing to sacrifice the good of the whole group for these selfish interests. A cohesive group is one in which all the members work together, get personal satisfaction from being a part of the group, and recognize their dependence upon each other. Cohesiveness leads to a group atmosphere referred to as climate or camaraderie. A group that has a good climate is characterized by a high morale, a lot of give and take, a sense of involvement, a use of disagreements to extend interaction and to clear the air, a commitment to the organization's goals, and a determination to move the task forward in an organized fashion.

GROUP MEMBERSHIP ROLES. The behavior of group members is as important as that of leaders. There are individuals who work to get the job done (task-oriented roles) and those who concern themselves with how the members get along together (process-oriented roles). People have special abilities—some like to collect, organize and coordinate information. Other task-oriented roles that members may assume in addition to information seeker are information giver, opinion seeker, opinion giver, ideas or procedures initiator, elaborator, summarizer, and coordinator of ideas. Some members may have a special knack for making people feel comfortable through empathetic listening and responsive feedback. These process-oriented behaviors help members get along with one another through cooperation and collaboration. Examples of process-oriented roles that members may assume to improve group interaction are listener (listens actively), harmonizer (encourages harmony), gate keeper (draws all members into the discussion), standard setter (supports others), and climate maker (encourages a group/team atmosphere).

Teaching small group skills. No matter what their role is, students should consider the following guidelines to effective small group participation:

- Share ideas and feelings openly.
- Listen to the content of messages as well as the emotions that lie beneath the messages.

- Provide feedback to what is heard so message senders can verify that their messages are understood.
- Keep discussions centered on issues rather than people.
- Develop goals for each small group session or activity.
- Work to solve the task or reach the goal established by the group.
- Evaluate the small group, "How did we do?"

The use of small groups in basic business classes multiplies the opportunities for pupil and pupil-teacher interaction. Many different types of small groups can be utilized in basic business classes—task groups didactic groups, tutorial groups, and brainstorming groups. To increase their effectiveness, task groups should have a clearly defined task that is understood by all the members, delineated roles and individual assignments for the members, a realistic time schedule to keep the group on task, access to necessary resources, and a plan for providing feedback to the entire class. Case problems and researching a topic are examples of tasks that small groups may address. Didactic, or instructive, groups allow the teacher or a student to instruct, to review, to clarify, and to interact with questions and comments in a small group setting. Didactic groups are commonly used for student reports and review sessions. Tutorial groups emphasize individual instruction, usually of a remedial nature. The teacher or a student may use tutorial groups to interact individually with each group member by reviewing information, motivating the learner, and evaluating assignments or projects. Brainstorming groups are problem centered and used to generate many possible solutions to a problem. The teacher's role in a brainstorming group is to motivate, to get the ball rolling, and then to step out of the way. These four types of small groups demonstrate the many possibilities available to the basic business teacher to increase student interaction and to better prepare them for the world in which they will live and work.

LEADERSHIP

Leadership development is always listed as one of the major purposes of vocational student organizations. However, every student in our classrooms needs to reach his/her fullest leadership potential, a potential that must often be realized by a student even prior to the leadership experiences he/she may have in a vocational student organization.

Many students do not see themselves in leadership roles. Also, many of them have little belief in their ability to gain or develop leadership skills. Basic business teachers should help prepare students for leadership roles in classroom activities, in student organizations and clubs, and in organizations outside of the school. The true value of developing leadership can be measured by the extent to which it creates an improved belief in "self" and in the ability to assume leadership.

Characteristics of effective leaders. Students need to realize that organizations expect and require active leadership if they are to function and achieve their goals. Discussions that focus on the characteristics of leadership and how they can be developed help students assess their own leadership potential. Also, they recognize that some of their peers already possess some of these leadership characteristics. A discussion of the following partial list of effective leadership characteristics will help students better understand the multifaceted dimensions of an effective leader.

An effective leader:[5]

- understands the principles of democracy
- respects the rights and dignity of others
- realizes that every person can make a contribution
- understands himself/herself
- accepts responsibilities
- does his/her part through work with the group
- gets along with people in a friendly manner
- is straightforward and agreeable with people
- is industrious
- praises individuals when praise is due
- is sensitive to basic trends and moods of the group
- is able to communicate thoughts and feelings in a clear and understandable manner
- is able to verbalize the ideas of the group
- is well informed on matters that concern the group
- arrives at decisions only after securing and studying pertinent information
- has confidence in developed abilities
- shows trust for fellow group members
- is optimistic
- believes that group action can overcome obstacles and solve problems
- works within the group with zest and enjoyment
- is open minded
- does not claim to have all the answers
- seeks the opinions of others
- supports the ideas of others if it is best for the group
- is willing to compromise on issues
- has strength of conviction
- will take a stand and be counted
- can be convinced to take another view if the evidence indicates the view held to be wrong
- shows initiative in getting a group started
- plans carefully to initiate action
- proceeds in group discussion with know-how rather than with reckless abandon

[5]The Center for Vocational Education, The Ohio State University. *Prepare Student Vocational Organization Members for Leadership Roles*, Module H-3, Professional Teacher Education Module Series. Athens: American Association for Vocational Instructional Methods, 1977, p. 9.

- is public spirited
- desires and works for those things that benefit the group
- expresses facts or offers possible solutions when participating.

Teaching leadership skills. Basic business teachers should utilize the following guidelines for developing student leadership skills through classroom and related instructional activities:

- Ensure that all students actively participate as leaders and/or followers.
- Have students observe/study characteristics of leaders and their leadership styles.
- Encourage students to determine why certain individuals become effective leaders and others do not.
- Ask students to describe the role delegation plays in increasing leader effectiveness.

A teacher's responsibility for developing *leadership should extend to all students*, not just the current officers of clubs and organizations. Students must understand their role in organizations—to promote the growth of the organization and work to accomplish its objectives by participating actively and by providing leadership. With the varied activities needed in organizations, it is possible for each member to develop leadership abilities. In addition to the officers, there are always committees and special projects through which students can test and develop their ability to communicate ideas, to initiate action, to inspire others to contribute, to display enthusiasm, to formulate and carry out a plan, to accept responsibility, and to get along with people. Students must understand that to become a leader, the first step is to have the first experience as a leader. A positive environment for student leadership growth is created when teachers: (1) encourage students to assume leadership roles and participate actively at various levels in classroom learning activities, in school-related organizations, and in organizations external to the school; and (2) give recognition to those who are involved.

Prospective student leaders should be encouraged to *observe successful leaders* and model their effective leadership techniques. There are three basic leadership styles: (1) the authoritarian leader who dominates or directs the group according to his/her own goals; (2) the democratic leader who considers all opinions and allows members to form their own goals; and (3) the laissez-faire leader who lets the members do whatever they wish. Different leadership styles may be necessary to meet the needs of different groups effectively. Furthermore, a group may require different leader behaviors depending on the task that must be accomplished.

Individuals become leaders for different reasons: (1) the person's status in the organization, (2) the person is perceived to have the most knowledge about the topic, or (3) the person possesses certain personality qualities. For whatever reason an individual emerges as the leader, the leader must be an effective communicator.

Whenever possible, a *leader should delegate* to others so they can assist in reaching the goals and feel that they are a part of the group. A good leader knows how to select the right people to do specific jobs. In addition, organizations usually have committees and projects that must have leaders also.

The number of students who have leadership experiences is directly related to the number of motivated leaders developed. Thus, delegation provides opportunities for others to be involved and develop leadership skills.

CONCLUSION

The primary purpose of basic business education is to increase students' business and economic understanding so they can function more effectively as consumers, workers, and citizens. As changes occur in society and in the workplace, has the content being taught in basic business courses been modified? In addition to teaching the basic business content, are instructional strategies being used that integrate critical thinking, goal setting, problem solving, conflict resolution, assertiveness, small group participation, and leadership skills into our curriculum? Do our teaching-learning activities enhance these important personal and workplace skills of our students? As basic business educators, we must be accountable.

CHAPTER 7

The Hidden Agenda for Communication

W. DALE BREWER and LINDA BLOOM

Pensacola Community College, Pensacola, Florida

In general, business educators do an excellent job of training students to be competent communicators. But unfortunately, business educators sometimes overlook certain aspects of communicating with which they are uncomfortable. Most of the instructional time spent in communication courses centers around written communication. In the business office of the nineties, however, the majority of communication is done verbally or through the use of intelligent pieces of equipment. Should not educators, therefore, reevaluate their courses to address the student needs of today and tomorrow? By providing a sound foundation upon which students can build, business educators provide their students with the skills necessary to succeed as they move toward the 21st century.

Four important areas commonly underemphasized in teaching students communication skills are

1. verbal communication

2. nonverbal communication

3. intercultural communication

4. communication through electronic equipment.

Failure is imminent if students are not competent in these areas when they enter the work force. To help ensure success, educators must address these areas which are traditionally hidden in business concepts.

VERBAL COMMUNICATION

One of Americans' greatest fears is having to speak before a group—a fear identified more often than the fear of death. Just exactly what happens during an oral presentation? In addition to the mental anguish a person feels, certain physical changes take place: heart rates increase, blood pressure rises, gastric juices flow, palms sweat, knees shake, and respiration becomes more rapid.

Unfortunately, many of the anxieties suffered cannot be overcome, but an individual can learn to deal with them effectively. Many public performers say that they are not prepared emotionally if they are not nervous before presentations. Anxiety is a good sign of emotional preparedness.

"Practice makes perfect" is certainly applicable in controlling stage fright, but are business educators providing students with enough practice to teach them how to deal with their anxieties effectively? Is the one-time only, five-to ten-minute speech before a business class sufficient? Educators must continually give students numerous opportunities to speak, both formally and informally before a group, regardless of the size.

Students must be taught to realize that the "pain" they associate with most oral presentations is short. Too, students must be taught to realize that most audiences do not recognize nervousness in presenters. In reality audiences may be more engaged in receiving the information than in analyzing the delivery of the speaker.

If students can be taught that they are speaking "with" a group rather than "to" a group, then they will have developed the skill necessary to communicate effectively in oral presentations. The purpose of the majority of presentations is to provide new information. As oral communicators, individuals are most effective when they speak on the level of the group and appear to be genuinely interested in sharing information.

Many business agreements are not completed because of miscommunication between the parties involved. Because of poor presentations, countless numbers of companies and executives have lost thousands of dollars. The ability to communicate significantly impacts on success or failure. Educators must, therefore, continually stress the value of effective communication to their students.

With the impact of technology, presentations are becoming more and more artistic. Overhead projectors are commonplace in today's meeting rooms. Transparencies are now easier to produce. Visual aids produced on equipment such as color photocopies and multi-faceted computers are within easy reach of the majority of persons faced with preparing an oral presentation. Most educators feel that using a visual aid eases the anxieties associated with presentations. Thus, students should be encouraged to supplement their oral presentations with visuals whenever possible. Students must be taught the art of developing and using visual aids effectively. Any presentation supported by research data can be enhanced by charts or graphs that visually demonstrate the data. Additionally, students should be taught how to prepare visuals emphasizing major points. The use of bullets, stars, and/or lines can add variety to a simple listing of key elements. Most people have a degree of creativity and will exhibit such when given the opportunity to do so.

Regardless of the subject being studied, teachers can provide students with opportunities to make better oral presentations. Subjects such as introduction to business, management, and business law offer these opportunities daily. Other subjects require a teacher to be creative in assigning topics for presentations.

Students are always interested in employment possibilities. Over a defined period of time (a month, for example), students can keep track of the want ads in their local newspapers. Salaries, educational or experience requirements, as well as any other information deemed valuable, can be recorded and presented to the class utilizing visual aids. Another important area of communication, working in small groups, can be developed by assigning specific tasks. A group of students can be assigned a project on a time basis determined by the instructor.

Another valuable opportunity for students to practice oral communication skills is through the use of current articles taken from business periodicals, newsletters, or newspapers. Within a given length of time, students can be instructed to read, summarize, and present the highlights of the article. If appropriate, visual aids can be used to enhance the student's presentation.

Educators can involve students in the teaching of a course by requiring presentation of a concept within a chapter/unit being studied. To develop and further sharpen true communicating skills, class discussion should be led by students. Again, visuals may be appropriate, but only if they add clarity to the presentation.

Many one-to-one communication situations occur daily in business. Students should be taught how to deal effectively with the many different personalities they will encounter. In business communication courses, as well as many other business courses, students are taught interviewing skills. Students should be given an opportunity to assume the role of an interviewer and should be required to formulate questions for a variety of situations. Finally, students should be taught how to analyze objectively the responses. Students will realize the sensitivity skills required to communicate successfully with potential employees.

Another one-to-one situation often ignored in business classes is that of evaluating another individual on some type of performance—for example, job performance. By creating mock performance appraisal forms and by providing the students with background information, an innovative teacher can give students the opportunity to recognize the value of praising as well as criticizing others.

Students must be given as many opportunities as possible to develop oral communication skills. It's the responsibility of the business educator to provide experiences that will help students sharpen and refine verbal abilities that will be most needed when entering the business world. Incorporating realistic activities that build oral communication skills should be an integral part of every business teacher's challenge—to provide the business world with competent, success-driven employees.

NONVERBAL COMMUNICATION

Most individuals communicate verbally with others daily. However, the most common form of communication is nonverbal. With the exclusive use of body movement, people were able to communicate long before words were used. Before verbal communication was a skill, people gritted their teeth to show animosity and smiled and touched one another to show affection. Today, people continue to use nonverbal cues to express superiority, dependence, disdain, reverence, respect, and love. These "silent expressions," so important in conveying feelings, account for about 93 percent of the emotional meaning exchanged in any interaction.

The clothes worn, the hairstyle chosen, the cars owned, the residential area selected—all are symbols that proclaim just as much, or sometimes more, than verbal speech. Individuals surround themselves with symbols that communicate information to others. From symbols people tend to stereotype others. Beyond the well-known stereotypes associated with certain common symbols (for example, a wedding ring), generalizing about what particular symbols communicate to others is impossible. Certainly symbols can and do communicate different things to different people. Another example of symbolic communication familiar to many people is the situation illustrated by the statement, "Stay away from Dr. Smith today; he's wearing his red tie!" The tie discloses something to other people. Stereotyping as in this example can cause much of the complexity and confusion in communicating.

People communicate more effectively if they are aware of and understand symbolic communication. Unless individuals are aware of what their symbols are communicating, they may be saying one thing while their symbols are communicating something else. For example, if individuals say that they do not need status symbols, but admit to driving Cadillacs, their symbols do not fit their words. When words and symbols do not agree, then mixed messages are sent that confuse rather than aid communication effectiveness. Effective communication occurs when both the words and symbols emit the same message. For effective communication, the moral seems clear—people need to find out from others what their symbols are communicating. They may or may not be communicating what is intended. Therefore, symbolic communication should be aligned with verbal communication.

Body language is another very important means of communicating. Evidence is overwhelming that peoples' bodies do communicate to other people. One form of body language that most people are familiar with is pointing the finger. The body communicates in numerous ways: facial expression, posture, touch, gestures, physical distance, physical appearance, and others. Communication effectiveness is increased as individuals learn more about what their body language communicates. Most body language is unconsciously exhibited and is, therefore, considered honest and effective communication of thoughts and feelings.

Human communication is complex: Everything a person says or does conveys a message to others. The most effective communication occurs when the receiver interprets the message as it was intended. To communicate effectively, verbal and nonverbal communication needs to be congruent.

INTERCULTURAL COMMUNICATION

How can Americans compete in the international marketplace when they do not understand the language spoken, do not know what the body language exhibited conveys, or do not know what the specific mores of a society might be? During the past decade, the study of intercultural communication has received much attention. However, intercultural communication is as old as civilization. Why, then, is there a resurgence in striving to understand the culture of others?

"When in Rome, do as the Romans do" is a familiar saying but often ignored by American business people. American business has failed in trying to sell many of its products and services overseas by not adapting to foreign ways and customs. A report from the President's Commission on Foreign

Language and International Studies suggests that over 6,000 American companies have foreign operations, and more than 20,000 businesses export products or services abroad. Many top-level executives have worked outside the United States—7 percent of the chief executive officers, 18.8 percent of the presidents, and 17.2 percent of the vice presidents. These individuals spent an average of about three years in a foreign country.

Demographers predict that at least one-third of the United States will consist of individuals associated with an identifiable minority group by the year 2000. American business transactions are steadily increasing in the global marketplace. As a result of these trends and developments, sensitivity to racial and cultural diversity is becoming increasingly important.

The ease of travel, the development of multinational organizations, and international tensions have made Americans realize that they must communicate and cooperate with others unlike themselves in order to succeed. Certainly barriers exist: the inability to speak and write the same lanuage, the numerous ways of thinking, the different value systems.

Stereotyping often occurs. Generalization are made as the usual customs and thought patterns of others are studied. However, just as no two people in Dallas, Texas, are identical, no two people from Japan, France, or Saudi Arabia are the same.

Unfortunately, educated people from other countries know more about the United States than people in the United States know about other countries. People outside this country have developed stereotypes about Americans, just as Americans have preconceived notions about people from other countries.

Cultural differences do exist among different societies—Eastern values are very different from Western values, but successful communication with others results not only from acceptance and objectivity, but also from patience and a sense of humor.

Nonverbal communication is very important because of language barriers and differing backgrounds and perceptions. Americans live by schedules and value promptness. Natives from many other countries "take time to smell the roses." Americans do not like to be kept waiting; however, a Latin American appointment may very likely be up to 45 minutes later than scheduled.

Americans get to the point of business quickly; this procedure is not expected in Latin America or the Middle East, where discussion is considered part of the spice of life.

Americans, British, and Northern Europeans feel uncomfortable when crowded together. Mediterraneans, Latin Americans, and Middle Easterners enjoy closer personal contact. In Saudi Arabia and other Middle Eastern countries, pushing and shoving in a public place is not considered impolite. Because of such differences, Americans may seem cold and distant to individuals from these areas.

Shaking the head to indicate yes or no is unknown in some countries, where different movements indicate yes or no. Arabs disapprove of using the left hand to take food—to do so is considered unclean. Eye contact differs according to particular cultures. Some people maintain eye contact to the extent that Americans become uncomfortable. Other cultures are taught to avoid direct eye contact in order to show respect.

What then can American educators do to help alleviate communication problems? Developing and teaching a new curriculum is imperative if students are to meet the challenges for global survival. In 1982, fewer than 1 percent of college students in the United States were enrolled in courses that taught about international complexities, and fewer than 2 percent of high school graduates studied a foreign language. Fortunately, many states are now requiring two years of foreign language study for high school graduates. With the world becoming more economically, politically, and socially inter-dependent, the importance of integrating intercultural communication into business-oriented courses increases daily. Students must be able to engage in conventional business communication without prejudice. Educators must help students to deal creatively with the effects of multicultural conditioning.

Three methods for integrating intercultural communication into existing programs are suggested. The first method is experiential. A student actually lives and interacts with individuals in their natural home environment learning the idiosyncracies of that culture. The second alternative is the behavioral strategy. Teachers have individuals from different cultures interact with one another in an educational setting to make comparisons based upon how people act under certain circumstances. The third alternative is informational. Readings are assigned by the instructor about peoples' customs or history.

Students must be taught to interpret episodes related to life events based upon cultural norms, mores, and customs. For example, in business communi-cation courses, students may be asked to compare cultural traits between a Japanese and an American business person.

To gain an understanding of intercultural impacts on business communi-cation, the following list of topics provides a source for comparison:

1. Body gestures, including touching
2. Facial expressions
3. Physical closeness
4. Eye-to-eye contact
5. Verbal pacing
6. Value of time
7. Customs (chatting over coffee)
8. Slang expressions
9. Gender and cultural prejudices
10. Professional etiquette/rules
11. Ideology

Learning about another culture includes studying the language, reading books and articles, and finding out about a country's subcultures, especially its business subculture. The best way to learn about another culture is to study more thoroughly and learn the language. If time does not permit a comprehensive language study, at least a few words should be learned.

Students should read books and articles about the culture and talk with people who have dealt with its citizens. Learning about the history, religion, politics, and customs, as well as studying the practical details, is very important.

A country's subcultures should also be researched. Does the business world have its own rules and protocol? Who makes the decisions? How are negotiations usually conducted? Is gift giving expected? What is expected in the exchange of business cards? What is appropriate dress for business meetings? According to Thill and Bovee, seasoned business travelers suggest the following:

1. In Spain, a handshake should last five to seven strokes because pulling away too soon may be interpreted as a sign of rejection. The French, however, prefer a single stroke handshake.

2. Liquor should never be given as a gift in Arab countries.

3. In Pakistan, business people often excuse themselves in the midst of meetings to conduct prayers, because Moslems pray five times a day.

4. In Africa, plenty of time should be allowed to conduct business so these people have the opportunity to get to know their visitor. Africans are very suspicious of individuals who want to finish business too rapidly.

5. In Arab countries, food and drink should never be turned down because Arabs consider refusing hospitality as insulting. However, acceptance should not be too speedy either. A ritual refusal ("I don't want to put you to any trouble") is expected before final acceptance.

6. The longevity of a company should be stressed with the Germans, Dutch, and Swiss. If the company has been established for a while, the founding date should be printed on business cards.

The above items are only a few examples of the variety of customs that make intercultural communications so interesting.

Americans can no longer ignore the influences of other countries, culturally or economically. Americans must learn to get along with others, to respect their cultures, and to realize that while other cultures are different, they are not right or wrong, better or worse. Rather than criticizing the differences, Americans, in order to compete in the international marketplace, must strive to study the languages, understand the cultures, and break the barriers that have separated nations for centuries.

TECHNOLOGICAL ADVANCES IMPACTING ON COMMUNICATION

The telephone is the most widely used piece of equipment in today's business office. Educators have always addressed the proper usage of the telephone; but because of technological changes, the telephone has taken on a new and exciting role. Now the telephone is used not only for one-to-one conversations, but also for communication between sophisticated computerized equipment. Survival in business in the 1990s depends upon a person's ability not only to communicate on a personal basis, but also to communicate efficiently and effectively through equipment that is becoming commonplace in today's business office. Business educators are being charged with the task of teaching their students about the technological advances that have greatly altered the role of today's business office.

Educators are realizing the value of including as much information as possible about telecommunications (the electronic transmission of information from one location to another) in their classrooms. Without actually having equipment available (video conferencing systems, for example), it is difficult for an educator to give students an understanding of the technology they may encounter when entering the work force. But by subscribing to publications (many of which are free), instructors can build a vast reference library containing information about the latest technological advances. Most articles contain pictures, charts, or diagrams illustrating the information, which further enhances a student's understanding. Students can be assigned articles for reading and then be required to report orally (or in writing) on their findings.

Equipment vendors see students as potential customers and are therefore eager to provide information. Inviting such people to address students ensures that students receive the latest information. If vendors are not able to visit the classroom, they will probably be willing to provide brochures and other printed information to the educator for use in the classroom. In addition to representatives from equipment vendors, the local telephone company will provide speakers and a wealth of printed information on the services they have available.

The following glossary of terms is offered as a foundation for informing students about the technological advances affecting business. If students can develop an understanding of these terms, they will have a background upon which to build when they enter the work force.

Cellular Mobile Telephone	Equipment using radio signals to transmit conversations between individuals in remote locations (such as an automobile).
Central Exchange System	A telephone system in a company in which each telephone has its own seven-digit number. A caller can dial this number directly, thus bypassing the switchboard. Internal calls can be made by dialing the last four digits of the telephone number.
Electronic Mail	Information distributed in an on-line computer system that would otherwise require a printed copy—such as a memo from one executive to another.
FAX (facsimile) machine	A type of electronic mail that uses imagery and telephone lines to transmit printed information from one location to another.
Local Area Network (LAN)	Computerized equipment within a building or buildings that are reasonably close linked together by cable for exchanging information.
Private Automatic Branch Exchange	A computer-controlled telephone system for large companies utilizing the use of a common switchboard for all incoming calls and then transferred to the appropriate extension.

Pager	A signaling device that notifies the holder of the "pager" to contact a predetermined number for a message.
Telecommuting	Being able to work at home and communicate with equipment at an office through the use of telephone lines and computers.
Teleconferencing	Using a telecommunication system, being able to conduct a meeting of three or more individuals in different locations via telephone lines.
Videoconferencing	Teleconferencing with the addition of special viewing equipment so that participants are seen in addition to being heard.
Voice Mail	A concept similar to electronic mail except that it does not require the caller to have a computer and it provides a spoken message as opposed to a visual one.
Wide Area Network (WAN)	A network utilizing telephone lines and computerized equipment to send and receive information between any locations throughout the world.

Students should realize that transmitting information can take many different modes—from the traditional telephone to sophisticated LANs and that an employee in a highly technical office environment needs to be thoroughly familiar with the concepts of telecommunication. Educators must continually stir an interest in their students to inquire about and investigate technological advances that can affect their lives—not only professionally, but also personally.

CONCLUSION

The purpose of business education is twofold: (1) to educate students about business, and (2) to educate students for business. Without good communication skills, people cannot achieve success in the business world nor can they be productive citizens. Students must be given the opportunity to

1. develop sound oral communication skills,
2. understand the impact of nonverbal communication,
3. appreciate other cultures and communicate successfully with persons outside their own culture, and
4. be familiar with and understand the technology that is affecting their lives daily.

Development of the above items cannot be accomplished by simply studying isolated chapters within textbooks. Educators must integrate these skills and concepts into all of their business courses. Students must continually be given the opportunity to employ the skills in which they will be expected to have competence when they leave the classroom.

Educators must realize that the content of their courses must be constantly analyzed and revised in order to keep up with the demands of business. Today's business educator must be more creative than ever due to the fast-changing business environment. As the 21st century approaches, the traditionally hidden and underemphasized communication skills of the past must be a part of business courses so that the American free enterprise system can continue to flourish. Such an emergence will ensure that America will remain *the envy* of many nations worldwide.

REFERENCES

Adelstein, Michael E. and Sparrow, W. Keats. *Business Communications.* Second edition. Orlando, FL: Harcourt Brace Jovanovich, Inc., 1990.

Chalupa, Marilyn R. "The Telephone Unit: New Services and Telecommunications." *Business Education Forum.* November, 1990.

Farrell, Thomas J. "Telephone Skills Reappear in Business Curriculum." *Business Education Forum.* February, 1991.

Jain, N. C. *International and Intercultural Communication Annual.* Chicago: International Press, Inc., 1982.

Kupsh, Joyce, Jones, Carol Larson, and Graves, Pat R. "Presentation Design Strategies." *Business Education Forum.* December, 1990.

Morrison, James L., and Morrison, Pamela P. "The Theory of Attrition Learning, Technology, and Intercultural Business Communication." *Journal of Education for Business.* January/February, 1991.

Motley, Michael T. "Taking the Terror Out of Talk." *Psychology Today.* January, 1988.

Mott, Dennis L. "Teaching Oral Presentation Skills." *Business Education Forum.* May, 1990.

Murphy, Herta A. and Hildebrandt, Herbert W. *Effective Business Communications.* Sixth edition. New York: McGraw-Hill, Inc., 1991.

Samovan, L. and Porter, R. *Intercultural Communication.* Belmont, CA: Wadsworth, 1988.

Thill, John V. and Bovee, Courtland, R. *Excellence in Business Communication.* New York: McGraw-Hill, Inc., 1991.

Tilton, Rita, Jackson, J. Howard, and Rigby, Sue Chappell. *The Electronic Office— Procedures & Administration.* Cincinnati: South-Western Publishing Co., 1991.

Treece, Malra. *Successful Communication for Business and the Professions.* Needham Heights, MA: Allyn and Bacon, 1991.

VanHuss, Susie H. and Daggett, Willard R. *Electronic Information Systems.* Cincinnati: South-Western Publishing Co., 1990.

CHAPTER 8

Listening: A Partner for Career Enhancement and Establishment

ANNA LAURA BENNINGTON
University of Arizona (retired), Tucson, Arizona

Communication is the most important skill in life. Definitions of hearing and listening as found in *Webster* are: *hearing*—the process or function or power of perceiving sound—opportunity to be heard; *listening*—to hear with thoughtful attention. We have spent years learning how to read, write, and to speak, but few can recall when and how they were taught to listen. What part of any curriculum includes training or education that enables our students to listen so that they really understand another human being?

What we communicate by listening. The first reaction of most people when they consider listening as a possible method for dealing with human beings is that listening cannot be sufficient in itself. Because it is passive, they think listening does not communicate anything to the speaker. Actually, nothing could be farther from the truth.

By consistently listening to a speaker a person conveys the idea that: "I'm interested in you as a person and I think that what you feel is important. I respect your thoughts and even if I don't agree with them, I know they are valid for you. I feel certain you have a contribution to make. I will not try to change you or evaluate you. I want to understand you. You are worth listening to, and I want you to know that I am the kind of person with whom you can talk."

The subtle but important aspect of listening is that it is the demonstration of the message that works. "Actions speak louder than words." Listening is definitely one action that speaks louder than words!

Listening behavior is contagious. Just as anger is usually met with anger, argument with argument, and deception with deception; listening can also be met with listening. Every person who feels responsibility in a situation can set the tone of the interaction, and the important lesson in this is: Any behavior exhibited by one person will eventually be responded to in a similar behavior by the other person.

Testing for understanding. Understanding other people is usually far more difficult than expected. "In business and in personal relationships, listen to people and understand them. When we really, deeply understand each other, we open the door to creative solutions and third alternatives."[1]

---

[1]Covey, Stephen R. *The 7 Habits of Highly Effective People.* Simon and Schuster. 1990. pp. 236-270.

We are the result of our experiences. Our experiences shadow our reflection and interpretation of that which we hear. Understanding another person's viewpoint would be an easy task if we could mirror the experiences. One solution to understanding is to role play—pretend we are that person.

STEPS INVOLVED IN LISTENING

The five steps involved in listening are: sensing, interpreting, evaluating, remembering, and responding. The sequence of the steps indicates people diagnose before they prescribe. Educators need to test themselves to be certain that they are using this process. Look at the physician, the opthalmologist, and the attorney. Diagnosing before prescribing is the mark of all true professionals!

Sensing. Physically hearing the message and taking note of it; it is necessary to tune out all distracting noises and focus on the message.

Interpreting. As listeners, we assign meaning to the words based on our personal experiences, values, beliefs, and needs. The nonverbal cues of the speaker will increase the accuracy of our interpretations.

Evaluating. As we sort through the speaker's remarks, separating fact from opinion, we evaluate the quality of the evidence. Evaluating requires effort.

Remembering. Good speakers assist the audience in remembering by clarifying their message with an introduction, transitions, and summaries. Retention is possible through note taking and a mental outline of the key points of the speaker.

Responding. An audience responds with applause, laughter, or silence. In one-on-one communication the initial response would be in the form of verbal or nonverbal feedback. Listening requires mental and physical activities including a mix of the environmental noises and conditions.

FOUR TYPES OF LISTENING

The four types of listening differ not only in purpose but also in interaction.

Active listening. Before replying to another person's comment with a point of our own, restate the ideas and feelings behind the comment to the other person's satisfaction. The goal is to appreciate another person's point of view.

Content listening. The goal is to understand the message and retain information delivered by the speaker. A good listener will identify key points and then listen for cues for summaries and enumerated points.

Empathic listening. Learning the speaker's feelings, needs, and wants is the goal in empathic listening in order to assist the speaker in solving a problem. The message is the vehicle for gaining insight into the speaker's feelings; listening helps individuals vent feelings as well as take steps to solving their own problems. Dr. Stephen Covey tells us empathic listening is powerful because it gives accurate data with which to work. Instead of projecting our own autobiography and assuming thoughts, motives, feelings, and interpretation, we are dealing with the reality inside another person's head and heart. We are listening to understand.

Effective listening. The effective listener is an active listener, one who creates an environment in which the speaker feels free to develop his/her thoughts. The active listener maintains the role of listener.

Effective listening is not simply doing what comes naturally; for, as Preston has noted, "Everyone has learned to talk, but no one has learned to listen."

WHY TEACH OR STUDY LISTENING?

The speech rate for many people is about 200 words per minute, yet most people think about four times that speed. During all the extra time the ineffective listeners let their minds wander. The brain takes detours thinking about the events of the previous day, makes plans for the next day or event, or sleeps.

WHY LISTEN?

What are the results of effective listening? Effective listening is the road map to improve communications. Listening encourages speakers to put forth their best efforts, helps participants to talk and solve problems, leads to positive attitudes, and provides information to share with others.

To be an effective listener
- find areas of interest
- judge content, not delivery
- listen for ideas
- hold judgment/fire
- be flexible
- work at listening
- resist distractions
- exercise the mind
- keep the mind open
- capitalize on the fact that thought is faster than speech.

Teaching students to be good listeners will provide them with living skills and particularly with the skills with which to interview (obtain a position) and to retain a position.

The "Six P's of listening" are:

Prepare: set the mind to the task of being an active listener.

Perceive: recognize when blocking occurs. Blocking is a barrier that interferes with objective listening.

Participate: focus thoughts on the task of listening well while receiving information.

Process: think about information heard to try to make sense of it.

Probe: ask questions to help to understand and process information we hear.

Personalize: fit information heard into our own needs and goals framework so that it becomes ours.

LISTENING: A PARTNER FOR CAREER ENHANCEMENT
AND ESTABLISHMENT

The Sperry Corporation, which has spent $5 to $6 million annually on listening research and training, reports that in schools where listening has been taught, listening comprehension has doubled in a few months.

How to listen. Active listening aims to bring about changes in people. To achieve this end, active listening relies upon definite techniques; however, educators should first understand why the techniques are effective. (To do so, we must understand how the individual personality develops.) Listen for total meaning.

A study of the 100 best listeners and the 100 worst listeners in the freshman class at the University of Minnesota has disclosed 10 guides to improved listening. Business people interested in improving their own performance can use these guides to analyze their personal strengths and weaknesses.

TEN STEPS TO BETTER LISTENING

Choose to listen. Educators must develop a stage for learning so the students will "choose to listen."

Listen actively. In passive listening the mind is only partially engaged; in active listening it is fully engaged, concentrating on what is being said and providing feedback (verbal or nonverbal).

An example of active listening is interviewing. The responsibilities of the interviewee and interviewer include preparing for listening, concentrating on verbal message, and concentrating on nonverbal message. As students enter the work place or change careers, one of the first steps is the interview. The classroom is responsible for preparing the students for this process.

The task of the interviewer is to find out whether a candidate will be able to do the job comfortably and to secure evidence that the person will fit into the organization. In the process of listening, both the interviewee and interviewer must learn to ask questions to be certain that the question has been understood and, therefore, interpreted correctly.

Listen for ideas and feelings. There are five levels of listening: cliches, facts, thoughts, feelings about one's self, and feelings about external events. The good listener is not afraid to listen for ideas and feelings.

Listen with the heart's ear. Hearing is a physiological process by which auditory impressions are received by the ears and transmitted to the brain. Listening refers to a more complex psychological procedure involving interpreting and understanding the significance of a sensory experience such as the roar of the ocean or the music of a great symphony. It is also important to accept our conversational partner as he or she is. If we can maintain an attitude of acceptance toward the person, we will be psychologically ready to listen.

Listen to the voice within. "Go to your bosom, knock there and ask your heart what it doth know," wrote William Shakespeare. When listening carefully to ourselves, we realize how others see/hear us. Discovery of negative or positive items about self could become the door to constructive change.

Know when to keep silent. There is power in silent, supportive listening. Ask questions and give people time to respond and to answer their own questions. Return a question with a question.

Be flexible when taking notes. The 100 worst listeners thought that note-taking and outlining were synonyms. They believed there was but one way to take notes—by making an outline. Efficient note-takers had equipped themselves with four or five systems.

Resist Distractions. Listeners MUST concentrate and control the environment.

Keep an open mind and exercise the mind. Good listening is challenging and requires effort.

Capitalize on speed. Use the lag time in the thought-speed process to summarize, anticipate, and think about the topic and what is being said. Make mental notes and/or written notes of items to challenge and/or question. Observe the body language as well as the voice or tone and volume of voice.

NONVERBAL LANGUAGE

The following checklist for evaluating nonverbal communication identifies many of the common positive and negative messages that people send without being aware of the nonverbal connotations of such behavior. Maintaining the appropriate professional image takes a conscious effort, but most people would agree that it is well worth the time spent if it is a determining factor in our professional advancement.

Facial Expressions

Positive Face	*Negative Face*	
smile	frown	mocking laughter
laughter	sneer	smirk
empathic face	cry	angry face
eye contact	glare	disgust

Voice Cues

Positive Voice		*Negative Voice*	
caring	satisfied	cold	blaming
warm	buoyant	tense	sarcastic
tender	cheerful	scared	angry
relieved	chuckling	hard	blaring
concerned	joyful	clipped	depressed

Body Positions and Movements

Positive Body	Negative Body
touching	neck or hand tension
distance reduction	rude gestures
attention	point
relaxation	throw up hands in disgust
forward lean	inattention.

Examining some examples of messages delivered through body language will help us understand the language. Touching is an important body-language sign. When people shake hands, it is a sign of self-assurance. Touching is used to define power relationships. Eye contact is crucial for good listening. The test is to stop in the middle of a sentence and notice whether the person to whom we are speaking looks away or is easily distracted.

Visitors appreciate being acknowledged when entering an office. Acknowledgments may be in the form of standing, walking from behind a desk, or joining another at a nearby table or chair. These gestures make one feel accepted and wanted; whereas, leaning back in a chair and remaining behind the desk may transmit an opposite message that says no time is available for further conversation.

MYTHS OF LISTENING

The following discussions of myths of listening reveal the mindset of the general population.

Myth one: Listening and hearing are the same thing. Fact: Hearing is the physiological process in which sound waves strike the eardrum, creating vibrations for transmission to the brain. Listening extends the physiological process to the assignment of meaning to sounds. Listening is, therefore, essential for message decoding.

Myth two: Listening and hearing are physiological processes. Fact: Hearing is a natural physiological process but effective listening extends the physiological process of hearing into the skill of accurate decoding and assignment of meaning. In fact, more people speak well than listen well.

Myth three: Everyone listening to the same message receives the same message. Fact: Understanding listening barriers, first described by Ralph Nichols (1957), is important for understanding individual habits that interfere with accurate message reception. Because listening involves individual decoding and assignment of meaning, listening will be different for everyone.

BARRIERS TO EFFECTIVE LISTENING

The six barriers to effective listening are: stress, "me" syndrome, brain speed, faking attention, failure to identify listening distractions; and emotionally resisting messages. To cope with the six barriers, we must understand them.

1. Stress makes it difficult to give full attention to another person or speaker.

2. Listeners with the "me" syndrome don't seem to care about the feelings of others and cannot see the legitimacy of any point of view but their own.

3. For most people, the thought speed/speech speed difference is not used to increase listening effectiveness but to think of other subjects while another is speaking. Listening experts tell us time would be better spent in internally restating the speaker's message, drawing analogies and examples related to the subject, and determining what questions to ask.

4. Faking attention is a habit of many and not related to whether the speaker is interesting or not. Obviously we miss most of the message and reduce our chances for accurate communication.

5. A failure to identify listening distractions contributes to ineffective listening. Listening for facts is distracting and difficult. Taking notes can distract from meaning. Physical noise, interruptions, and unidentified sounds are other distractions that keep us from receiving the speaker's message.

6. The sixth barrier is emotionally resisting messages. Often we react quickly to emotionally charged words or subjects as we relate them to personal experiences. In this process we often quit listening to what is being said. We make judgments and respond to those judgments as if the speaker's position were accurately known to us. We hear only the negatives and do not attend to ways to improve ourselves. This barrier parallels the "me" syndrome barrier.

Communication skills profile.

COMMUNICATION SKILL	ORDER LEARNED	EXTENT USED	EXTENT TAUGHT
Listening	First	45%	Fourth
Speaking	Second	30%	Third
Reading	Third	26%	Second
Writing	Fourth	9%	First

MANAGEMENT IN THE 90S

The key to success in the 90s is people. Business will need to alter its management style as it shifts the power to people. As this transition takes place, the communication skills profile is important. More time needs to be spent in teaching listening skills in the public schools K-12, at the post-secondary levels, and in training and development within business and industry.

Managers need to be equal-opportunity listeners. Some managers lend their ears only to those who occupy higher salary brackets. This is not listening. Listen to the one hired yesterday; it is a rare manager who tunes in so democratically. Some managers have a weekly listening breakfast or dream up a suggestion-of-the-week award. We must do something about what we hear. A sincere, speedy response is what counts. When an employee or staff member dares to suggest a better way, the courteous and smart thing to do is respond fast!! Use e-mail (electronic mail) or a written short thank-you note, since small acknowledgments carry weight.

Leaders pay attention. Leaders authorize people to think, and they make that clear by listening. Listening says: "You are smart and have important things to say—you are worth my time—go ahead; what a good idea!"

SUMMARY

Despite the popular notion that listening is a passive approach, clinical and research evidence clearly shows that sensitive listening is a most effective agent for individual personality changes and group development. Listening brings about changes in people's attitudes toward themselves and others and also brings about changes in their basic values and personal philosophy. People who have been listened to in this new special way become more emotionally mature, more open to their experiences, less defensive, more democractic, and less authoritarian. Listening is very important in all aspects of life.

When people are listened to sensitively, they tend to listen to themselves with more care and make clear exactly what they are feeling and thinking. Group members tend to listen more to each other, become less argumentative, more ready to incorporate other points of view. As listening reduces the threat of having one's ideas criticized, the speaker is better able to see the ideas for what they are and is more likely to feel the contributions are worthwhile.

Another important result of listening is the change that takes place within the listener. Because listening provides more information than any other activity, it builds deep, positive relationships and tends to alter constructively the attitudes of the listener. Listening is a growth experience.

Skills for active listening are as follows:

Self-control
1. gain positive attitude for listening
2. stop talking
3. control own emotions
4. empathize with others
5. avoid mental arguments
6. avoid assumptions, conclusions, stereotypes

Mental processing
1. summarize main points
2. identify and evaluate facts and evidence
3. prepare questions
4. avoid interruptions

Verbal skills
1. paraphrase others' positions
2. question for clarification
3. summarize main points and meanings.

The first step in being a top manager is to listen. We must try to change the way people manage their work. Smart managers (teachers are managers of learning) empower their staff on a well-prepared stage.

Summarize your traits as a listener by taking the short quiz which follows. *Ask yourself the following questions and answer with: "A" = Always; "D" = sometimes; "E" = rarely; and "G" = never. Assign the following points: A = 7, E = 3, D = 5, and G = 1.*

1. Do you let the speaker completely express ideas without interruption?
2. Do you stop yourself from becoming upset or excited when the speaker's views differ from your own?
3. Are you able to prevent distractions from disrupting your ability to listen?
4. Can you listen without making continuous notes on everything the person says?
5. Are you able to read between the lines and hear what a person is saying even when there are hidden messages being conveyed?
6. When you feel that the speaker or topic is boring, do you keep youself from tuning out and daydreaming about other matters?
7. Are you able to tolerate silence by sitting quietly and allowing the speaker time to gather thoughts and go on with the message?
8. As you listen, do you find yourself trying to pull together what the speaker is saying by thinking of what has been said and what seems to be coming?
9. As you listen, do you note the speaker's body language and try to incorporate this into your interpretation of the message?
10. If you disagree with what the speaker is saying, do you refrain from providing immediate feedback by shaking your head?
11. Do you sit quietly instead of moving around a great deal when listening, changing your posture, crossing and recrossing your arms and legs, and sliding back and forth in your chair?
12. When you listen, do you stare intensely into the speaker's eyes and try to maintain this directness throughout the time the person speaks?
13. When the other party is finished speaking, do you ask pointed and direct questions designed to clarify and amplify what was said?
14. If the speaker has been critical of you, do you refrain from trying to put down the speaker before addressing the substantive part of the message?

Scoring interpretation:
88-98 = Excellent. An ideal listener.
78-87 = Very good. You know a great deal about listening.
65-77 = Good.
50-64 = Average. Typical of most listeners.
Below 50 = Below average. You need to work on effective listening habits.

HOW TO REMEMBER MORE OF WHAT WE HEAR

The following list has tips to help improve retention of what we hear.

1. Give our undivided attention to what is being said.

2. Use imaging whenever possible.

3. If possible, repeat back what has been said to verify that you understood what was said.

4. Use the difference between speech speed and thought speed to:
   • mentally summarize what the speaker says
   • try to anticipate what the speaker will say next
   • evaluate the speaker's support or evidence
   • distinguish between facts and opinions
   • determine what is unsaid
   • try to identify the speaker's organizational patterns.

5. Apply appropriate mnemonic devices.

6. Write it down if possible.

7. Expose our mind to the information in a variety of ways—hear it, write it down, read it, and say it.

8. Repeat what we want to remember.

Listening is a skill. The keys to effective listening are: be flexible; listen for ideas; work at listening; resist distractions; exercise the mind; keep an open mind; judge content not delivery; practice restraint; and capitalize on thought speed.

"The problem with communication is the illusion that it has been accomplished." George Bernard Shaw.

REFERENCES

Alexander, Wilma Jean and Echternacht, Lonnie. "Developing Business Skills Needed in the 1990's." *Strategic Planning for the 1990's. NBEA YEARBOOK NO. 28.* p. 43-54.

Austin, Nancy K. *Working Woman.* New York. March 1991. pp. 46-47.

Birch, David L. "The Coming Demise of the Single-Career Career." *Journal-of-Career-Planning-and-Employment.* 1990. V50 - pp. 38-40.

Dychtwald, Ken. *Age Wave.* Tarcher. 1989.

Epstein, Cynthia Fuchs. "Symbolic Segregation: Similarities and Differences in the Language and Non-Verbal Communication of Women and Men." 1986. *Sociological-Forum;* winter, pp. 27-49.

Fennimore, Todd F. *The Helping Process Booklet for Mentors. Dropout Prevention Series.* 1988. Ohio State Univ. Natl Center for Research in Voc Ed.

Fireside, Bryna. *Choices, A Student Survival Guide for the 1990's.* 1989. p. 119.

Gall, M.D.; Gall, Joyce P.; Jacobsen, Dennis R.; Bullock, Terry L. *Tools for Learning.* ASCD. 1990. pp. 86-109.

Hanley, Nancy M. "Power, Sex, and Nonverbal Communication." *Journal of Sociology - Berkeley.* 1973-74. pp. 1-26.

Hodgetts, Richard M. *Modern Human Relations at Work.* The Dryden Press. 1987. pp. 387-393.

Lindner, A. Frances. *Life Skills Workbook: A Guide to Personal Growth, Career Survival Kit for Teen Education and Employment.* Wisconsin Univ. Vocational Studies Center. Order No. CSK201. 1987.

Pearce, C. Glenn; Figgins, Ross; Golen, Steven P. *Business Communication Principles and Applications.* John Wiley & Sons. NY. 1988.

Sheppard, Sharon. "The Informational Interview as a Tool for Sharpening Oral, Written, and Interviewing Skills." *Bulletin of the Assoc. for Bus. Communication;* V 52. June 1989. pp. 19-20.

Shockley-Zalabak, Pamela. *Fundamentals of Organizational Communication.* Longman. 1988. pp. 148-150.

Sweets, Paul W. and Peale, Norman Vincent. *The Art of Talking So That People Will Listen.* Prentice Hall. 1983.

Willmington, S. Clay. "Oral Communication for a Career in Business." *Bulletin of the Assoc. for Bus. Communication;* V 52. June 1989. pp. 8-12.

CHAPTER 9

Evaluation: A Tool for Learning and Identifying Talent

BETTY A. KLEEN

Nicholls State University, Thibodaux, Louisiana

Evaluation in the classroom is recognized as an integral part of the total instructional program, incorporating assessment of cognitive, affective, and psychomotor objectives. Davis reminds educators that evaluation and testing are *Not* synonymous, although many students and teachers typically think of tests and grades when the word is mentioned.[1] Within evaluation, it is important to remember that test scores are just one measurement. As business teachers at the middle school, high school, or postsecondary level plan evaluation, numerous techniques should be selected and used throughout the teaching/learning process.

As part of the instructional process, evaluation should be both formative and summative. It should be used for diagnosis, as well as a basis for determining grades. Formative evaluation, sometimes referred to as "informal" evaluation, should be used as the teacher and students progress through a topic of study. Formative evaluation provides feedback; it does not necessarily result in a grade. This category of evaluation techniques, used during a given lesson, helps a teacher determine if students are grasping concepts, processes, etc. Summative evaluation, often referred to as "formal" evaluation, is then used as a culminating evaluation.

An effective business teacher at any educational level recognizes the importance of evaluation as part of the entire instructional process involving both the teacher and the student. Educational evaluation is useful only to the extent that it helps the teacher, student, or administrator make sound educational judgments and decisions. If it is to help the student, then the student must be an active participant in the evaluation techniques.

As a teacher plans a course and accompanying evaluation, consideration must be given to the integration of basic skills into vocational education. A 1989 statement by the Policies Commission for Business and Economic Education concerning the role of business education as a component of general education supports the need for business educators to ". . . integrate the teaching of both academic and employability competencies throughout the

---

[1]Davis, Rodney E. "Construction of Evaluation Devices and Interpreting Results—Subject Matter Areas." *Evaluation and Accountability in Business Education,* NBEA Yearbook No. 16. Reston, VA: National Business Education Association, 1978. pp. 152-169.

business curriculum."[2] In a similar vein, a 1988 joint report from the U.S. Secretaries of Commerce, Education, and Labor, "Building a Quality Workforce," called for curriculum changes in order to achieve excellence in basic skills areas such as reading, writing, and oral communication.[3]

Numerous articles written in the last few years cite a need for students to develop critical thinking skills in the classroom. As Stone and Poole have stated, "To learn the theory of basic skills is only one component in the process of educating students. Critical thinking plays an important role, as students must take basic skills instruction and apply that instruction to solving problems in the world of work."[4]

Carefully planned evaluation techniques can go a step beyond helping educators determine if students have learned. Carefully designed, evaluation can be both a tool for learning and a tool for identifying talent. Evaluation techniques can be planned to assist students in developing their individual talents in all the areas identified above, although this is not always an easy task. Evaluation is more difficult in the higher levels of learning. Effective evaluation techniques should be selected for their educational impact, not merely for the purpose of teacher convenience.

A main goal of this chapter is to challenge the business educator to go beyond the basic level of evaluation for understanding and to select evaluation techniques that challenge and encourage each student to think and develop his or her own individual strengths. Carefully planned evaluation can help each student develop individual talents and abilities in such areas as thinking, reading, writing, calculating, following instructions, producing quality and quantity work, and being punctual and maintaining regular attendance.

ARE WE USING THE MOST EFFECTIVE EVALUATION METHODS?

John Goodlad's 1984 book, *A Place Called School: Prospects for the Future,* reports a dominance of student passivity at the high school level. Goodlad reported that students spent most of their in-class time listening, doing written work, and preparing for assignments; fewer activities involving active modes of learning were evident. Both academic and vocational classes were recipients of Goodlad's criticism.[5] Whether one agrees with Goodlad's educational reform ideas or not, his description of what is happening in the vocational classroom indicates a need for more active learning and more time devoted to instructional and evaluation activities.

Weber's recent study of vocational classrooms reported business education classroom activities differing somewhat from Goodlad's findings.

---

[2]"This We Believe About the Role of Business Education as a Component of General Education." *Business Education Forum* 44:7, October 1989.

[3]Sticht, Thomas G. "Functional Context Education." *Business Education World* 70 (Winter 1990): 25, 27.

[4]Stone, James R., and Vicki Poole. "Reinforcing the Basics Through Business Education." *Business Education for a Changing World*, NBEA Yearbook No. 25. Reston, VA: National Business Education Association, 1987. pp. 145-152.

[5]Goodlad, John. *A Place Called School: Prospects for the Future,* New York: McGraw Hill, 1984.

The dominant student activity, practice/performance of physical tasks, involved students in an active way. In addition, it appears that discussions, simulations/role playing, and reading occurred somewhat more frequently than was noted in the classrooms studied by Goodlad and his associates. Furthermore, in a majority of cases students appeared to have sizable control in carrying out their assigned tasks/activities.[6]

Weber further reported that questions posed by teachers often required an evaluation or judgment on the part of the students; students were also more frequently required to use higher-order thinking skills. Learners were more often involved in an active way, individually or in groups, and evaluative feedback was greater than that reported in Goodlad's earlier study.

Both Goodlad's studies and the Weber study identify room for improvement in evaluation techniques used in the vocational classroom if an instructor is to better facilitate the development of students' functional skills and talents and critical thinking skills. While Weber's study indicates that changes are being made in some vocational classrooms, more can be done to enhance the evaluation component of the learning process.

EFFECTIVE EVALUATION

As noted earlier, effective evaluation involves the learner and addresses cognitive, affective, and psychomotor domains. Carefully designed, it can serve as a sound motivational tool and can incorporate learning competitively, individually, and cooperatively in the classroom environment. Effective evaluation can lead the learner toward routine self-evaluation of learning or task completion. Crucial to the success of planned evaluation is that it is appropriate for the lesson content.

When a teacher employs alternatives to objective testing, many doors are opened. Students become active participants in the evaluation process rather than passive participants. The teacher also opens the door to covering neglected areas of instruction and incorporating a learner's awareness of his/her own performance. This ability to conduct self-evaluation is a necessary trait students need not only to enter the work force but also to take advantage of upward job mobility.

Student-centered methods of evaluation may be perceived as more attractive by some students. They replace activities such as filling in worksheet blanks. Student-centered methods, as opposed to teacher lecture followed by rote questioning where students are required to "throw back" facts presented during the lecture, help motivate students. Student-centered methods may sacrifice efficiency, but they can generate effectiveness.

INDIVIDUAL, COMPETITIVE, AND COOPERATIVE EVALUATION TECHNIQUES

An instructor charged with the task of evaluating students should use individual, competitive, and cooperative techniques. The lesson content,

[6]Weber, James M. "Instructional Methods in the Business Classrooms." *Journal of Education for Business* 63 (May 1988): 341-351.

number of students involved, number and type of instruments used, scoring techniques used, and time factors (time of actual evaluation and time away from routinely planned activities) must all be considered when selecting an appropriate evaluation technique. While costs and benefits of various evaluation methods must be weighed, effectiveness is often more important than efficiency.

Certain skills courses may by nature require more evaluation techniques based on the individual student. It is important that each student master keyboarding of letters or manuscripts. Likewise, it is important that each student understand how to complete an accounting worksheet accurately. Other courses such as basic business, business law, information processing, and office practice present greater opportunities for cooperative learning and evaluation of those cooperative learning activities.

Johnson, Johnson, and Holubec, strong supporters of cooperative learning, state, "Cooperative learning promotes a greater use of higher reasoning strategies and critical thinking than do competitive and individualistic learning strategies."[7] Elements of cooperative learning evaluation help develop positive interdependence, face-to-face interaction, interpersonal and small group skills, and group processing. At the same time, cooperative learning also requires individual accountability for each student within the group. Students can be required to evaluate both the entire group and individual members at the end of a group activity.

In the sections which follow, numerous individual, competitive, and cooperative learning evaluation techniques are presented. When used correctly, they allow students an opportunity to develop their own talents in thinking, communicating, planning, and decision making, and provide opportunities for students to practice reading, writing, and speaking skills.

QUESTIONING: AN EFFECTIVE EVALUATION TOOL

Questioning is an interaction-oriented evaluation technique that gets the students involved. Evaluation is achieved through questioning, probing, and responding. This type of evaluation is more appropriate for advanced objectives such as application, analysis, evaluation, and synthesis, and for the affective domain. Questioning activities can stimulate thought and creativity within each individual. A student can be challenged to open his/her views for critical analysis, as well as be challenged to develop more effective communication skills.

The teacher must plan in advance to ensure that questioning techniques get the best results. As questions are prepared, the following points should be considered:

1. Ask logically sequenced questions rather than only random, spontaneous questions to help students drive toward full understanding. If only spontaneous, factual questions are asked, students have no model of questions that stimulate critical thinking.

[7]Johnson, David W., Roger T. Johnson and Edythe Johnson Holubec. *Cooperation in the Classroom.* 3:18. Edina, MS: Interaction Book Company, 1990.

2. Ask questions requiring deeper thought, rather than "yes" or "no" answers. A successful questioner utilizes different categories of questions to challenge students. Action questions call on students to respond to "What would you do if you were . . . ?" Extension questions ask a student to elaborate or explain ramifications. Synthesis questions require a student to explain how a comment relates to the previous comment. Challenging questions ask a student, "so what?" Hypothetical questions of "suppose that" or "let us assume that" require analysis and evaluation. Summary questions such as "what can we conclude?" require evaluation and synthesis.

3. Ask questions to which students respond based on their own understanding and for their own benefit, rather than asking leading or teacher-centered questions.

4. Wait for a response from someone in the class rather than supplying the answer for the students. This also discourages shallow thinking on the part of the students.

5. Allow student/student dialogues rather than insisting on only teacher/student dialogues. Allow students to talk more (in a controlled and directed manner) rather than the teacher talking too much.

While clearly challenging students, teacher questions should also guarantee a good chance of success. Giving slower students an opportunity to respond to recall questions while providing opportunities for brighter students to analyze, summarize, or debate points can meet the needs of all students. The entire class should have an opportunity to participate—a careful teacher can draw even the introverts into the activity. Correct answers and partially correct answers should be acknowledged. Positive feedback promotes self-esteem; the instructor must always consider the effect of teacher response on a student's dignity.

While using the questioning technique for evaluation, the teacher must remain alert to prevent monopolization of the conversation by a few, glibness on the part of other students, and talking without saying anything pertinent by others. Although this method may pose difficulty if trying to assign a grade, it can be most beneficial in determining if a lesson is "getting across."

A well-planned questioning session provides feedback to the teacher and to the student, gets the students actively involved, and is more interesting than rote response questions. Teachers must recognize that a key first step in teaching students how to formulate their own questions is to serve as a model of good questioning behavior.

OBSERVATIONS

Observation using checklists or rating scales can be a very valuable tool for process evaluation. Keyboarding teachers have relied on observation sheets for many years to assist in evaluating students' techniques in the classroom. The observation sheet markings then serve as a diagnosis vehicle and a focus for subsequent attention to modifying process. The observation sheet provides a means to evaluate the students at work rather than being the final product.

To be most effective, observation of process should be controlled, organized and systematic. In a course such as keyboarding, specifically designed checklists should be prepared to ensure that all necessary process factors are observed. Students should be observed for a particular process on a particular day; another process should be systematically observed on another day.

Observation as an evaluation tool need not be limited to skills courses. Used as an evaluation technique for activities such as preparation of an oral report, a checklist can focus on factors such as content, form, and delivery.

Observation of work habits can be through anecdotal records, behavior diary records, behavior summaries of observations over a period of time, or behavior rating or attitude scales. Observation sheets can include habits such as beginning work promptly, having materials available, planning work effectively, using equipment correctly, following directions, being cooperative, displaying initiative, and maintaining a neat work area. Rating sheets with scales from 1 to 5 or descriptors such as excellent, good, fair, and poor can be designed.

Valuation of work habits as an actual component of a student's final grade, however, should only be used if the learners clearly understand at the beginning of the semester what constitutes good work habits. This requires a full explanation by the teacher. If used as a component of the student's final grade, specific incidences of less than desirable work habits and continual anecdotal evidence must be recorded to substantiate any final grade given for work habits.

Another way to assign points for work attitudes is to give all students a certain number of points at the beginning of the semester. An infraction of classroom rules, poor work habits such as borrowing supplies, etc., would result in the loss of a certain number of these points. Students typically do not like to lose points and will strive to maintain good work habits and abide by classroom rules.

While checklists and rating scales are helpful in keeping observations focused on key points or allowing observational data to be used in making quality judgments as well as quantitative judgments, they take time and effort to construct and can be clumsy to use if too complex. Checklists measure only the presence or absence of a trait or behavior. When designing such checklists or scales, the teacher should plan to keep the form short, make each item clear, focus on only observable characteristics or behaviors, include only important characteristics, and arrange the form for easy use.

CASE STUDIES

Use of case studies for evaluation purposes can help a teacher determine if students have grasped basic concepts. Case studies present a prime opportunity to encourage students to develop critical thinking skills. Students are required to zero in on the problem, examine contingencies and consequences, and make a decision. This can be done either individually or within the framework of cooperative learning. Students receive additional practice in refining organizational skills and analyzing and interpreting relevant facts.

Interpersonal skills are also polished when the case study technique is structured as a group project.

If students are unfamiliar with the case study method, initial use of this method can include a guided design by the teacher. Going through the case step by step and guiding the discussion, asking "what is the problem?" "what caused the problem?" etc., helps prepare students for future case work with less teacher guidance. Closure could be from several groups presenting ideas while the teacher or other students critique the presentations. In a guided design, the teacher then gives the final closure, seeking to reemphasize major points related to the intended lesson.

To further assist learners in practicing basic functional skill development, each student should be required to take individual responsibility for the analysis. Each must be prepared to contribute to the discussion, must be responsible for sharing ideas with classmates, and must be responsible for subjecting ideas to debate and criticism. The teacher can require the students to complete any necessary mathematical calculations, draw upon their own experiences as they consider consequences of various alternatives, and tie in content from other courses.

Students can be challenged to bring originality into the classroom presentation of a case. Originality should be rewarded; there is more than one way to get a right answer and sometimes more than one right answer. If brainstorming activities are used while identifying alternatives, no suggestion should be labeled unacceptable during the brainstorming time.

Case study work can also be a basis for formal evaluation (grade assignment). Qualitative participation should be analyzed for this purpose, including a thorough analysis, proper substantiation of position, extension of knowledge, getting to the heart of key issues, and distinction between fact and opinion. If used as a regular part of class work, a grade can be assigned to each student each day the case analysis method is used. By referring to a seating chart, the teacher can make notes, record special comments, and later post daily grades in the gradebook. Some cases can be done in class and some can be take-home cases, providing additional variety to the case approach and dividing group and individual work.

ORAL AND WRITTEN REPORTS

Oral and written reports present an opportunity for students to demonstrate initiative and creativity, as well as expand their understanding of lesson or unit concepts. A short oral report may be assigned to individual students or to a group. The report can be based on findings from a homework activity or an in-class activity such as case analysis. Likewise, written reports may be required of individual learners or groups.

If a grade is to be assigned, oral report evaluation can focus on delivery, content, and form. For assignment of a grade to written reports, depth of coverage, number and types of sources consulted, ability to summarize and synthesize, concern for accuracy, and neatness should also be incorporated into the evaluation scheme.

INDIVIDUAL STUDENT CONFERENCES

Teacher-student conferences provide an additional evaluation opportunity. Whether the conference is a very brief and in-class conference related to improving a process, or a somewhat longer and private conference, this evaluation method allows the evaluator to show personal interest in the student's progress, a personal interest that may not be evident to the student in other evaluation activities. As always, the instructor must be conscious of respecting a student's individual dignity during the conference. An individual conference may be the best means of assisting a student in improving affective domain skills.

ROLE PLAYING

Role playing allows students to participate in acting out a situation to illustrate points or better understand a concept. During early stages of studying a topic, the teacher can choose to provide a highly structured role-playing situation. As the class studies a topic in more depth, the teacher can switch to moderately structured situations. Relatively unstructured situations may call upon students to do the deepest level of thinking as they are involved in the role play. Those not actually involved as "players" can serve as evaluators; this ensures that those observing are exercising good listening skills and developing their own critical thinking skills.

DEBATES

Debates provide yet another means for student involvement and participation. When debating, students further develop skills in presenting ideas, listening, organizing thoughts, interacting with others, and thinking critically. While it is usually impossible to involve all students in the actual debate, even if teams are formed, those in the audience can be called upon to act as a jury and make a decision as to which team debated best. This also requires listening skills, organizing thoughts, thinking critically, and some interaction with others while the jury is reaching a decision.

HOMEWORK EVALUATION

Homework can be an effective learning tool if planned feedback is reasonably comprehensive. Completeness and accuracy of homework, or lack of completeness and accuracy, can identify areas of understanding or non-understanding. Any assigned homework should contribute to a student's achievement, and the purpose of any homework should be clear. When appropriate, homework assignments can be individualized. If homework is used as a true diagnostic tool, immediate feedback should be provided to the student.

Picking up homework and returning it three days later with an assigned grade may do virtually no good. Simply checking answers as right or wrong or giving a numerical grade is not the solution, either. To allow students to benefit from homework as an evaluation tool, papers should be checked in class. Answers and explanations of answers should be provided. Students can always check each other's papers if some type of homework grade is to be assigned.

Spot-checking homework and giving a grade may be more effective than giving pop quizzes on homework. This can benefit the student who has at least tried the homework but does not know it well enough to pass a quiz. Some teachers may prefer to offer an option of dropping the lowest quiz grade and replacing it with a 100 percent if all homework for the grading period has been submitted. This gives an additional incentive for completing the homework and attending class.

PRACTICE SETS AND SIMULATIONS

Practice sets or simulations, whether completed individually or as a cooperative activity, call upon the student to plan work, draw upon previous learnings, make decisions, complete the work, and evaluate the product. Completion of a practice set requires interpretation of data in order to arrive at an appropriate solution. Both personal skills and technical skills can be evaluated as students complete a practice set. Supplemented by teacher discussion and follow-up, as well as worksheets when required, they serve as effective ways to evaluate the learner's progress in the course.

Today's computerized practice sets designed for accounting, recordkeeping, office practice, etc., seemingly increase opportunities for undetected copying. This copying results in no learning by the student who has copied the work. Teachers must regroup to evaluate in other ways, such as giving quizzes to reveal knowledge of printed data and *requiring completion* of practice sets rather than *grading* the completed set.

STUDENT SELF-EVALUATION

Students are helped to grow to maturity by accepting responsibility. Truly effective evaluation in the business classroom will provide students an opportunity to learn self-evaluation. Letting the learner out of the classroom with very little ability to judge his or her own work is doing a great disservice to that individual. Employers are looking for those who can evaluate their own work for accuracy, completeness, and overall quality.

Students can learn to do this by serving on grading or proofreading committees, or at minimum exchanging papers with other students in the class to evaluate others' work. A grading committee could be established to evaluate both daily work and more comprehensive written reports and projects. Individual self-evaluation sheets can also be used in instances where students have completed a "job." Students often progress to a higher degree of mastery when they perform self-evaluation during the learning process and prior to the formal, terminal evaluation of the teacher.

MAKING CLASS TIME COUNT

Although each lesson is planned carefully, business teachers at all levels recognize that some class time is routinely lost to administrative activities. This administrative time can also be used for student formative evaluation. A brief quiz on previous lessons can be projected on a transparency at the beginning of class. By routinely being given only a specified period of time and no extra allowances for tardiness, students soon learn to be on time. Restricting the time limit also requires the teacher to handle administrative details efficiently. While all quiz grades may be recorded, perhaps only the top 10 of the 15 or 20 given would be averaged for a grade. This serves as an additional reward for good attendance. Checking and explaining answers in class provides immediate feedback of understanding of key points.

Keyboarding teachers have long noted the value of warm-up drills at the beginning of class. After making certain that early in the semester students understand the procedures, this time is not wasted as attendance is taken, homework returned, etc. Students use the time to assess their individual skill levels.

DIFFERENT EVALUATION TECHNIQUES FOR DIFFERENT COURSES

Business education encompasses a variety of courses, and not all evaluation techniques can be used successfully in each course. The type of evaluation method selected should relate to the teaching aimed at, whether that teaching be knowledge, analysis, or synthesis oriented, or whether it be cognitive, affective, or psychomotor domain. The evaluation technique selected should fit the teacher's style, the nature of the subject matter, the size of the class, and the students' abilities.

In the sections that follow, sample evaluation techniques are identified that can assist the teacher and the individual student in determining if learning is taking place. At the same time, these evaluation techniques can help individual students develop their thinking and problem solving skills. Many of the techniques require communicating, planning, and decision making, either individually or in a cooperative learning situation. While not all-inclusive, the courses listed below reflect key areas of administrative support, basic business, and accounting.

Accounting and recordkeeping. Application exercises, problems, and/or production work are typical homework activities in an accounting class. To enhance learner self-evaluation, comprehensive and immediate feedback related to homework assignments is needed. Questioning sessions must require students to go beyond rote memorization of facts, procedures, and processes. Observation checklists focusing on work habits may be completed by the instructor as students complete practice sets or simulations. Students should also critique their own work for accuracy, completeness, neatness, etc.

Basic business and business law. Checklists, attitude inventories, simulations, case studies, reports, role playing, questioning sessions, student self-evaluation, oral or written reports, and debates can all be incorporated into individual classes and serve as a basic for formative evaluation. Some of these activities, scheduled at the end of a topic of study, can also serve as summative evaluation activities. Basic business offers many opportunities for both individual and cooperative learning activities as a means of formative evaluation.

Business English and business communication. Although the content of this course may vary significantly from state to state, instructors may find an activity such as requiring students to keep a personal journal on business-related topics an effective way to encourage independent and critical thinking. Teachers may find it difficult to find time to read the journals, but they must be read if the activity is to become an effective evaluation tool. Other formative evaluation activities may include either cooperative or individual efforts relating to letter, memo, and report writing.

Cooperative education and office practice. As an effective means of encouraging and refining student self-evaluation, students can be asked to complete weekly report forms and periodic self-assessment forms, identifying problems faced and solved on the job, areas needing improvement, and overall progress on the job. These evaluation activities can be conducted in addition to formative and summative evaluation conducted by the teacher in the related classroom instructional environment. Problems and/or production work can be used for both formative and summative evaluation in office practice class. Performance appraisals of in-class work can focus on personal traits, ability, skill performance, business techniques, and attendance. Students can be provided opportunities to work in committees to solve various office problems.

Information processing. While this is another course for which content may differ significantly from state to state, the instructor once again has many opportunities for selecting evaluation techniques that encourage the student to further develop basic skills while working either individually or in a cooperative activity. By requiring students to make presentations on how to complete certain computer tasks, an instructor can evaluate the student's understanding of process and procedures while also providing an opportunity for practice in planning, decision making, organizing, and communicating.

Keyboarding. Robinson, Erickson, Crawford, Beaumont, and Ownby remind instructors to make more frequent use of formative evaluation—not for a grade but to focus on specific learning activities necessary for progress toward performance goals.[8] This formative evaluation should occur on a daily basis in keyboarding classes to enhance instructional effectiveness. Rating sheets can be used for recording and quantifying work habit levels. Technique evaluation can be measured by teacher observation and completion of checklists or rating sheets. Basic skill development can be monitored through straight copy and statistical copy timings, problems, and/or production work. Grading in keyboarding classes is conducted only periodically to determine the level and quality of student performance. Summative evaluation in

---

[8]Robinson, Jerry W., L. W. Erickson, T. J. Crawford, L. R. Beaumont, and A. C. Ownby. *Typewriting: Learning and Instruction.* Cincinnati: South-Western Publishing Company, 1979.

advanced keyboarding requires the learner to demonstrate skill and knowledge in use.

CONCLUSION

Evaluation is an integral part of the total instructional program in the business classroom. As such, evaluation must be both formative and summative, informal and formal. To prepare our students for tomorrow's world of work, instructors must give attention to the integration of basic skills and employability competencies. Students must be helped to develop critical thinking skills. Business classroom evaluation techniques must provide opportunities for students to think, communicate, plan, and make decisions. The evaluation techniques must incorporate reading, writing, and oral communication.

Individual, competitive, and cooperative learning techniques may be used for formative evaluation. Questioning sessions, observations, case studies, oral and written reports, individual student conferences, role playing, debates, homework, practice sets and simulations, and student self-evaluation all provide effective means for the teacher and the learner to work together to evaluate learning. A variety of carefully chosen evaluation techniques properly administered can help each student master content, strengthen basic skills, and improve critical thinking skills. Evaluation *can* be a tool for learning and for identifying talent.

CHAPTER 10

Characteristics of Learning and Associated Outcomes

H. DALTON DRENNAN and JOE E. SAWYER

Middle Tennessee State University, Murfreesboro

Observers of the educational scene over the years will probably agree that there are three constants that must be considered when developing teaching strategies and learning activities. These are—

1. How students learn
2. What teaching strategies facilitate meaningful learning
3. Relevancy of material used in the classroom.

The purpose of this chapter is to reexamine the most basic of these education components: the teacher's desire to make learning more meaningful. Teachers realize that there is no one best way of teaching all students. Students and teachers have different perceptions and learning styles, and often, they assimilate and process information in different ways.

When teachers realize that students have different learning styles, they are in a position to teach students in ways they learn best. Teachers will then be able to develop an integrated framework of instructional strategies and classroom activities that they feel fit their students, their own teaching styles, and content areas. Only then will the goal of integrating learning skills into the curriculum become a reality.

SOME BASIC LEARNING CHARACTERISTICS AFFECTING STUDENT BEHAVIOR

As shown in Chart 1, there are a myriad of factors that influence learning outcomes. The backbone of any model of instruction that promotes student participation and motivation, however, is an understanding of the education taxonomy that Bloom and Associates used to classify learning in categories (or domains). These domains are—

1. Cognitive learning: relating the knowledge, analyzing, understanding, and decision making
2. Psychomotor learning: muscular (or motor) and manipulative skills
3. Affective learning: forming attitudes and values that influence actions.

Based on the writings of Benjamin S. Bloom and others, the educational taxonomy is organized into six major classes: knowledge, comprehension, application, analysis, synthesis, and evaluation. Many times the objectives in one class are built on the behaviors found in the preceding classes. The following information is based on some of Bloom's ideas.

Knowledge. Knowledge more often than not is the only educational objective that involves the psychological processes of remembering; however, it may also include the processes of relating and judging. Much is taught in business subjects that could be classified in this area—especially in general business and economics, where there are isolated bits of information. Knowledge, however, is always partial and relative since we are now told that each seven years knowledge doubles.

Business teachers have always taught many subjects that would come under the classification of knowledge. This may be justified because as a person increases the amount of information he or she knows, that individual becomes more familiar with and more capable of being involved in the day-to-day activities in life. Some of the knowledge that is gained in business subjects is reasonably stable, yet many of the topics change rapidly.

In most business subjects, the teaching of knowledge is usually basic to the subject, because that is the prerequisite for a higher level of learning. One cannot continue to learn accounting without the basic knowledge of the content of the preceding chapter. All of the other classifications of educational taxonomies make use of or are based upon knowledge.

Business teachers realize that it is easier to learn and retain knowledge related to other classes or subjects than isolated facts. Examples of knowledge include—

1. Important accounting terms
2. Economic concepts
3. Correct forms of usage in business writing and speaking
4. Rules of punctuation
5. Factors that determine economic trends
6. Characteristics of the various forms of business ownership.

Comprehension. Most writers seem to believe that the largest general class of intellectual abilities and skills are those that involve comprehension. The emphasis here is on communication, where the teacher expects students to be able to use the information and ideas communicated—whether the communication be oral, written, or in some symbolic form. For example, business teachers will lecture in an economics class, require typewritten assignments after a demonstration, and expect students to be able to write shorthand after the symbols have been demonstrated and practiced.

In addition to reading comprehension, other types of comprehension are considered in this category—that of translation, interpretation, and extrapolation. At the comprehension level, one may understand what is being communicated without necessarily relating it to other materials or understanding its fullest implication. Examples of comprehension include—

1. The translation of shorthand symbols into printed form
2. The ability to take a business report and translate it into an abstract
3. The ability to take a graph and explain it

4. The ability to translate relationships expressed in symbolic form such as maps in economic geography, graphs in economics, etc.

5. The ability to prepare graphical material from raw data

6. The ability to comprehend and interpret financial statements with depth and clarity

7. The ability to predict an economic trend.

Application. Application builds upon knowledge and comprehension. A student moves from comprehension to application when the student can take a situation, demonstrate what has been learned, and actually apply it correctly in another situation where the solution is not specified. The majority of what is taught in business classes appears to be application. Examples of application include—

1. The ability to use research procedures to answer questions about marketing or advertising

2. The ability to apply business laws to practical situations

3. The ability to take information from bids made for equipment and place it on a bid summary

4. The ability to change an alphabetic filing system into a geographic system.

Analysis. Analysis is an even more advanced skill than comprehension and application; analysis may be an aid to fuller comprehension. One finds that lines cannot be clearly drawn to indicate an ending point for comprehension and the beginning of analysis. Comprehension involves content; analysis involves content and form. For example, analysis may be subdivided into three parts:

1. To identify or classify the *elements*

2. To show the *relationship* among the elements

3. To recognize the *organizational principles,* the arrangement, and structure

Examples of analysis include—

1. Ability to recognize unstated assumptions after reading a business report

2. Ability to distinguish a conclusion from statements which support it in a business report

3. Ability to comprehend the interrelationships among the ideas presented in a business letter

4. Ability to distinguish the relevant from irrelevant in all business subjects

5. Ability to understand the persuasive parts of advertising materials

6. Ability to recognize bias in business research.

Synthesis. Synthesis is the bringing together of all elements and parts to form the whole. In many instances, synthesis provides the student an opportunity for creativity. Within this opportunity for creativity one still finds certain limitations that may have been set based upon each particular problem.

Less uniqueness and originality exist in comprehension, application, and analysis than in synthesis because synthesis requires that elements be combined. Synthesis is unique because it allows students to put their own ideas, feelings, and experiences into an assignment. Examples of synthesis include—

1. Ability and skill to write various types of business letters—goodwill, bad news, application, etc.
2. Ability to make a business speech and relate a personal experience to the topic
3. Ability to make an investigative study, then take the results and be able to offer a solution to the problem
4. Ability to plan a course in international business communication
5. Ability to draw a layout of a business department in a secondary school according to specific information, which may be furnished by administrators.

Evaluation. Evaluation may be defined as making a judgment about the value of ideas, works, solutions, methods, and materials. It involves the use of criteria that may either be determined by the student or given to the student by the teacher. Evaluation, considered the last stage of the process, involves some combination of the knowledge, comprehension, application, analysis, and synthesis.

Even though evaluation may be listed as last in the cognitive domain, it is not the end of thinking or problem solving. One might consider the evaluative process as the forerunner to the acquisition of new knowledge, a new effort at comprehension or application, or a new analysis and synthesis.

Business teachers seem to be involved very heavily in evaluations on the basis of internal standards; yet, those standards may not be in agreement with external standards. A student may produce a flawless document in word processing, yet the document itself might not be of much value to business personnel because of its content. Examples of evaluation include—

1. Comparisons of American and Japanese management styles
2. Decisions as to whether students need to be taught keyboarding skills on typewriters or microcomputers
3. Questions about the conclusions listed in a business report—whether they follow logically the content found in the report
4. Questions as to whether the standards used in word processing and shorthand classes are compatible with business standards.

OTHER LEARNING CONCEPTS FOR TEACHER APPLICATION

Today, there appear to be two major families or groupings of learning theory and many subgroupings within these families; but for business teachers it is usually enough to be aware only of the two families of theory.

One learning-theory position stresses stimulus-response association. It includes all the reinforcement and conditioning theories of learning. Experience appears to be a major factor in these theories.

The second of the two learning-theory families contains the Gestalt-Field, cognitive-field, and perceptual-field points of view. This view suggests that behavior is a function of perception and that meaning within the person determines behavior.

Numerous learning concepts exist in education that have the capability of developing research findings that may aid teachers in synthesizing learning theories. Eight of these concepts have been identified and are enumerated below for teacher consideration:[1]

1. *Identification.* Students learn by and through identification with others, including their parents, peers, and teachers. Thus it is important that they have good models.

2. *Learning by discovery.* Obtaining knowledge for oneself by the use of one's own mind frequently has advantages in terms of motivation, organization of what is learned, retention, and meaningfulness.

3. *Empathy.* Openness, trust, and security in human relationships free intelligence and enable students and teachers to learn more and to be more successful in joint activities.

4. *Culture potential.* Anthropological studies have emphasized that different societies and cultures cultivate different qualities and capacities. Learning experiences that build on the cultural capacities of individuals and groups are particularly successful.

5. *Knowledge about learners.* Research has shown that students learn more when teachers know them as individuals.

6. *Methods of increasing transfer.* When the teacher points out the possibility of transfer and develops and applies generalizations with the learners, transfer is more likely to occur.

7. *Zeal for learning and knowledge.* Students like learning from teachers who love knowledge, from communities that provide resources for learning, and from a home environment that supports the search for knowledge by example and by the materials provided.

8. *Sex differences.* Too little attention is given to the differences in interests, needs, and problems of students in the school curriculum.

Of specific interest to business teachers are six types of learning outcomes that have grown out of educational theories that are especially relevant for business education.[2] Five of these outcomes are described below:

1. *Associated learning.* Associated learning occurs in every business course since each subject area has its unique vocabulary and its essential factual content that students need to know and remember.

2. *Pure-practice learning.* Like associated learning, pure-practice learning is common to every business course. Pure-practice learning means that the student already knows how to perform a task and is merely doing additional practice to make the process automatic and to increase the ease and efficiency of performance.

3. *Discovery-cognitive learning.* Thinking and understanding learning, to some extent, pervades all learning as the student is expected to act with some degree of intelligence about the content of any course.

---

[1]Hass, Glen, and others. *Readings in Curriculum.* Second Edition. Boston, MA: Allyn and Bacon, 1970. pp. 195-96.

[2]Calhoun, Calfrey C. *Managing the Learning Process in Business Education.* Bessemer, AL: Colonial Press, 1988. pp. 20-27.

4. *Appreciational-humanistic learning.* Appreciational learning, which seeks to develop positive attitudes, appears in every business course because the student consciously or unconsciously makes value judgments and adopts certain attitudes and behavior patterns.

5. *Perceptual-motor learning.* In perceptual-motor learning, perceptual learning relates to analysis and organization of sensory experiences for the eyes, ears, and muscles. Motor learning consists of the coordination of muscular responses. This type of learning is most evident in skill development.

IMPLICATIONS OF LEARNING FOR TEACHER CONSIDERATION

Business teachers who realize that learning outcomes and student involvement are not structurally dissimilar will add depth, totality, and realism to their classroom activities. Effective teachers have their own styles of teaching. They also respect the individuality of their students in the realization that students learn through their own perceptions.

Teaching is at its most efficacious when sound learning tactics are inherent in each classroom activity. Some of these basic learning principles are listed below to provide business teachers with a frame of reference in designing and revising their classroom activities.

1. Students must build from things they have experienced or understand.

2. *How* a course is being taught should receive as much emphasis as *what* is being taught.

3. The integration of teaching strategies and learning activities provides the relevancy needed for a positive transfer of learning.

4. Motivation is best achieved through realistic classroom activities that allow students to play active roles in the learning process.

5. Effective teacher modeling is required for establishing and maintaining a classroom ambiance conducive to learning.

6. Classroom instruction utilizing a variety of teaching strategies and materials provides more opportunities for students to experience the success of meaningful learning within the range of their abilities.

SUMMARY

In the final analysis, the hidden agenda of an instructional program is the development of learning objectives and effective learning environments that recognize students' needs in constructing meanings and relationships. Emphasis should be placed on both the process and the product. A successful infusion of learning strategies into the classroom will develop student understandings that are transferable to other classes, daily activities, and work activities.

REFERENCES

The American Heritage Dictionary of the English Language. Boston: Houghton Mifflin Company, 1980.

Bloom, Benjamin S., *et al. Taxonomy of Educational Objectives.* New York: David McKay Company, Inc., 1956.

Calhoun, Calfrey C. *Managing the Learning Process in Business Education.* Bessemer, AL: Colonial Press, 1988.

Gartner, William B., Mitchell, Terence R., and Vesper, Karl H. "A Taxonomy of New Business Ventures." *Journal of Business Venturing* 4:169-186, May 1989.

Hass, Glen, *et al. Readings in Curriculum.* Second edition. Boston: Allyn and Bacon, 1970.

Reeves, Francis M. "An Application of Bloom's Taxonomy to the Teaching of Business Ethics." *Journal of Business Ethics* 9:609-616, July 1990.

Van Wyk, Rias J. "Technology Analysis and R & D Management." *R & D Management* 20:257-261, July 1990.

106

CHAPTER 11

Active Learning Through Structured Grouping in the Classroom

GALEN MILLER

Formerly of California State Polytechnic University, Pomona

CAROL MONTHEI

Colorado State University, Fort Collins

The ultimate goal of any business education program is to prepare students for the world of work. In earlier times, preparing students for work meant teaching them the technical skills needed to perform specific tasks on the job. However, in today's modern workplace, workers need much more than the technical skills to do the job. Today's workers also need skills in effective communication, problem solving, creative thinking, decision making, and human relations.

In many traditional classrooms, students sit quietly in assigned seats in neat rows, working individually and competitively with little or no inter-action. Business and industry experts point out that this is not conducive to preparing students for today's work environment. In the modern workplace persons are not expected to sit quietly for long periods of time, solve problems quickly and privately, and provide a finished product with little or no feedback. Rather, persons are expected to work as a team using creative thinking and logical reasoning to solve complex, conceptual problems.

To prepare students for the modern workplace and to improve the educational learning process, innovative teachers are using an instructional strategy called active learning. Active learning is the process of consistently engaging the learner's mind through learning by doing.[1]

One method of involving students actively and successfully in the learning process is to group students. However, *proper* grouping is essential to the success of grouped learning activities. Too often teachers use random grouping—grouping students with no consideration for the goals and expected outcomes of the learning activity. Random grouping can result in the failure of an otherwise well-planned lesson. In contrast, structured grouping is an organized, efficient, planned procedure for grouping students.

Structured grouping is not a new concept. For example, the authors remember grouping experiences during elementary school. Being a member of the bluebirds, working diligently to "fly up" to the redbirds, and praying

---

[1]California Business Education Subject Matter Project.

you wouldn't become one of the dreaded sparrows is a not-so-fond memory of learning to read. This type of grouping is structured, organized, efficient, and planned. But, it is homogeneous in nature, that is, students of the same ability are grouped together, and the homogeneous approach often creates poor self-esteem, ridicule, and labeling of students.

A more modern and socially beneficial approach—heterogeneous, structured grouping—is used by teachers who are aware of the importance of celebrating students' diversity. Gender, race, ethnicity, and ability are represented in the groups; therefore, labeling of students—one of the most detrimental causes of low self esteem—is reduced and/or eliminated.

Structured grouping is not a panacea for all instructional ills. Structured grouping is appropriate when outcome goals are related to improving the intellectual thinking and social skills of students, or enhancing classroom management.

WHEN TO USE STRUCTURED GROUPING

Intellectual Thinking. One of the most serious criticisms of today's school curriculum is the lack of opportunity for students to learn creative problem-solving techinques.[2] Business and industry are demanding workers who are able to synthesize abstract ideas and to think in a creative, analytical, and logical manner. Nevertheless, teachers often, after introducing a new concept, check for students' understanding by requiring written papers and seatwork. Assigning isolated, individual projects does not promote nor teach the type of higher-order thinking skills required in today's work environment.

A basic premise of vocational education is hands-on application so students can practice and reinforce their technical skills (i.e., hard skills). Structured grouping activities can be used as a hands-on technique to let students practice and reinforce their conceptual, analytical, and creative thinking skills (i.e., soft skills). Structured grouping activities give students an opportunity to actively engage in debate, discussion, consensus, the democratic process, concept attainment, and synthesis. As students practice these conceptual processes, they become more adept in using these soft skills—just as they become more adept in using their hard skills through practice and reinforcement activities.

Social Skills. When a prospective employee is interviewed for a job, very little interview time is spent determining the technical expertise of the candidate. Technical expertise can be determined easily by school transcripts and reference checks. The vast majority of interview time is spent attempting to determine if the interviewee has the interpersonal and social skills necessary to become a successful member of the organizational team. Furthermore, according to business and industry experts, persons seldom get fired from their job because of a lack of technical knowledge or expertise. Rather, workers who are fired often lose their jobs because they do not have the social skills to interact with their coworkers and supervisors.

---

[2]Cohen, Elizabeth. *Designing Groupwork: Strategies for the Heterogeneous Classroom.* New York: Teachers College Press, 1986.

Strategy grouping is an ideal way to help students learn social and inter-personal skills at the same time they are learning content and intellectual thinking processes. Research has shown that interracial relationships among students are improved through the interaction provided by structured grouping activities.[3] Also, when a teacher delegates authority to a structured group, the group has the opportunity to actively control the learning environment as opposed to the passive teacher-directed environment of a traditional classroom. Students are able to practice active listening techniques, to learn how to work with and accept other peoples' ideas, and to accomplish team-identified goals (as opposed to individualistic goals).

Using strategy grouping gives students the opportunity to practice oral language skills. Many students need the opportunity to practice expressing themselves in a clear and concise manner. The active learning atmosphere of a small group is much more conducive to practicing language proficiency than a teacher-directed activity.

Classroom Management. A great deal of valuable time is wasted when students are allowed to sit idly while the teacher completes administrative paperwork (e.g., taking role, passing back homework, etc.). If a teacher does not begin instructional class activities for the first five minutes of a 50-minute class period and stops instructional activities three minutes before the end of the period, 16 percent of the instructional time has been wasted.

Structured grouping is one method to engage students in learning activities immediately upon entering the classroom. Predetermined groupings and a previously assigned activity will engage the students in active learning while the teacher completes administrative paperwork. Students need to be taught that wasting time is not acceptable or productive. After all, business and industry expects more than an 84 percent effort from workers!

Also, educational experts are concerned with the amount of time students are actually engaged in learning. Often, when seatwork is assigned, the students who need to work the hardest to learn the material are the students who are doing everything but the assigned work. These unmotivated students see no relevance in seatwork assignments. They have no motivation to stay on task except the teacher's continual admonishments to "get to work." However, the peer-dominated, interactive nature of structured groupwork is more likely to capture and hold the interest of the less motivated student. Furthermore, group accountability is a strong motivator to keep everyone in the group actively engaged in the task at hand.

A big frustration for many teachers is how to deal effectively with the wide range of student ability. Research shows that homogeneous ability grouping and individualized seatwork are not particularly effective.[4] However, heterogeneous-ability grouping can benefit both low and high achievers. Low achievers can receive additional exposure to the material through the verbal interaction that takes place during the group activities. High achievers can

---

[3]Ibid.

[4]Ibid.

benefit from the heterogeneous group structure by having an opportunity to explain and verbalize the material. By using strategy grouping, teachers can intellectually challenge all students rather than teach down to the lowest common denominator.

Although using structured grouping is a positive way to promote diversity, to encourage socially acceptable behavior, and to expose students to conceptual thinking, it is not a method that should replace all other instructional strategies and delivery methods. For example, structured grouping is not meant to replace teacher-directed instruction. However, a structured group activity following a teacher-presented new topic is an effective way to reinforce instruction.

Structured grouping is not appropriate when the goal is for students to memorize facts and rules, to compute answers to problems, or to complete a quiz reciting facts. Under these circumstances, groups of students will do what any group of sensible adults would do—copy the answers of the group member who best knows the facts or who is best at the computation. When the final goals of instruction are to promote intellectual thinking, to enhance socialization behavior, or to improve classroom management, structured grouping is extremely effective.

HOW TO GROUP STUDENTS

The first consideration for grouping students is to determine the desired performance objectives for the activity—the same basic rule for any well-planned learning activity. The performance objectives will help the teacher determine the type of training students will need in order to work in groups, how many students should be in each group, and what strategy to use to mix the students heterogeneously.

Groups should be balanced in a number of areas. The groups should be of mixed academic ability—low-, medium-, and high-ability students. Also, teachers need to ensure heterogeneity of gender, race, ethnicity, etc. If it is determined the groups are homogeneous in any area, students can be switched until the desired heterogeneity and balance are obtained.

TRAINING STUDENTS FOR GROUPWORK

Students should not view groupwork as play. Teachers need to explain to students that in the world of work, social and interpersonal skills are as important as technical knowledge. Therefore, the outcome objectives of the group activities need to include various socialization skills as well as intellectual and conceptual learning.

Teachers cannot assume that students have the skills necessary to interact as members of a group. Students need to be trained in how to interact cooperatively so they can work as group members with little direct teacher supervision. Depending upon the performance objectives, tasks may require social skills such as coming to group consensus, working in a collegial manner, showing each other how to do a manipulative task, or discussing concepts and issues. Consequently, teachers must decide what new behaviors students need to learn so they can accomplish the groupwork task.

Using hands-on exercises and games is an effective way of introducing new socialization concepts and allowing students to practice the skills. To merely expose students to socialization skill practice is not enough. Debriefing after the activity, through class discussion, is essential to the effectiveness of the exercise. It is during the postgame discussion that students gain insight into the needs of others and how those needs fit with the needs of the group.

During the initial stages of group interaction, conflict may occur. Often, teachers are uncomfortable when they see conflict occurring and rush in to fix the problem. In reality, group conflict is a normal part of the group process. Learning to work as a team member includes learning how to deal with conflict within the group. Therefore, teachers should refrain from intervening too quickly. Helms and Haynes explain that "conflict that prohibits cohesion is not altogether a bad thing; out of conflict a broader range of ideas and options may be addressed. Creativity is dependent on conflict."[5]

TYPES OF GROUPS

Many types of strategy groupings can be utilized for groupwork activities. Again, it is important for the teacher to identify the performance objectives so that an appropriate group structure is formed that will enable students to complete the assigned task.

Forming groups to "retell" is an effective and efficient way to expose students to a variety of material on a subject. A group of students are assigned different reading material on the same subject (e.g., newspaper article, brochure, pamphlet, etc.). After they have silently read the material, the students retell, in their own words, what they have read. Other group members can add to the discussion by sharing what they learned through their assigned reading.

Dyadic learning groups can be used to study content material. Students form partner groups. Both students read a few pages of the text. Next, one partner orally summarizes from memory what was read. The other partner listens, corrects, clarifies, and elaborates on the material. After the oral summary, both students read the next few pages, and the procedure is repeated with the partners changing roles.[6]

Cooperative groups can be formed to help students of mixed-ability levels be responsible for each other's learning. Group members are expected to help each other learn the material and assist in editing and reviewing each other's assignments. Usually students are held accountable both individually and as a group. That is, students are held accountable for their individual effort, but they also have a stake in the success of the group as a whole.

---

[5]Helms, op. cit., p. 6.

[6]Wood, Karen D. "Fostering Cooperative Learning in Middle and Secondary Level Classrooms." Journal of Reading. October 1987.

Although a major objective of groupwork is to promote cooperation, competitive team grouping should not be ruled out completely. Competitive team grouping works well when reviewing for a test or when a learning activity is needed on a day when traditional instructional strategies are ineffective (e.g., the day of homecoming, the day before vacation, etc.). The tasks should be fun and the rewards should reflect the nature of the activity— "goofy" prizes, certificates, or even applause. Competitive groupwork should not be based on serious awards for winning (e.g., the winning group receives a better grade than the losing group).

Base groups are formed on a long-term basis, and students are asked to work together at appropriate times throughout the term. For example, using base groups for an assigned activity while the teacher is doing administrative paperwork at the beginning of class is an efficient use of instructional time. Even though long-term base groups may be used, students can be formed into other short-term groupings for a variety of other activities. Students benefit from interacting in a number of groups during a time period. The coexistence of base groups and short-term groups enhances the learning environment.

EVALUATING GROUPWORK

Two types of evaluation are involved when determining the degree of success for groupwork: evaluation of the students and evaluation of the group process.

Teacher Evaluation of Students. Teachers are often concerned about how to evaluate students who are participating in group projects. There are two types of evaluation—feedback and graded evaluation. The purpose of feedback is to determine if students are on the right track—not to formally evaluate their work. One form of feedback is individual upgraded worksheets that will help indicate whether the performance goals of the activity are being accomplished or not. Another method of feedback is oral questioning. With a few well-designed questions, teachers can determine quickly if students understand the concepts that underlie the task. Bringing the class together for a large group discussion at the end of the period is another effective method of feedback.

Feedback on groupwork activities is not always necessary. Some groupwork activities innately provide feedback information. For example, a group is assigned to design an electronic worksheet on the computer that will produce a graph. If the graph is produced, feedback has been provided. That is, students know they are on the right track.

For some conceptual ideas, it will take several group activities before all group members understand the concept. In this case, it is not necessary to get feedback on each activity. Obtaining feedback after several activities designed to teach the same concept is acceptable and more time-efficient.

Proponents of groupwork have differing views about graded evaluation. Some teachers grade students on an individual basis and as a member of the group. Other teachers believe that the purpose of groupwork is to provide practice and reinforcement. They do not grade the groupwork project itself. These teachers opt for individual testing to determine whether students have grasped the content or conceptual ideas that were represented by the groupwork task. Other teachers initially do not evaluate the group decision (no right answer is expected). They evaluate the group interaction during the first several grouping activities. Once students have exhibited appropriate groupwork behavior, then these teachers evaluate the outcomes of the task.

Questions about evaluation procedures are a big concern for students. From the very beginning, students should understand the criteria for evaluation. Also, this is an appropriate time to remind students that learning to work effectively in a group is a vital skill needed in the business world. Businesses do not profit based on one person, one idea, or one right way. Although the value of each individual within the organization is important, how the individual interacts within the organizational structure is critical for both the individual's and the organization's success.

Evaluation of the Group Process. The second type of evaluation involves determining the effectiveness of the groupwork process. Three categories of participants are important in effectively evaluating the success of the groupwork: teachers, students, and impartial observers.

Teachers who choose to use strategy grouping devote many hours to planning and implementing the activities. Perhaps for the first time they are moving out of the comfort zone of traditional instructional strategies to test the waters of new and innovative techniques. Even though the last thing these innovators may want to discover is that the groupwork process needs adjustment, it is vital that educators critically and objectively analyze the activities from beginning to end. Often, in the beginning, adjustments need to be made so that the groups can function. Sometimes it is too late for adjustments, but by taking good notes, the next groupwork activity can be improved. Even though the process was initially well planned, there is always room for improvement and adjustment.

Feedback from students is very important. A questionnaire designed to gather student reactions to the activities is not difficult to design or interpret. Insights from the groupwork-activity participants are invaluable when planning a sequel.

Finally, impartial observers are a good source of feedback. Observers need to follow a clearly defined, detailed feedback process. During a preconference meeting between teachers and observers, the objectives of the observation are identified, and the methods of observation are determined. It is important that observers understand the concepts underlying structured groupwork so that teachers receive helpful information that will contribute to their professional growth.

When using observers, it is critical that a safe, nonthreatening environment is established. The observers' role is not to make critical evaluation. Teachers who are trying new and innovative instructional strategies should not be subjected to formal evaluation of the procedures. Rather, observers should be considered coaches whose only agenda is to help teachers improve the process.

EXAMPLES OF GROUPING ACTIVITIES

Here are a few examples of structured grouping activities.

- After giving teacher-directed instruction on the critical thinking process, set up the structured groups as juries. Give the groups the facts as presented in court of a real-life trial case, including the jury instructions to come to a certain verdict (e.g., instructions to arrive at a murder verdict or a manslaughter verdict). Identify one member of the group as an observer and have that person record the process that the jury uses to come to a verdict. Instruct the group to use the critical thinking process that has just been presented to them.[7]

- After teacher-directed instruction on the difference between fact, opinion, and personal preference, give the groups a list of statements that include statements of fact, opinion, and personal preference. Have the groups discuss the statements and determine what type of statement is represented. Ask them to identify sources they could use to defend the fact statements and what questions might be raised about the opinion and preference statements.[8]

- After the teacher has given the ground rules for critiquing group members' work, heterogeneously group the students and have them share the writing they have done for a previously assigned writing activity. Each group member's written work is rotated, and each member writes nonjudgmental comments on a separate piece of paper that will help the writer improve and clarify his/her writing.

- A competitive "Family Feud" type activity is a way to help students review for an exam. Heterogeneously group students into teams. Choose a master of ceremonies (or the teacher can be the MC). Keep score and give some type of reward that is fun and not related to the students' grades.

SUMMARY

Structured grouping, an instructional strategy that promotes active learning in the classroom, is an organized, efficient, planned procedure. Heterogeneous grouping of students is a way to promote students' intellectual thinking, to improve students' social skills, and to enhance teachers' classroom management.

Teachers are the key players in establishing the environment for group success. Teachers identify the performance objectives, train the students, ask the questions, determine the groupings, provide the feedback, and evaluate the success of the group process. Teachers are actively involved in the groupwork by monitoring, encouraging, and facilitating the activities.

Groupwork does not always produce a cohesive, problem-free group. However, when students are allowed to make mistakes and to work out their individual differences, they are experiencing the real-world environment of today's modern workplace.

Business educators have a responsibility to prepare students for the world of work. Structured grouping is another tool in teachers' instructional delivery toolboxes to enhance learning experiences of students.

---

[7]Ennis, Robert H. "Goals for a Critical Thinking Curriculum." In Arthur L. Costa (Ed.) Developing Minds: A Resource Book for Teaching Thinking. Association for Supervision and Curriculum Development, 1985.

[8]Ruggiero, Vincent Ryan. Critical Thinking. South Dakota: College Survival, Inc., 1989.

CHAPTER 12
Lifelong Learning

DONNA J. COCHRANE
Bloomsburg University, Bloomsburg, Pennsylvania

This chapter explores the concept of lifelong learning as part of the hidden curriculum. The major topics are workplace changes, the increase in corporate training, lifelong learning skills, and ways to include lifetime learning skills in the business education curriculum.

THE FUTURE WORLD OF WORK

As society moves toward the 21st century, a number of factors are changing the workplace. The information industry is becoming a dominant force in the economy, and technological advances are rapidly changing the employment picture. Not too many years ago, business educators could safely predict that a high school graduate equipped with sufficient business skills, such as bookkeeping, could be gainfully employed in an entry-level position in business. This graduate would have the opportunity to grow in the field with little or no additional education. This is no longer true. "Few vocational skills learned in the teenage years will continue to serve the individual over a lifetime of work."[1]

Today a secretary no longer has to type one, two, or three drafts. With a desktop computer, there are opportunities to be creative and innovative. A bank teller's job used to consist of a series of repetitive tasks. Now competitive pressures to be the one-stop bank have enlarged the bank teller's job to include advising customers on the variety of financial services. The teller has access to information previously in the domain of middle management and is also charged with making judgment calls at the point of customer contact. Both the teller and the secretary are linked to data via computer terminals, requiring a new range of skills to operate the equipment and to access relevant data speedily. What were once considered to be fairly routine skilled business jobs have expanded to include a good knowledge of a wide variety of skills. A comparison of factory-type jobs will reveal an even more startling discovery. Years ago an unskilled worker could be taught to operate a turret lathe and to be productive. Today the turret lathe is being operated

---

[1]Clark, Marilyn and Others. *School Textbooks and Lifelong Learning: Textbooks as Tools for Learning How To Learn. An Exploratory Case Study.* United States of America Northwest Region Educational Lab, Portland, Oregon, May, 1980. p. 28.

by numerical control equipment, and that unskilled worker could easily be out of a job.

Even new college graduates with skills matching the needs of industry and business today may find those skills obsolete within five years or less due to the progress of technology. Estimates indicate that 75 percent of the work force will require retraining by the year 2000. Some experts predict that many employees will need to undergo major retraining efforts two or three times throughout their careers; areas such as financial services, law, insurance, and data processing will require almost constant updating.

WORK FORCE CHALLENGES FOR BUSINESS

Businesses today are having increasing difficulties in finding qualified, trained workers. The Labor Department has developed a scale that shows that the average young adult reads at a level of 2.6 on a 6-point scale, far below the 3.6 level necessary to function in the estimated 26 million new jobs that will have been created between 1984 and the year 2000. This problem is especially acute in metropolitan areas, where many businesses are located. An advertising firm in Chicago found that only one in ten applicants was able to meet minimum literacy skills for mail-clerk jobs. In 1988 New York Telephone Company received 117,000 applications when several hundred jobs opened up. Fewer than one-half of the applicants were qualified to take the basic employment exam, and of those, 2,100 passed. Today's high schools are graduating 700,000 functionally illiterate young people, and 700,000 more drop out each year. The Labor Department estimates U.S. jobs will require at least one year of college education by the year 2000.

Not only is the quality of work force entrants declining but businesses are also faced with a shrinking work force. Eighty-five percent of the workers in the year 2000 are already at work today. People between the ages of 16 and 24, the new entrants to the work force, will have declined by three million by the year 2000. The average age of the work force will go from 36 years old today to 39 years old by the year 2000. With the shrinking and aging work force, businesses are having to look for solutions to their employment needs. They have no choice but to retrain the work force they already have as well as to hire underskilled workers and supply training to them.

THE CORPORATION AS TEACHER

Corporations have been in the business of training for quite some time, but now it is even more necessary. According to the American Society of Training and Development (ASTD), American corporations spend $210 billion each year on formal and informal training of employees. This amount is very close to the national budget of $238 billion for K-12 education which includes staff, facilities, materials, and training. Training in business is on the upswing for a number of reasons. More and more jobs have expanded responsibilities requiring intensive training. In addition, organizations are recognizing the need for employees to be cross trained.

116

Aetna spends $40 million annually for training on what could be considered basic skills—reading, writing, critical thinking, math, and learning to learn. The purpose of this training is to enable employees to improve their skills. Some corporations are also functioning as degree-granting institutions: IBM, Xerox, and AT&T provide education that leads to bachelor's degrees. McDonald's Hamburger University offers associate degrees in applied science. High school and postsecondary students must be made aware of the necessity of retraining in the workplace, and these students must also be equipped with specific strategies to cope successfully in the changing workplace.

LIFELONG LEARNING DEFINED

The definitions of lifelong learning are broad and center around continuous education from early childhood through adult life. One definition of lifelong learning is that it "refers to the purposeful activities people undertake with the intention of increasing their knowledge, developing and updating their skills, and modifying their attitudes throughout their lifetimes."[2] Other definitions include lifelong learning as a component of a learning society and relate it to adult and continuing education. None of these concepts are really new. Opportunities existed back in the 17th and 18th centuries in North America and around the world for adults to participate in organized learning activities. At the close of the 18th century, continuing education began to move from what was primarily a religious or localized orientation to some formats stimulated by the advance of industrialization. The 20th century saw some new forms of continuing education evolve. For example, the Agricultural Extension Service was begun in 1914. Several other aspects of adult and continuing education began at about this time, for example, adult literacy and vocational training programs. Today there are quite a number of popular learning activities that can be pursued into retirement, such as the learning networks and the Elderhostel movement.

Today the domains of learning sources include schools, nonschool organizations, and individually-used sources. In the context of a life span, the school-based learning occurs during the years of childhood and youth, while nonschool learning occurs in the work place in the adult years. Learning by means of individually-used sources may occur at any age. Education can be further distinguished by whether it is formal, institution-based or informal, nonschool based. Nonformal educational activities are offered by nonschool organizations such as churches, agricultural extension services, trade unions, professional associations, and private industry. Examples of individually-used sources are travel and print and electronic media, including accessing data services from a home computer. All of these examples show intentional learning; however, unintentional learning can take place in the home, at work, with friends, from the mass media, and through community activities.

---

[2]Advisory Panel on Research Needs in Lifelong Learning During Adulthood, 1978. p. 17. In Cross, K. Patricia. *Adults as Learners.* San Francisco: Jossey-Bass Publishers, 1981. p. 258.

LIFELONG LEARNING IN THE CURRICULUM

What would the lifelong learning concept mean in a traditional school setting? Some writers advocate the abolition of schooling, while others argue for the abolition of the distinction between schooling and living. To fully institute lifelong learning curricular changes in the schools would involve drastic changes. The emphasis would be on the qualitative rather than the quantitative aspects of schooling. A lifelong education-oriented curriculum would be much concerned with developing pupils' willingness to learn, acceptance of learning as a natural and desirable activity, positive definition of oneself as a learner, and so on.[3] Skager and Dave developed criteria for a school curriculum incorporating lifelong education.

> The school curriculum should recognize the importance of the essential unity of knowledge and the interrelationship between different subjects of study and emphasize self-directed learning, including development of readiness for further learning and cultivation of learning attitudes appropriate to the needs of a changing society.[4]

The aim of schooling in a lifelong education-oriented framework is to develop people who are capable of functioning under minimal supervision and are willing to adapt to a changing world. The curricula will be required to foster the development of independence, self-responsibility, self-critical analysis, and flexibility. The world of rapid change will foster intellectual and emotional insecurity; thus, the curriculum will have to stimulate sensitivity to problems and innovative skills. The curriculum should also promote decision-making skills, skills in coping with organizational structures, and skills in the communication and reception of ideas. The curriculum will need to give everyone the ability to face what is new as a challenge and not with fear.

When lifelong learning is addressed in the curriculum, content versus process learning should also be studied. Content learning is the learning of selected facts, whereas process learning is learning that enhances the ability of students to cope effectively with their future lives by increasing their ability to deal effectively and autonomously with novel situations. The following are the skills a student should have:

- Possessing or being able to locate information
- Possessing highly general cognitive skills
- Possessing general strategies for problem solving
- Setting one's own objectives
- Evaluating the results of one's own learning
- Being appropriately motivated
- Possessing an appropriate self-concept[5]

---

[3]Cropley, A. J. *Lifelong Education.* Oxford, England: Pergamon, 1977. p. 115.

[4]Skager, R., and Dave, R. H. *Developing Criteria and Procedures for the Evaluation of School Curriculum in the Perspective of Lifelong Education.* Oxford: Pergamon, 1977. In Cropley, *Ibid.*, p. 130.

[5]Biggs, J. B. "Content to Process." *Australian Journal of Education*, 1973, 17, 230-233. In Cropley, *Ibid.*, p. 137.

The first three of these conditions involve cognitive skills, while the remaining four are concerned with attitudes, motives, values, and emotions.

Other skills that should be included in the curriculum to foster lifelong learning would be the introduction of adult development and learning patterns. Educators could help prepare students for the stages and transitions they are likely to experience by including how adults deal with life changes as well as the support services available to them. The students could learn about the educational services available to them in school and after graduation. This will help the students prepare to be intelligent consumers of these services in school and nonschool settings.

LIFELONG LEARNING SKILLS

If the concept of lifelong learning is to be incorporated into the business education hidden curriculum, then it is necessary to direct classroom efforts toward preparing students for a rapidly changing world where a lifetime of learning is a requirement for survival. Even after defining lifelong learning, it is still difficult to name which skills should be taught in business education classes. Ideas of what constitutes lifelong learning skills may well come from the businesses themselves. Examining what training businesses are offering their employees will give some clues to what types of abilities create valuable employees in the changing workplace.

As mentioned earlier, Aetna teaches problem-solving skills and learning how to learn. Another insurance company, Aid Association for Lutherans, extensively trains employees who process applications and claims. The training for its nearly 500 employees focuses on helping the employees work together in self-managing teams. At its Blacksburg, Virginia, plant Corning, Inc. hired employees who expressed a willingness to work in a team setting and had problem-solving ability. Their training included interpersonal skills and technical skills. In addition, Corning's entire work force went through quality training as well as training in problem solving and decision making, communication and group dynamics, and statistics.

Additional sources of information about which skills will be needed for the changing work force include current studies and the literature. Presently there is a great deal being written about what tomorrow's workplace skills will be. A joint study conducted by the ASTD and the U.S. Department of Labor resulted in an overview of which workplace skills are essential. Employers want not only the basic three R's but much more. "Employer complaints focus on serious deficiencies in areas that include problem solving, personal management, and interpersonal skills. The abilities to conceptualize, organize, and verbalize thoughts, resolve conflicts, and work in teams are increasingly cited as critical."[6]

---

[6]Carnavale, Anthony P.; Gainer, Leila J.; and Meltzer, Ann S. *Workplace Basics: The Skills Employers Want.* The ASTD and U.S. Department of Labor Employment Training Administration, 1988. p. 8.

119

From a report entitled "Countdown 2000: Michigan's Action Plan for a Competitive Workforce" come five categories of a new work-readiness definition of literacy. The categories are language/communication skills, quantitative skills, problem-solving skills, interpersonal/attitudinal skills, and job-seeking/self-advancement skills.[7] Charner and Rolzinski identified some areas that need to be taught including critical thinking, abstract reasoning, and learning to learn.[8]

In light of this evidence from business and the literature, certain areas will be addressed as important strategies/skills to enable students to cope with the changing workplace and to develop a positive attitude toward lifelong learning. The skills to be discussed are problem solving and decision making, creative and critical thinking, team building, and learning how to learn skills.

Problem-Solving and Decision-Making Skills. An important lifelong learning skill for the changing work place is problem solving. Problem solving can be defined as the ability to reason and solve practical problems, follow complex written or oral instructions, and deal with situations in which there may be several variables.[9] Some educators associate this type of behavior with critical thinking, problem solving, or reasoning. They typically refer to teaching students to use their learning in new situations to solve problems, to reach decisions, or to make evaluations. In order to foster behavior of this type, the students must be prepared to use the five-step problem-solving process.

First, students must be taught to recognize problems when they see them. Second, students will have to be able to state the problem in the form of a question. Third, students must be taught to collect information from many sources to find solutions. Fourth, students are to evaluate possible solutions and select those that are likely to succeed. Fifth, the students should try out the solutions and decide which one is the most feasible. Using this process, a teacher can encourage good problem-solving methods in any business class whether it is a social business or a skills class.

There are at least three elements of teaching that seem to make a difference in student gains when using these learning and thinking skills. First, the teacher should encourage students to verbalize why they are taking each step in the problem-solving process; second, the teacher should encourage student discussion and interaction; and third, the teacher should emphasize problem-solving procedures using varied examples. Case problems are useful when teaching the problem-solving strategy. Another exercise where this process can be used is the selection of an appropriate solution to a problem with a software package or the production of a complicated document. When instituting problem-solving strategies, students may start with a very simple problem containing only a few variables and then progress to more compli-

---

[7]Bowsher, Jack E. *Educating America.* New York: John Wiley and Sons, Inc., 1989. pp. 213-14.

[8]Charner, Ivan and Rolzinski, Catherine A. *Responding to the Educational Needs of Today's Workplace.* San Francisco: Jossey-Bass, Inc., 1987. pp. 89-90.

[9]Bowsher, *Op. Cit.*, pp. 213-14.

cated problems. As students become adept in using the problem-solving process, they will also improve their information-gathering abilities as they set out to find possible solutions.

Creative and Critical Thinking Skills. Both business organizations and the current literature emphasize the importance of creative and critical thinking skills. There is an important distinction between these two skills. Critical thinking skills emphasize assessment of existing problems using a prescribed process with established criteria. Creative thinking skills encourage examination of problems applying a free-form flow of ideas to generate a solution. Another way of describing these two skills is the examination of what is versus the examination of what could be.

A number of researchers in the area of critical thinking have found the importance of the group process in developing critical thinking. In a classroom situation the experience of group projects stimulates this type of thinking. Critical thinking is composed of two interrelated processes: identifying and challenging assumptions and imagining and exploring alternatives. Critical thinking is a continuous process composed of alternating phases of:

- reflecting on a problem or theme;
- testing new solutions, strategies, or methods on the basis of that reflection;
- reflecting on the success of these actions in particular contexts; and
- further honing, refining, and adapting these actions according to alternative contexts."[10]

Thinking is action, not a passive armchair activity. In his book about critical thinking, Brookfield explores some guidelines for being a facilitator of critical thinking. Although his book was intended for teachers of adult learners, most of the ideas can be applied to secondary and postsecondary classrooms. Diverse materials and methods are necessary to accommodate different learning styles when encouraging critical thinking. Expect that the students engaging in critical thinking will at times encounter periods of frustration. Because the teacher becomes a facilitator, a helper of learning, he or she will address the question, "How does what I am doing contribute to my students becoming critical thinkers?" Developing critical thinking has been described as a learning conversation. "Some of the most effective contributions toward developing critical thinking come through facilitators' designing exercises or written materials that prompt students to engage in this process without needing teachers standing over them directing their activities at each stage of the proceedings."[11] Brookfield found that creative thinking is fostered in small group work when the teacher is a consultant, not a group participant. Role playing, games, and simulations can be appropriate exercises to develop critical thinking.

How can creative thinking be described? Creative thinkers reject standardized formats for problems. They use trial-and-error methods when finding

---

[10]Brookfield, Stephen D. *Developing Critical Thinkers.* San Francisco: Jossey-Bass Publishers, 1987. p. 230.

[11]*Ibid.*, p. 236.

new approaches. "They have a future orientation; change is embraced optimistically as a valuable developmental possibility."[12] Creative thinkers have self-confidence and trust their own judgment. Unfortunately, students have been socialized in the typical classroom toward thinking convergently rather than divergently. In convergent thinking there is only one right answer whereas in divergent thinking there is no right answer but often equally acceptable solutions. Students soon learn, however, that divergent thinking is not necessarily rewarded, and it is often regarded as a disturbance or annoyance in class. Students then generalize that this is not a useful or rewarding type of behavior in school. However, when divergent thinking is stimulated in the classroom, the quality of thoughts is judged in terms of the quantity, variety, and originality of the responses. Divergent thinking has become equated with creativity although there is far more to creativity than a high level of divergent thought.

When engaging students in an exercise designed to stimulate creative thinking, the facilitator must be sure the group understands that contributing and listening share equal importance. This advice is true for the facilitator, too. There is an element of surprise when using a creative thinking exercise, so one must expect risk, surprise, and spontaneity. Encouraging creative thinking invites disagreement, a diversity of opinion that is central to the process. Brainstorming is a common exercise to stimulate creative thinking. Group members are allowed to generate wild ideas without fear of reprisal. Another exercise to encourage creative thinking is to assign a question like "What would you do if you inherited enough money so you would not have to work?" This fantasizing stimulates creative thinking.

Team Building Skills. For the past two decades, businesses have been using the team approach. The team approach has been linked to higher productivity and product quality as well as to an increase in quality of worklife. The ability to work with people in a teamwork setting is an important lifelong learning skill. Problem-solving strategies can be instituted through the team approach, a popular creative method used in business. Creative problem solving is characterized by effective teamwork, the examination of a problem in new ways, and the invention of new solutions to existing problems. Group work is not a new teaching tool in the business education classrooms; however, the ground rules for creative brainstorming must be set in place. In other words, no idea is to be eliminated in the initial phases because it is too simple, stupid, or crazy.

The concept of teamwork can be introduced by assigning projects to the entire class rather than to individual students. The students become the bosses and workers working together in deciding the priorities, the division of jobs, and the setting of the deadlines. The class would also be responsible for monitoring the progress of the job and handling interpersonal problems. This type of activity would work well in an advanced class such as office practice.

---

[12]*Ibid.*, p. 116.

The teamwork concept can be used in social business classes in a real or simulated activity of starting or operating a business. Managing the school store is one way to apply the teamwork concept.

Learning How To Learn Skills. Employers and researchers alike cite the ability to learn as an important characteristic of a lifelong learner. In the previously mentioned ASTD and Department of Labor study, it was found that learning how to learn is considered a basic workforce skill. It is the most basic of all skills because it is the key that unlocks future success. Without this skill, learning is not as rapid nor as efficient and comprehensive. In business, learning how to learn means discovering how an employee best absorbs information—for example, find out if an employee learns best through visual, auditory, or tactile means and then design the training to incorporate that preference. "Training in this skill also means exposing the employee to various learning strategies and analytical approaches and providing instruction on how best to apply these tools."[13] In an educational setting the teacher can implement the same strategies and encourage students to discover their own learning styles. The teacher is instrumental in teaching how to learn skills by providing a wide variety of instructional methods and the opportunity for individualized learning. The goal of learning how to learn is to give students the tools for investigation, making them self-sufficient learners. The next section of this chapter explores this aspect more fully.

LIFELONG LEARNING AND THE ROLE OF THE TEACHER

The image of the teacher has long been associated with an individual standing at the head of the class lecturing to a captive audience. This image of the teacher as the exclusive bearer of knowledge will have to change. In order to incorporate lifelong-learning concepts into the curriculum, the teacher must first become a lifelong learner. Since teachers are living in the same changing society as the students, it will be necessary for teachers to continually adapt and adjust. "In short, both teacher and pupil will be engaged in a program of lifelong learning so that they will, in fact, become 'co-learners'."[14] For some educators, the possibility of becoming a learner along with their students can be frightening or at least disconcerting. Teachers can be excellent role models for change by sharing with their pupils their enthusiasm toward learning new areas and by admitting that they do not always know the answer.

The teacher in a lifelong learning curriculum has several major roles influencing the attitudinal, motivational, and cognitive domains. In the attitudinal domain, the teacher will help students to develop a creative attitude toward new situations, to deal with them effectively, and to experience satisfaction from such coping. The teacher's role in the motivational domain

---

[13]Carnevale, *Op. Cit.*, p. 9.

[14]Dave, R. H. *Lifelong Education and School Curriculum.* UNESCO Institute Monographs, 1973, Whole No. 1. p. 44. In Cropley, *op. cit.*, p. 132.

will be to arouse the students' desire to face change and to profit from it rather than to avoid change. The teacher's task in the cognitive domain will be to equip each student with skill in gaining skills and the development of a feel for the structure and methods of knowledge. This will be done through building an understanding of the sources of information that are available. "The teacher's fundamental job will be to foster students' ability to carry out their own investigations of knowledge, relating what they learn to their own existing knowledge and future needs, and analyzing and evaluating their own learning as they go."[15]

Some writers suggest that the teacher's role will change to one of a co-learner, coordinator of learning activities, educational consultant, and facilitator of learning. In a truly lifelong-learning classroom, the teacher would not simply impart knowledge but would help learners diagnose their own learning needs and suggest the appropriate resources and solutions. The teacher will have to become an expert in the appropriate resource for the particular learner.

INDIVIDUALIZING THE LEARNING EXPERIENCE

Because learners come from highly diverse backgrounds regarding pace of learning, readiness to learn, and styles of learning, learning programs need to be highly individualized. While the technology is forcing job changes and requiring the learning of new skills, it also facilitates individualized learning. This is the beginning of the era of distributed learning—learning that is fundamentally independent of time and space. Through the use of computer and communications technology, it is now possible for a person to learn when and where he or she wants.

Examples of computer and communications technology are interactive instruction, electronic mail, video conferencing, and videotex systems. These technologies put vast amounts of information at the fingertips of any individual as well as provide for interaction between students and instructors who need to share information. Learning would shift from a largely passive role in the classroom to active participation because of interactive instruction. Rigid classes will give way to individualized learning programs. "Computer-based instruction provides drills, tutorials, or simulations that generate unique learning sequences based upon the student's specific responses. Computers can be used to test the understanding of other self-study materials or to manage self-study programs."[16] The chief advantage of employing electronic methods of learning is that distributed training tends to focus on higher-level learning skills such as problem solving and decision making rather than lower-level skills such as memorization or concept learning.

---

[15]Cropley, *Ibid.*, p. 132.

[16]Kearsley, Greg. *Training for Tomorrow*. Reading, MA: Addison-Wesley Publishing Co., Inc. p. 4.

WHERE AND HOW LIFELONG LEARNING CONCEPTS
ARE BEING TAUGHT

While lifelong learning concepts might not be addressed directly, some of the previously mentioned strategies are currently being introduced into business textbooks. For example, a recent high school text about the world of work devotes several chapters to problem-solving techniques, group dynamics, and dealing with change. Teachers should examine their teaching materials to determine if they incorporate some lifelong learning strategies. Textbooks should be examined to determine if they include examples of independent learning, utilization of resources in the community for learning, and relationships among disciplines. Do the exercises require the use of problem-solving skills? Does the content relate to careers in its field and to information about preparation for adult life roles? Does the text material encourage an approach to life with openness and curiosity and recognize the need for and value of education throughout life? Is the student required to set goals or set standards of accomplishment and engage in self-evaluation? Does the material consider alternative points of view and examine values?

Several states are already incorporating topics related to lifelong learning into their syllabi. Some states are including problem-solving strategies, recognizing the need for lifelong learning, and preparing for career changes throughout life. Vermont's State Department of Education syllabus for the Personal and Professional Development Competency and Task List has a section marked "Demonstrate the Ability to Apply Decision Making Skills." This section requires the demonstration of problem-solving procedures and the decision-making process. The student must be able to explain brainstorming, preview a list of tasks, and set priorities. The Division of Vocational Technical Education of the Oregon Department of Education has identified essential learning skills to be taught and tested for the office systems cluster. These skills include reasoning skills and generating ideas. The Nebraska syllabus includes problem-solving strategies in the applied communication section.

School districts may already have in place some type of career-education curriculum. But examination of a number of career-education curricula showed no direct mention of lifelong learning. Very few of the characteristics needed to become a lifelong learner are actually included under the heading, "career education." Career education skills deal more directly with job information, basic education skills, and occupational opportunities. There is no reason, however, why lifelong learning techniques could not be included under this area if there is a program in place throughout the primary and secondary grades. It is preferable, however, to integrate lifelong learning concepts throughout the curriculum rather than in one course.

BENEFITS OF LIFELONG LEARNING

What would be the benefits of lifelong learning if, indeed, people in general were to become lifelong learners? The benefits could be grouped into four major categories: (1) individual benefits, (2) societal benefits, (3) personal or noneconomic benefits, and (4) economic benefits. For an individual there are the noneconomic benefits such as intellectual benefits, the skills/knowledge for effective living, and personality benefits such as self-esteem, self-worth, meaning, and fulfillment. Some selected noneconomic benefits of lifelong learning to society would be a literate population and informed, skilled citizens. For the individual, the economic benefits include entry-level training, on-the-job advancement, and occupational flexibility. For society, the economic benefits consist of availability of trained manpower, increased job satisfaction, an increased general standard of living, and high employee productivity.

SUMMARY

Secondary and postsecondary educators have an important role to play in teaching lifelong-learning concepts to their students. If business educators are indeed preparing students for employment, they have an obligation to provide students with strategies that will enable them to adapt and grow in their work lives. Understandably, there could be some reluctance by educators to add another area to an already overcrowded curriculum. The inclusion of the lifelong learning skills, however, requires a change in methodology more than adding another subject area into the curriculum. Strategically, there is no better place to teach lifelong learning skills than in business education classrooms.

CHAPTER 13

The Need To Incorporate the Work Ethic and Ethics into Business Education Curricula

F. STANFORD WAYNE

Southwest Missouri State University, Springfield

PATRICIA H. CHAPMAN

University of South Carolina, Columbia

All teachers have heard a number of employers lament, "They just don't make employees today like they did in previous times." Employers also express a range of perceptions such as, the work ethic is alive and well; the work ethic is badly bruised; the work ethic is dead.

These feelings should concern employers, educators, and trainers because if a deterioration of a strong work ethic is really occurring in this country, it will contribute to lower productivity in organizations throughout this nation.

People seek to find ways to decrease low productivity in business by implementing obvious tools such as time management techniques and various technological devices. However, the implementation of the work ethic as a tool to curb low productivity occurs less frequently because it is often a less obvious cause of low productivity, and it is not always understood.

Thus, this article explores how the work ethic evolved to its current state and answers these specific questions: What is it? How has it evolved? Has it been modified? Has it been replaced? Does it compete with other ethics? Is it dead? What can employers, educators, and trainers do to strengthen a work ethic in employees and students?

Generally, two extreme schools of thought exist on the part of employers, educators, and trainers toward the work ethic: The work ethic is in serious trouble and almost dead, or, the work ethic is strong and alive. Those adhering to both schools of thought can benefit from making a concerted effort to have the work ethic emphasized more in various business education curricula. A variety of instructional strategies/techniques is offered for all groups for this purpose.

Related to the issue of work ethics are the issues of how students should conduct themselves in an ethical manner on the job when using computer technology and when writing business correspondence. Some of these concerns are summarized, and additional strategies/techniques are provided to help instructors prepare students to come to grips with and respond to these issues that will likely affect them on the job.

BACKGROUND

The Work Ethic Defined. An ethic by its very nature is a collection of internally consistent values which both describes and guides the activities of individuals. More specifically, the work ethic is an obligation imposed on individuals by society. It refers to the usefulness, importance, or general worth that these individuals assign to some behavior or conception related to work (e.g., the physical effort required or the length of time spent on a particular task or job) and nonwork activities (e.g., leisure time).

The work ethic has become part of the cultural legacy. Americans are a work-oriented people. When they first meet someone, one of the first questions asked is, "What do you do?" If the other person does nothing, the implication is that there is something wrong with that person—a character defect.

Old and New Values. The Protestant work ethic refers to an identifiable, established collection of values that is internally consistent and imposes obligations on individuals by the society adhering to this ethic. As part of this ethic, individuals have a moralistic basis for choosing work as a calling under which they meet obligations to God, thereby earning a place in heaven.

In modern times, however, new values have appeared whereby individuals feel right about work in terms of individual choice and self-determination, rather than being made to feel righteous through work that is seen as the fulfillment of societal obligations.

Wayne conducted research to explore whether or not the new and old values fit together to form a singular new work ethic. He identified a number of values that are different from those established for the Protestant work ethic. Depending upon level or type of job, career, or work activities of individuals, an assortment of new work ethics may emerge in contrast to the old Protestant work ethic or a single new work ethic. The end result of this research was an instrument to help identify individuals' work values orientation.

Historical Development of the Concept of Work. The business system and its rapid growth are very dependent on people's attitudes toward work. In today's society individuals tend to assess more critically the importance of work in their lives and their attitudes toward the business system than did individuals of earlier generations.

No matter how rapidly society changes, current attitudes and values regarding work have their roots in history. How people work in the present and future can be very much influenced by particular values and attitudes. Studying past values and attitudes toward work can thus provide insight for current and future values and attitudes.

A review of work and attitudes toward work from classical Greece's worker-slaves to the medieval laboring monks to Calvin's adopted Protestant ethic to Max Weber's secular nature of work shows how definition of work and attitudes toward it have changed over the past several thousand years.

Work Values During Ancient Times. During ancient times work was done to meet basic survival needs. The ancient Greeks considered work demeaning and necessary only for the mere sustenance of life. At the time of the Benedictine monks, work became more respected in terms of giving meaning and integrity to life. To them prosperity and work could not be separated; however, work was part of the religious life and far from being valued in its own right.

Work Values During the 15th and 16th Centuries. During the 15th and 16th centuries, Calvin and Luther stressed that work was to be done for biological survival and as a sacred duty to God. Work was seen as the right or moral thing to do instead of strictly as a means of livelihood. A definite value was now being placed on work. A person's emphasis in living was on being economically productive. Leisure was cosigned a lesser status, to be indulged in in one's spare time. Leisure was viewed as a means to refresh one's self before returning to one's real purpose for existence—work.

Work Values During the 19th Century. Toward the end of the 19th century, the word *work* took on a broader connotation and included all forms of effort—work of art, farm, and factory. Before this time, if one worked, one primarily labored and toiled.

Max Weber described the divorce of work from its former function as service to God. Work became accepted as having equal dignity with religion and as having value in itself.

Work Values During the 20th Century. In modern industrial societies, particularly up to the 1950s and 1960s in the United States, work supposedly has had these functions: (1) a source of subsistence; (2) a regulator of activities; (3) a provider of patterns of association and friendships; (4) a provider of identity; (5) a provider of meaningful life experiences; and (6) a determinant of social status.

According to the American Newspaper Publishers Association, which underwrote a ten-year study conducted by the opinion research firm of Yankelovich, Skelly, and White, old work values are those that are based upon several beliefs: One of primary concern is that the land holds unlimited potential; another is that each individual is capable of moving up the socio-economic ladder. Each generation of a family was expected to achieve more than its past generations. By achieving more, the family would accumulate more of society's rewards (e.g., money, possessions, and status). All the individual had to do was work hard, be dedicated to the task, and conform to the rules, and the family would reach a higher standard of living. In the 1950s technology was expanding, and many believed the standard of living was increasing precisely because hard work was paying off.

However, in the 1960s people began to think differently, and values began to change. Some of the major causes cited for the shift in values orientation were the women's movement, the popularity of developmental psychology, and the impact of television. The old values of upward mobility, materialism, the Protestant ethic, and strictly defined social roles were challenged by new values of self-entitlement and a focus on one's self.

During the middle 1970s, many people were finding and believing that hard work did not always pay off. The American Publishers Association report summarized several value clusters evolving from the traditional homogeneous values population. While traditionalists held to their old beliefs and refused to accept any new ideas, some people were found to maintain the old values but allowed others the privilege of changing. Still another group was seen as holding the traditional values but reinterpreting them as being a way of finding self-fulfillment. Others went further into self-actualization, seeing it as a more important goal than money and material possessions, while another group saw affluence as a way of paying for the luxuries and expenses of the full work life. Another group seemed to have no purpose or goals in life; they lived one unstructured day at a time. The newspaper publishers' report concluded that U.S. society has become a pluralistic society in which choice becomes the byword.

By the end of the 70s decade, individuals wanted to choose their own personal goals, to choose appropriate rewards for achievement, to choose individual roles within relationships, and to choose lifestyles within the greater organization of society. Many individuals tried to feel guiltlessly free to do their own thing while maintaining that everyone else could do the same.

Finally, in the 1980s several authors predicted the coalescence of the diverse values groups. According to Peggy Haney of J.C. Penney Company, a small segment of the population appeared to still hold the old values, and another small group appeared to remain purposeless. Through the 1980s the new values evolved and are currently held by two large groups within U.S. society—those who strive for self-fulfillment and those whose ultimate goal is pleasure. According to a number of authors, the largest, fastest-growing group would become the one that is primarily pleasure-oriented. An array of comments in the literature of the 1990s confirms that this prediction has come true.

EMPLOYERS COMMENT ABOUT EMPLOYEES' WORK VALUES

Newspapers, journals, and conversations with business persons make people aware of the work ethic dilemma facing the United States as it moves toward the 21st century. Within American industry the push is on for workers and companies to be more productive and competitive in national and international markets. Top managers alone cannot make companies more productive; employees must share this objective. Thus, employers, educators, and trainers have responsibility for ensuring that future employees can become productive, contributing members of the work force over a lifetime.

Studies Suggest Strong Work Ethic Exists. Many individuals in American society do not agree that the country is facing a work-ethic dilemma. For example, the Public Agenda Foundation and several other organizations suggest that the work ethic is now in surprisingly good health and may even be growing stronger. Various studies by the foundation indicate that a majority of workers (as many as 52 percent) align themselves with a strong form of the work ethic: "I have an inner need to do the very best job I can, regardless of pay." Three out of four workers surveyed believed that they could be helpful in improving the quality and efficiency of their work, and a majority believed that under the right conditions, they could significantly increase their performance. Interestingly, nearly two-thirds said that they prefer a boss who demands high-quality work.

Studies Indicate a Decline in Work Ethic. However, many other studies completed during the past few years have consistently shown a decline in positive attitudes toward work. Many of these studies have indicated that employers are concerned with employee work characteristics in a changing work environment. A summary of these studies and comments of employers frequently appear in the newspaper, and several examples are now presented to illustrate a decline in a positive attitude toward work.

David Hopkins, an associate professor of business and public administration at the University of Denver, surveyed recent college seniors before graduation and 18 months after graduation while they worked at their first jobs. He found these young workers valued work, but not more than family, health, and happiness. More than ever, they valued free time and sought jobs that allowed them to be self-actualizing. Although these new workers were willing to work hard and wanted challenging jobs, they placed equal importance on the quality of life their jobs allowed them to lead. The data suggested that they actively sought out jobs that provided the attributes, fringe benefits, hours, and travel requirements they desired. Hopkins also found out that if the younger workers didn't get what they wanted from their jobs, they were very willing to pick up and move on. These new workers clearly valued self-satisfaction, the chance to use their skills, opportunities for personal development, and adequate salaries. However, they expressed even more interest in direct compensation and insurance benefits, freedom of expression, creativity, and comfortable working conditions.

Wyatt Company found in surveying its workers that only 43 percent of them with less than a year on the job viewed their companies as "more than just a place to work," and even that rate dropped to 32 percent after five years on the job.

In another scathing indictment of today's workers, three of four engineers surveyed by the Institute of Industrial Engineers agreed "the loss of a strong work ethic in this country has contributed to low productivity and clearly hampers this nation's competitiveness in the global marketplace." These engineers worked in service industries, government, and academia. By wide margins they believed employees don't work as hard or as well or are as loyal or motivated as 10 years ago. Moreover, the engineers indicated workers in this field are often ill-educated, unenthusiastic, and resistant to change.

Yet another group of employers, restaurant owners and managers, has been appalled by the work habits of their employees. They have summarized their observations of the new generation of workers with these comments: "They typically engage in 'gamesmanship' (dragging out tasks to avoid additional assignments) and 'scamming' (getting something done with little effort or conning someone else to do the work." "They also frequently play 'baiting the man,' the 'man' being management." "They deliberately do things to provoke customers into demanding to see the manager." "Sometimes they mix up orders; sometimes they deliberately slow down the line, especially during peak buying times."

According to these restaurant owners and managers, theft is rampant among restaurant workers, particularly at drive-in windows. Workers often shortchange some customers to steer extra food items to friends, and they have no skills whatsoever in terms of customer service. As an example, one employee who spoke rudely to a customer was fired. Within a week another employee did the same thing and was fired. Today's workers do not seem to learn a lesson or to grasp that in business workers must try to accommodate customers, even if they're obnoxious. It is very important to note that these owners and managers of restaurants indicated their observations of employees are not unique to the restaurant industry.

Further, a recent Roper Organization survey implied that workers are coming up short in their commitment to work. It showed that for the first time in the 15 years that the question about work and leisure has been asked, leisure was put ahead of work by 41 percent of Americans as "the important thing" in their lives. Only 36 percent put work first. Among college students, 47 percent put leisure ahead of work.

Even Douglas Fraser, who worked his way up from a Chrysler assemblyline worker to a six-year stint as president of the powerful United Auto Workers union, acknowledges that people's attitudes toward work have changed radically. "The newer generations are more interested in time off from their jobs than their fathers and grandfathers were," says Fraser, now a professor of labor relations at Detroit's Wayne State University. "They have other values—living a fuller life with their family, having more time for recreation, more time to socialize."

Ed White, an industrial engineer at Abbott Laboratories in Libertyville, who describes himself as a buffer between management and productive workers, observes that "people want to do a very good job, but they are often frustrated when they see things that aren't done smart or efficiently by management. Then they feel that if management is going to do dumb things like that, what incentive do they have to do a good job?"

Ed White and other industrial engineers at Abbott Laboratories state the work ethic probably is not as good now as it was 20 years ago. Life is much more complicated today, and the nature of the workplace has changed. People, even production workers, have to know a lot more to do jobs that seem simple.

The Gallup Organization surveyed a sample of working adults last year and indicated that while the vast majority (89 percent) said that they were satisfied with their jobs, those whose jobs gave them a sense of identity work harder and longer than those who regard work as little more than an economic necessity. Members of the postwar generations who have entered the workforce since the 1960s are significantly less satisfied with their jobs than older workers. Gallup also noted that in a similar poll taken 16 years ago, today's middle-aged workers—who were then under age 60—expressed similar dissatisfaction.

EMPLOYERS MUST SHARE THE BLAME

The literature reveals that employees are not entirely to blame for a decline in positive attitudes toward work. This section explores how employers must share the blame and what they can do to help reverse negative attitudes about work.

Employers Must Insist on Quality Work. If workers' attitudes about work are not acceptable to employers, employers need to revise some of their management practices that only work for those individuals who still adhere to the old Protestant work ethic. Management practices must be implemented that also appeal to employees with new work values.

St. Lawrence University's Stuart Hills, author of *Corporate Violence*, believes that "management has scapegoated the workers for shabby work when in reality American workers are capable of turning out top-flight products if management insists."

American management historically has paid much less attention to quality control than other cultures such as the Japanese. American corporate enterprises seem to be more interested in short-term profits. With the mass volume they've had and the relatively little competition until recently, they could get away with producing shabby products. Nothing corrodes the work ethic more than the perception that employers are indifferent to quality. Strict, even harsh emphasis on the highest standards of quality reinforces the conviction that work has intrinsic worth and meaning. Improving standards as a means of reinforcing the work ethic may involve the restructuring of jobs.

Employers Must Implement Productivity Programs. Employers have also lacked the commitment to implement productivity programs for employees, again because of more concern for financial gain and less concern for long-term investment in productivity and quality. Many times workers are not consulted before decisions are made. In the musical "Camelot," King Arthur pauses several times to wonder: "Does might make right?" This question should be as relevant for management today as it might have been for medieval monarchs. Managers may have authority to make decisions and to command, but there is never a guarantee that commands will be followed enthusiastically by the workforce or endorsed by peers in management. Thus comes a gut-level realization that people can be more productive when they have a stake in the outcome. To win workers' commitment, it is important to place greater responsibility for quality on the workers.

A major deterrent to employee commitment has to do with status, authority, fairness, and prerogatives in the workplace. In a high-decision workplace, symbols of status and privilege that are not distributed in accordance with performance are likely to undermine both the work ethic and high levels of performance. High commitment requires a sense of shared responsibilities, goals, and burdens, and this means that those lower in the hierarchy must be able to see themselves and their supervisors as sharing the same destiny.

Employers Must Provide More Individual Freedom. Another reason for a decline in the work ethic may be that employers have not given today's workers more individual freedom. According to the College Placement Council, today's workers want to be interdependent and dependent at the same time. It takes creative management to find the balance between "do my own thing" and collaboration. Today's employees are also no longer willing to surrender their autonomy in exchange for material rewards, unlike

133

those individuals who adhered to the old Protestant work ethic values.

Employers Must Update Their Skills Through Training. Managerial skills and training simply are not keeping pace with the many changes occurring for workers. Existing incentive and managerial systems are often out of sync with the changing realities and values of the workplace. This is clearly reflected in resulting problems with employees' work behavior. Rather than increasing their efforts in response to the new competitive realities, workers' behavior is deteriorating, and they simply aren't working as hard as they used to. Employers will have to update their approaches in order to inspire changes in workers' behavior on the job.

Employers Must Train Employees. Employers must provide training for employees to help them cope with technology-oriented business; to help them properly use company information, sources, equipment, and other assets; to help them develop good decision-making skills; and to motivate them to work harder.

The American work force is aging; many workers today have been in the work force for 30-35 years. Workers who refuse to learn and use new technology are robbing employers of increased productivity. This, in turn, makes business less competitive in the world markets. "Being good" at the job one performs should be a source of pride for workers. In business today, one cannot "stay good" at a job without initiative and retraining to help provide employees with a willingness to accept new ideas, new methods, new management techniques, and new responsibilities.

Since research and development is such a costly part of business, unethical use of information may cost companies billions of dollars a year. Newspapers, TV, and other media highlight abuses of confidentiality and computer technology for personal gain. Computer programs and other types of company information are being accessed and used by employees. Workers need to be trained to evaluate their use of information, equipment, and other assets. Through training, they must realize the importance of keeping all types of business information confidential and of using company equipment, software, and materials only for business functions. This subject will be discussed more fully in the computer ethics section of this article.

Poor decisions result from inadequate training, poor basic skills, lack of attention to projects, and failure to study situations and plan accordingly. Supplies are wasted, and work has to be redone because of poor decisions.

Employees seem to be less motivated to work, and if they do work, they are less motivated to do a good job and to strive for outstanding performance. A tendency exists among workers to do enough to just get by. Realizing that the best motivation is intrinsic, employers should be concerned with developing new ways of motivating employees, including motivational seminars.

Employers Must Hire the Right Employees. Employers must take care in the hiring process to hire the right persons for the right jobs. Additionally, more attention should be given to employee orientation so that employees know and understand company expectations. Some of these expectations include appropriately using leave time, assuming responsibility, and maintaining a serious work attitude.

Deliberate abuses of paid work time by employees cost American businesses billions of dollars a year. Time theft may take the form of calling in sick when not ill, extending break and lunch times, arriving late, leaving early, using company time for personal calls and personal business, excessive visiting with co-workers, and goofing off. Productivity is greatly diminished by these abuses, and employers no longer feel they are getting a full day's work for a full day's pay. Many employers are concerned that this practice is growing into a national epidemic. Thus, employers must make these expectations known during the hiring process and enforce them after employees are hired.

Employees are also less willing to assume responsibility for particular jobs. Psychologists report that attitudes are molded through facing challenges and successfully reaching goals. Because employees shun responsibility for accuracy, dependability, good public relations, and employee-employer relations, the proper work ethic and attitudes are not being developed by many of today's employees. Employees seem willing to pass the buck for work errors and fail to assume responsibility for errors and corrective actions. Each employee needs to ascertain his or her area of responsibility and actively maintain that responsibility to help the company meet its goals. Employers must help employees to develop responsibility, dependability, and good people skills.

Employers should be able to expect the persons they hire to be mature individuals who use their training to perform in a competent, disciplined manner. Employers, however, cite that employees are not serious about the jobs they perform. One employer stated that she no longer hires 18-20 year olds. She stated that her business did not have time to wait for them to grow up and realize they were hired to perform a job, not to socialize. While the work atmosphere should be pleasant, it must also foster appropriate business-like behavior and attitudes. Again, managers must make their expectations known from the very beginning, enforce them when necessary, and provide training and counseling when necessary to provide employees with desired skills and behaviors.

Employers Must Challenge Employees. Surveys show that many employees are bored with their work. Those who adhere to old Protestant ethic work values did even repetitive and boring work without question; however, today's employees seek more interesting and challenging work. With today's technology executives must figure out how to use technology to perform repetitive and boring tasks and tap into employees' needs to be involved in more creative and challenging work.

The U.S. Office of Technology Assessment substantiates the fact that there is a great need and desire on the part of new employees to learn. They need continuous growth, challenge, job enrichment, and greater levels of responsibility that fit their age, maturity, and level of experience.

Employers Must Communicate Expectations. Employers must communicate more with employees, reward performance, and maintain discipline (draw the line, take a tough stand, hang tight, define perimeters, and maintain a cohesive group). They must also balance discipline with rewards, be decisive, stage decisions for maximum impact, and make sure all employees know that change is best for all concerned. Employers must actively create enthusiasm and not be negative to the point where followers lose faith and become listless.

Employers Must Provide Fair Compensation for Work. Many employees receive messages from their jobs that run counter to their own work-ethic norms. First, studies summarized in newspapers suggest almost half of the workforce believes there is no relationship between how good a job they do and how much they are paid. They also see little connection between any increased organizational productivity and their pay. More than seven out of ten workers say they want more recognition for good work.

Frequent attempts have been made to structure incentive systems to provide greater support for the work ethic, but they have often failed to distinguish between satisfaction with a job and effectiveness in doing it. A focus on job satisfaction does not necessarily enhance work-ethic values; indeed, it may even undermine these values. If executives want to capitalize on the considerable human potential that already exists in the workforce, they must focus on motivators as well as satisfiers and not confuse the two.

CHANGES IN THE WORKPLACE HAVE AFFECTED WORK VALUES

In recent years three specific changes in both the workplace and the workforce have dramatically altered employers' past attempts to minimize the amount of freedom of choice and action permitted by workers. These attempts are acceptable to those workers who adhere to the Protestant work ethic values.

One of the most significant changes is a marked increase in the amount of control or discretion that individuals have over their work. Discretionary effort, which varies widely from job to job and from person to person, refers to the difference between the maximum amount of effort and the care individuals could bring to their jobs and the minimum amount of effort required to avoid being fired or penalized. A workplace that requires high discretionary effort has emerged, based on three specific developments; new jobs, new technologies, and new values.

The shift toward white-collar jobs has increased the amount of discretion in the workplace. A second industrial revolution has begun, a revolution that will increase the amount of discretion in the workplace and will take a course opposite that of the first industrial revolution, which served to make the individual worker less important. Close to half of American workers (44 percent), according to one newspaper study, say they have experienced significant technological changes in their jobs during the last five years. Just under three quarters of this group say the changes have made their work more interesting; more than half say technological changes have given them greater independence. Today, with higher education levels, dramatic changes in family responsibilities, and the rise of new values emphasizing self-development over sacrifice, many employees are no longer willing to surrender their autonomy in exchange for material rewards.

A second change is that lifelong learning has become an economic necessity. As Alvin Toffler predicted in *Future Shock* nearly 20 years ago, the illiterate in the year 2000 will not be those who cannot read and write but those who cannot learn and relearn. A recent report from the U.S. Office of Technology Assessment, "Computerized Manufacturing Automation: Employment, Education, and the Workplace," comes to a similar conclusion. "The challenge for employers, educators, and trainers will be to design and deliver instruction that develops skills with which individuals can better deal with the unknown—i.e., with future changes in skill requirements brought on by possible increased use of programmable automation and other factors." The implication is that trainers and educators should be aiming at developing strong basic skills in reading, math, and science. They should be teaching analytic and problem-solving skills that will enable people to operate effectively in a changing environment. Further, they should be building a broad base of occupational skills that will, in turn, broaden career choices and serve as a foundation for developing additional skills. Because employees are likely to have three to five careers during their working lives, commitment to lifelong learning is crucial for the adaptability that will be necessary.

The third change is a result of the "Sesame Street" generation that has been brought up to require a lot more mental, visual, and emotional stimulation; employers aren't doing as good a job in this area as they should be.

One concern addressed earlier regards the issue of computer ethics. The next section discusses more specifically what educators and trainers can do to bring this topic into the classroom.

TEACHING COMPUTER ETHICS IN THE BUSINESS EDUCATION OR TRAINING CLASSROOM

The Department of Labor has said that by the year 2000, the number of U.S. systems analysts and programmers will double. Computer use will continue to increase because computers will do in minutes what would take hours to do manually. With this increased use of computers comes the accompanying temptation to decrease ethical standards.

Ethics are learned either from direct experience or from someone who teaches them. Thus, business educators and trainers are in an ideal position in the classroom to teach individuals how to use computers in an ethical manner.

Hilton wrote an excellent article on how to help instructors advance computer ethics in the classroom by linking a clear definition of business ethics to computer use, providing four categories by which to classify unethical computer use, describing a research-based model for teaching ethics rules, and describing a research-based model for teaching attitudes. He also provided numerous additional resources that can help teachers become involved with computer ethics.

The first step in ethics instruction for computers would be to discuss generally the concepts of ethics, values, and attitudes. These concepts can then be applied directly to business ethics and, more specifically, computer ethics.

Next, instructors might find useful a discussion of specific abuses that occur as they relate to computer usage and subsequently lead to unethical activity. Among these are the improper access, use, creation, and destruction of data or programs. Although not unique to computers, the concepts of vandalism and theft of both hardware and software can be discussed.

Hilton suggests that teachers next teach the rules of computer ethics and then attitudes about computer ethics. Individuals can know a rule as it relates to the use of either hardware or software. In other words, they can distinguish what is right or wrong. However, attitudes toward the rule must be taught so individuals can distinguish what is right or wrong when they are in a situation that requires them to apply or not apply the rule. Hilton provides detailed objectives and steps for teaching both computer rules and attitudes.

A number of individuals have also made the point that instructors must be a model for those using computer hardware and software in the classroom. Instructors must demonstrate proper attitudes consistently over time. Unfortunately, the literature suggests that students often observe and imitate their instructors who illegitimately obtain software for illegitimate purposes.

Individuals should be taught to use computer technology to accomplish goals of the organization. In their capacity as employees, workers should use the technology only for business purposes. Copying programs, using personal (and personnel) information without authorization, and allowing others such as friends to use equipment and programs are unethical behaviors.

Many times the media cite crimes involving unauthorized use of computer technology as well as entering and altering programs of private companies and government agencies. Many states have enacted legislation establishing penalties for such activities. When possible, instructors should bring in real-life examples from the news and use them for discussion purposes. Teachers might invite speakers such as vendors, attorneys, and other business personnel to discuss a variety of topics such as copyright infringements, legislation, penalties, and the like. Some of the strategies/techniques suggested at the end of this article might also be appropriate for computer ethics instruction.

TEACHING COMMUNICATION ETHICS IN THE BUSINESS EDUCATION OR TRAINING CLASSROOM

The purpose of this section is to suggest how to implement ethics instruction pertaining to individuals' oral and written communication, primarily by using the case study method.

The component of ethics instruction would take the form of oral and written communication where individuals could respond initially to ethical-based personal situations and then proceed to the creation of company policy regarding appropriate ethical responses to business problems. Situation role playing might also sensitize people to realities of ethics in their personal lives and in business.

Using short case problems that present ethical implications can provide a useful framework for the examination of ethical beliefs and practices. Starting with simple cases and proceeding to more complex ones can not only help identify individuals' present value systems as they determine how they can best handle each case but also provide an opportunity to expand the development of thought processes. Some cases can be designed to elicit a response to a personal ethical dilemma, while others can target organizational ethics.

Cases should be adapted to fit age, experience, knowledge, and interests. Furthermore, cases can also provide important opportunities for open discussion. This discussion can take the form of oral interaction, written responses to a series of ethical dilemmas, or a combination of the two. For example, individuals can first discuss the dimensions of a case and then summarize in writing what they would do in a particular situation. Such practice will help to sharpen both their oral and written communication skills. Simplistic exercises can lead to more challenging cases and writing assignments. The October 1991 issue of *Business Education Forum* provides several examples of short ethics cases as a basis for writing and discussion.

Numerous other possibilities exist for business educators and trainers to implement ethics instruction into their classes by having individuals create their own case situations for verbal interaction in groups or with the instructor having them research and write individual papers on assigned topics. For example, instructors can provide individuals with opportunities to include information in correspondence that is objective and verifiable. They can provide numerous examples of how unverifiable information can lead to court action. Unverifiable statements include those often made in recommendation letters such as "Most individuals did not like to work for him," and "He was totally unreliable." In these cases, individuals might write, "On five occasions, I had to discipline him for fighting with others," or "She was late for work 22 times during the last four months."

Instructors can also teach how to handle information concerning ethical situations when this information is passed along in confidence. Perhaps the situations have to do with someone else reporting phony figures on a budget, padding an expense account, or drinking on the job. Should individuals nod and forget the discussion, tell the person he or she is wrong, or report the situation to someone else? Business educators and trainers might lead individuals to know that it is appropriate for others to confide in them, but they must tactfully expect others to resolve the problem in an appropriate way. Listening should not end up as an automatic approval of unethical behavior.

Instructors can demonstrate how to respond in an ethical manner on resumes, letters of application, and during job interviews. They should stress the need for precise and factual information about job qualifications and experience. Individuals should be cautioned not to distort information in order to present themselves in a better way; for example, they should not credit themselves with a degree that has not been earned or omit a previous job from the resume or letter of application because they want to avoid questions, particularly if they were terminated. Are these actions ethical since many firms have a policy of immediately terminating employees whose resumes or letters of application have been falsified in some way?

139

Instructors can also teach how to act in an ethical manner when engaging in situations that require persuasion (such as sales)—both orally and in writing. For example, a seller puts it in writing and tells a prospective buyer that a car is in excellent shape because it has 35,000 miles on it. In fact, the car has 155,000 miles on it, but the seller has rolled back the odometer, a practice banned by federal law. The buyer later learns this fact, sues, and wins the case. Ethics guidelines to be stressed here are for individuals to always communicate honestly with relevant facts and not to promise more than can be delivered. One might also be advised to consult an attorney in some cases to ensure good, ethical conduct.

The business education or training classroom presents an ideal opportunity to teach how to conduct research in an ethical way—to be honest about the purposes, to respect confidentiality of information, to share results if promised, to avoid manipulating respondents, to be honest about analyzing and interpreting data, and to respect respondents' rights and feelings.

Another area that lends itself to discussion in a business education or training classroom concerns the consequences of plagiarism, using reproduction equipment for copying when materials are protected by copyrights, and illegally pirating software, videotapes, and other materials.

Finally, the business education or training class is the perfect place for instructors to help instill in individuals a sense of proper work ethics. Examples of possible topics for written and oral assignments are presented in the final section of this article.

Many challenges are inherent in teaching ethics in the business education or training classroom. The task is not easy but cannot be ignored or left to chance. Business education and training instructors can and should have an influence on the perceptions that individuals form toward appropriate business ethics.

Business education instructors and trainers must recognize their responsibility in creating an instructional environment in which individuals become aware of the ethical concerns that face individuals and organizations while meeting goals. They must help individuals identify the choices that will contribute toward a positive image of both themselves and their organizations.

STRATEGIES/TECHNIQUES FOR TEACHING WORK-RELATED STUDIES

This last section details further specific strategies/techniques for teaching the work ethic. Educators and trainers who prepare individuals for careers should provide them with skills and knowledge that prepare them for the world of work. Included in this transfer of skill and knowledge is an obligation for educators and trainers to develop individuals' potential for work, with work attitudes being an important part of that obligation. The development of proper work attitudes cannot be ignored, neglected, or left to chance since the majority of this paper supports the fact that the work ethic in many individuals in society is severely lacking.

Educators and trainers spend a great deal of time with those they teach. They have ample opportunity to affect individuals' work conduct by devising ways to teach the work ethic and reinforce positive work attitudes. Many opportunities exist in business education curricula to teach proper work attitudes. Although no magic formula exists for teaching these attitudes, they can and should be infused into activities that are already present in instructional lesson plans. Wayne provided a number of strategies/techniques and several resources that educators and trainers could consult for additional ideas. Educators and trainers can use these strategies/techniques in their classrooms in order to help instill the work ethic in those they teach. They should

1. seek to instill by example the traits they hope to develop in individuals they teach.
2. return assignments promptly since promptness is an important part of the work ethic.
3. help students, through example, to learn the difference between a day's work for a day's pay and just putting in eight hours.
4. help students develop concern for people.
5. require students to perform to the exacting standards of business, and not accept marginal work.
6. design curricula and courses with success in mind. Successful experiences in the classroom will lead students to repeat desired behavior.
7. design courses so each component has an absolute relationship to the real world.
8. require students to choose objectively between conflicting needs rather than allowing them to make choices based on what others want.
9. establish early and clearly in students' minds an understanding of rules, and enforce them.
10. provide learning sequences that will condition students to perform under increasingly rigid time standards.
11. experiment with approaches that "turn on" students. Provide ample outlets for students' creative abilities and involvement.
12. use visual aids to teach abstract qualities such as tact, trustworthiness, dependability, diplomacy, and loyalty.
13. videotape students to emphasize appropriate business dress and grooming and to reinforce good enunciation, pronunciation, grammar, pitch, and tone.
14. use resource individuals from business to speak to students about the expectations in business and to conduct mock interviews.
15. use bulletin boards to help students develop pride in their work. Display a picture of the student of the week, excellent work, or memorable quotes about the value of quality work.
16. use news stories that directly relate to work, work attitudes, work ethics, job satisfaction, work behavior, as a springboard for class discussion.
17. use newletters and other media to publish information about school programs and student achievements.
18. use simulations to develop a spirit of cooperation and teamwork, responsibility, the necessity of accuracy, the satisfaction of completing assignments that meet business standards, and the wise utilization of time.

19. encourage students to become involved in student organizations as a workshop for understanding human relations, promoting citizenship, instilling occupational pride, developing desirable traits through experience, and promoting respect for hard work and healthy competition.

20. teach work ethics through a variety of assigned written and oral communication activities. In addition, students will gain much-needed practice of these communication skills.

Educators and trainers can also pay close attention to the concerns of employers as they relate to inappropriate work behaviors and target instructional efforts to meet these concerns. Many of these concerns have been summarized earlier.

SUMMARY

Many of today's employers are concerned that employees do not have proper attitudes about work and that they often act unethically at work, particularly when computer technology is involved. Such attitudes and actions can have detrimental effects for both employees and the firms where they work.

This article is intended to help those reading it to better understand what the work ethic is and what employees, employers, educators, and trainers must do to promote a healthy work ethic. By bringing together the varied ideas and suggested resources, all groups can help to strengthen the work ethic in society and promote the ethical performance of various work tasks. This effort can lead to more success for employees on the job and ultimately to increased productivity for organizations.

REFERENCES

Bernstein, P. "The Work Ethic: Economics, Not Religion." *Business Horizons* 31:8-11; May-June 1988.

Boone, J. L. "A Call for a Modern Work Ethic." *The Vocational Education Journal* 63:53; September 1988.

Brown, T. L. "Bridging the Value Gaps." *Industry Week* 230:1; July 1986.

Cannon, Mark W. "What Business Educators Can Do To Help Prevent Crime: Teach Values." *Business Education Forum*; December 1981.

Chapman, Patricia H. *Comparison of Business Ethical Beliefs Among High School Senior Business Education Students, College Seniors in Business Education Teacher Training, and Non-Managerial Office Workers."* Doctoral Dissertation. Columbia, SC: University of South Carolina, 1986.

Church, G. J. "The Work Ethic Lives! Americans Labor Harder and at More Jobs Than Ever." *Time* 130:40; September 7, 1987.

Chusmir, L. H. and Koberg, C. S. "Religion and Attitudes Toward Work: A New Look at an Old Question." *Journal of Organizational Behavior* 9:251; July 1988.

Ciner, B. "U.S. Work Ethic Fading?" *Management Review* 77:10-11; November 1988.

Curtis, G. "American's Work Ethic—Old and New." *Advertising Age* 55:18; September 1984.

Dow Jones & Company, Inc. "A Special News Report on People and Their Jobs in Offices, Fields, and Factories." *The Wall Street Journal* A:1; May 15, 1990.

Dow Jones & Company, Inc. "A Special News Report on People and Their Jobs in Offices, Fields, and Factories." *The Wall Street Journal* A;1; July 3, 1990.

Furnham, A. and Rose, M. "Alternative Ethics: The Relationship Between the Wealth, Welfare, Work and Leisure Ethic." *Human Relations* 40:561; September 1987.

Geber, B. "The Myth of the New Worker." *Training* 24:108; January 1987.

Gottlieb, L. "Sloppy Work Ethics Must Cease." *Restaurant Business* 129:56-58; January 1987.

Half, Robert. "High Cost of Time Theft." *Dun's Business Month* 25:23-24; January 1985.

Half, Robert. "Beating the System: How Time Theft Costs $137 Billion A Year." *Personal Journal* 60:10; October 1984.

Henderson, Floris S. "Instill the Work Ethic in Students." *Business Education Forum;* April 1979.

Hilton, T. S. E. "A Framework for Teaching Computer Ethics." *Instructional Strategies: An Applied Research Series* 5:3; Summer 1989.

Hosmer, L. T. "Adding Ethics to the Business Curriculum." *Business Horizons* 31:9; July-August 1988.

Lipset, S. M. "The Work Ethic—Then and Now." *The Public Interest* 9:61; Winter 1990.

Ludeman, K. "The Work Ethic: Eight Strategies for Leading the New Work Force." *Library Journal* 114:87; May 1989.

Lutz, R. P. "The New Work Ethic?" *Industrial Management* 29:1; January-February 1987.

"Managers Fail to Support the Work Ethic." *Advanced Management Journal* 49:57; Summer 1984.

Miller, P. F. and Coady, W. T. "Teaching Work Ethics." *Education Digest* 55:54; February 1990.

Powers, F. E. "A Team Approach to the Work Ethic." *The Vocational Education Journal* 63:55; September 1988.

Rogers, D. T. "The Work Ethic in Industrial America, 1850-1920." *Monthly Labor Review* 103:57; October 1980.

Sheehy, J. W. "New Work Ethic is Frightening." *Personnel Journal* 69:28 June 1990.

Stein, B. "Bosses Unite! It's Time to Demand the Work Your Employees Owe You." *Business Month* 135:54; April 1990.

"Survey Finds Change in Work Ethics and Attitudes." *Advanced Management Journal* 48:7; April 1987.

Wayne, F. S. *The Development and Validation of an Instrument to Measure Adherence to Protestant Ethic and Contemporary Work Values.* Doctoral Dissertation. Tempe: Arizona State University, 1984.

Wayne, F. S. "An Instrument to Measure Adherence to the Protestant Ethic and Contemporary Work Values." *Journal of Business Ethics* 8:793; 1989.

Wayne, F. S. "Teaching Work Ethics in the Classroom: Instructional Resources and Ideas." Delta Pi Epsilon *TIPS* 4:1; Winter 1988.

Wayne, F. S. and Scriven, J. D. "Teaching Ethics in Business Communication Classes." *Business Education Forum;* October 1991.

Weber, M. *The Protestant Ethic and the Spirit of Capitalism.* Trans and Ed. T. Parsons. New York: Charles Scribner's Sons, 1958.

Yankleovich, D. "Tracking the Attitudes of the Public." A Study conducted for the American Newspaper Publishers Association; 1979.

Yankleovich, D. and Immerwahr, J. "Put the Work Ethic Back to Work." *Association Management* 36:149; May 1984.

CHAPTER 14

Social and Personality Development

LILA L. PRIGGE
University of North Dakota, Grand Forks

CHARLES M. RAY
Ball State University, Muncie, Indiana

Teachers teach students a great number of technical skills to prepare them for business careers. However, they often fail to teach students how to deal appropriately with the intangible aspects of their jobs such as maintaining positive self-esteem, coping with stress in the work place, developing suitable attitudes, using common courtesies, and learning proper business etiquette.

To help students succeed in their careers, teachers must teach more than course content and skills. Students must be given opportunities to build self-esteem, to develop strategies for coping with the negative consequences of stress in the work place, and to exhibit suitable attitudes, common courtesies, and business etiquette. In order to provide such opportunities, teachers must be aware of what is involved in building self-esteem, the negative consequences of stress, and possible strategies for coping with those negative consequences. They must also be able to identify what constitutes suitable attitudes, common courtesies, and business etiquette.

SELF-ESTEEM

People who have high self-esteem usually are better able to cope with stressful situations than people who have low self-esteem. Students who have low self-esteem are more likely to be the students who exhibit delinquent behavior. These students generally have a poor relationship with teachers and parents. In a longitudinal study, Kaplan, Johnson, and Bailey showed that:

> Negative self-attitudes as measured by felt rejection by teachers, felt rejection by parents, and self-derogation were positively correlated with the frequency of committing several delinquent behaviors that were measured concomitantly with these self-attitudes or measured two years afterward. . . . positive correlation between negative self-attitudes and delinquent behaviors that were measured concomitantly may be explained by the fact that delinquent behavior violates internal values and evokes negative responses from others.[1]

---

[1]Kaplan, H. B.; Johnson, R. J., and Bailey, C. A. "Self-Rejection and the Explanation of Deviance: Specification of the Structure." *Social Psychology Quarterly* 49:118; June 1986.

Importance of self-esteem. High self-esteem is imperative for students because it is so vital in the development of good mental health, social relations, and a productive lifestyle. When students have low self-esteem, it is not easy for them to change, because their self-esteem is the result of all their life experiences since earliest childhood. Therefore, educators need to provide positive experiences to make students feel successful. Such positive experiences will help students increase their self-esteem. The relationship between positive and negative experiences and a person's self-esteem has been documented by Youngs, et. al.:

> The relation between self-esteem and the number of life events experienced seems to suggest that the mere experience of an event, positive or negative, threatens an adolescent's self-esteem. . . . Perhaps negative events decrease self-esteem, whereas positive events increase it. . . . As the number of negatively experienced events increased, there was a statistically significant decrease in the level of self-esteem.[2]

These findings suggest that students' low self-esteem may be reinforced by life events that are perceived to be negative. Unless these students are able to improve their self-esteem, they will have difficulty succeeding in the work force.

Students' self-esteem does not affect just their relationship with others; it also affects how they feel about themselves. Part of improving self-esteem is helping students develop a self-awareness, or knowing who they are. It is important for students to experience learning situations that help them identify the special characteristics that make each person different from everyone else.

Signs of low self-esteem. How students see themselves will affect their decisions. If they have a realistic and positive opinion of themselves, they will make effective decisions. Therefore, it is important for teachers to recognize students who exhibit behavior associated with low self-esteem. Such behavior might include one or more of the following signs: self-dislike, social withdrawal, pessimism, a sense of failure, complaints about one's body, feelings of worthlessness, loss of interest in and about life, psychosomatic symptoms, feelings of distress, higher anxiety, inferiority, self-consciousness, lack of self-confidence, tension, alienation, nonconformity, or depression. Identifying students who exhibit one or more of these signs and helping them improve their self-esteem will prepare them to succeed in the work force.

One important element associated with low self-esteem is stress and its negative effects. Research studies agree that there are many individual factors related to stress in the work place. They include low self-esteem, family and/or marriage obligations, workaholic tendencies, hidden agendas, submissive conformity, impatience and overagressiveness, ambiguity, financial constraints, emotional health, competitiveness, rigid personality, frustration, inability to ventilate or let go, lack of control, a feeling of being threatened, and a fear of success or failure. The relationship between self-esteem and

---

[2]Youngs, George A., Jr.; Rathge, Richard; Mullis, Ron, and Mullis, Ann. "Adolescent Stress and Self-Esteem." *Adolescence* Vol. XXV, No. 9:337; Summer 1990.

the negative consequences of stress needs to be considered carefully. According to Youngs, et. al.:

> If stress has a negative impact on self-esteem for adolescents, it becomes an important concern for parents and for counselors who work with adolescents. . . . The experience of negatively perceived events appears to be the primary contributor to lowered self-esteem. . . . persons working with adolescents must pay special attention to the impact on self-esteem of events which adolescents perceived to be negative.[3]

A person's level of self-esteem can be related directly or indirectly to the negative consequences of stress.

NEGATIVE EFFECTS OF STRESS

Parker and DeCotiis define job stress as "A particular individual's awareness or feeling of personal dysfunction as a result of perceived conditions or happenings in the work setting."[4] Employees who are under continuous stress at work cannot function efficiently. But the negative effects of stress are not confined to the work place; employees' personal lives also suffer as they become increasingly unhappy due to stress at work. Continued stress may make the employee edgy and easily upset.

When employees see their jobs as unimportant because they cannot see how what they do fits into the total organization, they do not see themselves doing anything worthwhile, and their self-esteem suffers. As stress increases, employees become more inclined to evaluate themselves negatively. This can result in such feelings as being dissatisfied, tired, frustrated or anxious, of believing work as boring, meaningless, or irrelevant. These feelings are magnified when employees feel they have no control over the situation. When they think there is nothing they can do to improve the situation, they no longer have any incentive to be conscientious.

A major concern for educators is the negative consequence of stress as they relate to adolescents. Research indicates that stress in adolescents' lives can result in low self-esteem, low-achievement in school, and delinquent behavior.

Sources of Stress. Society today is complex and filled with contradictions. Work organizations have become increasingly complex as new technologies require constant change. All these elements contribute to increased stress in the work place.

The degree of stress experienced in the work place has been found to be related to psychological expectations of the work. If employees are wrong about what their work is or will do for them, they may be disappointed and not realize their psychological expectations. In such a situation, they will feel more stress than in a situation in which their expectations are met.

Not only do employees have expectations of their work, but employers also have expectations of the role employees will play. When the expectations

---

[3]Ibid., pp. 334 and 339.

[4]Parker, Donald F. and Decotiis, Thomas A. "Organizational Determinants of Job Stress." *Organizational Behavior and Human Performance* 32:161; October 1983.

of the employee and employer do not agree, role conflict occurs. If the role conflict is not resolved, employees begin to experience stress.

In addition to work-role expectations, another potential source of stress is the state of working conditions of the organization. Most organizations today take care of the obvious expectations of the worker such as a fair salary, vacations, health insurance, and sick leave. The expectations related to the higher psychological needs such as esteem and recognition are less often met. If employees are not able to find ways to satisfy their higher-level needs, stress and frustration will grow.

Another source of work-related stress is conflict; when competitive or opposing ideas are set against one another the situation can be very stressful for everyone involved. Conflict can be either internal or external. Internal conflict occurs when an employee is expected to do something that does not agree with personal beliefs or values. External conflict occurs when people working together view work situations from different perspectives based on their personal beliefs or values.

No matter what the source of stress, its negative effects result in inefficiency at work and are also reflected in the employee's personal life. For example, to get a desired job, the employee might have to give up living in a preferred area or might have to work hours that interfere with personal life. Such situations contribute to feelings of stress both at work and at home.

Along with the concern about the negative effects of stress, it must be recognized that a certain degree of stress is inevitable and, indeed, even necessary and helpful. Most people actually need some stress or tension to perform their best.

Symptoms of Stress. Shirom indicated that, "Individual perceptual filters, a result of different personalities and experiences, influence the way in which situations are assessed."[5]

That explains why a certain event may be perceived as negative by one individual, while for another individual the same event may be the necessary requirement that stimulates action or improves performance, and thus may be perceived as positive.

Too much stress, however, can be disastrous. It can exact a heavy toll on physical health, emotional stability, relationships with people, ability to think clearly, and sense of purpose in life.

Any stress that is perceived as negative and causes a person to run away from a situation or fear trying new things is detrimental to the employee as well as to the organization. As pointed out by Langemo:

> If work-related stress is not acknowledged and dealt with effectively, it could lead to institutional and individual dysfunction, decreased productivity, decreased quality of instruction, and of individual well-being, and increased turnover and potential failure of individuals and/or institutions.[6]

---

[5]Shirom, A. "What is Organizational Stress? A Facet Analytic Conceptualization." *Journal of Occupational Behavior* 3:26; 1982.

[6]Langemo, Diane. *Relationship of Hardiness, Exercise Activity, Organizational Variables, and Work-Related Stress In Nurse Educators in Public Comprehensive Higher Education Institutions.* Unpublished Ph.D. dissertation, University of Minnesota, pp. 20-21; 1987.

Work-related stress is becoming a subject of increasing concern to health officials. Some even consider stress to be the number-one health problem today.

People who suffer from unrelieved stress develop such physical health problems as high blood pressure, migraine headaches, heart disease, ulcers, asthma, alcoholism, drug abuse, anxiety, etc. Emotional problems can also be caused by stress: insomnia, anger, depression, fatigue, cynicism, inflexible opinions, being easily upset, growing distant from friends, crying easily, etc. All of these symptoms can also relate to the person's development of low self-esteem. Therefore, as Youngs, et. al. concluded, "Parents, counselors, and others dealing with adolescents must be alert to the negative impact that stress appears to have on self-esteem."[7]

No cure exists for stress, because stress is not a disease. Stress is a condition of life itself. It can be a constructive or destructive force, depending upon how it is managed. Thus, it is imperative that educators teach students how to manage stress. The effective management of stress includes reducing stress and/or developing strategies to cope with stress.

Strategies for reducing the negative effects of stress. A review of current literature resulted in the following suggestions for reducing stress: making a daily "to do" list, organizing work before doing it, anticipating what tasks will need to be completed, learning as much as possible about the company, developing decision-making skills, eliminating or solving the problems causing it, modifying the situation, avoiding stressful situations, increasing physical activity, finding relaxing things to do, going directly to the source of the stress, or seeking counseling.

The review of literature also provided these additional suggestions for coping with stress: setting priorities, taking some immediate action based on the present understanding of the situation, finding out more about the situation, thinking objectively, keeping feelings under control, letting people know where they stand, working harder and longer, wherever possible giving opinions about how things are done and the way things are going at work, talking things over with spouse at home, leaving the problem and trying to solve it later, facing the situation knowing that family members will provide help and a sense of proportion to the problem, taking some of the work home and working on it there, forgetting work when finished for the day, ignoring the problem until ready to handle it, taking a break and coming back to the problem later, tackling routine work to cool down and regain composure, getting as much rest as possible to be fresh and alert at work, becoming more involved in nonwork activities, taking a day off, leaving the office to go home early, thinking of the good things in the future, letting the feeling wear off, giving up and accepting what's happening, doing nothing and trying to carry on as usual, and trying not to worry or think about it.

To reduce stress, workers must know as much as possible about their work. Ideally, workers should understand how their work fits into the work

---

[7]Youngs, et. al., op. cit. p. 339.

organization, what interaction there is with other workers, what recognition it receives, and how these factors compare with what they had hoped to gain from their work. If these conditions are met, employees will have job satisfaction because they will know they are doing worthwhile work and doing it well. Everyone likes to feel that they are somebody and that what they do is important. Thus, a good fit between employees and their work conditions will enhance self-esteem and improve physical health.

POLITICS AT WORK

One factor associated with working conditions is the role of politics at work. Do employees have to be competitive to succeed? Must they become involved in office politics? Psychologists differ as to the importance of office politics. Many psychologists believe that employees do need to be competitive and learn how to function within the political atmosphere in the office in order to succeed in their careers. These psychologists would tell students that they must win friends and influence people to be successful in business. They would also tell students that knowing the right answers or having good ideas is only part of what is necessary to succeed. Students who enter their first job may be disillusioned when they first realize the impact of office politics.

They would also urge educators to help students understand the importance of working within the system and being aware of the politics that are occurring within their work environment. Karp provides the following suggestions to help students avoid some of the ruder awakenings of corporate life: "Never embarrass your boss; honesty is the best policy; don't brag to strangers; pick your friends carefully; right or wrong, the boss is the boss; collect chips, but not too many; avoid end runs; and give credit when credit is due."[8] These suggestions should show students that it requires a certain amount of sensitivity to organizational dynamics to get things done.

On the other hand, some psychologists have begun to question the importance of competition and office politics. They are finding that hard work combined with highly developed skills makes employees successful even when they are not competitive in their jobs. Highly competitive people are often viewed by their peers and supervisors as being unfeeling and insensitive to the needs of others. Highly skilled, hard-working employees don't have to be concerned about outdoing other employees in order to be successful. As educators have begun to realize, self-competition is a better motivator than competition with others. Self-competition prompts people to strive to improve their performance with each new assignment. They tend to reach for higher levels of achievement; each time individuals succeed in reaching that higher level, they feel good about themselves and gain confidence that they can accomplish even greater levels of achievement. On the other hand, people who are highly competitive are mainly concerned with doing better than the other employees. In some cases, the other employees may not be very capable

---

[8]Karp, H. B. "Avoiding Political Pitfalls." *Management Solutions.* 33:10. October 1988.

so the competitive person does not have to perform at a very high level to be better.

With or without an involvement in highly competitive situations or political atmosphere in the office, employees will always experience some degree of work-related stress. To counteract the negative effects of stress and maintain a high level of self-esteem, employees need to develop effective methods of coping with stress.

THE IMPORTANCE OF A HEALTHY LIFESTYLE

Although it is impossible to eliminate stress completely, there are several positive strategies that can be employed to reduce stress. One effective coping strategy is the development of a healthy lifestyle that includes physical fitness and proper nutrition. While a healthy lifestyle alone does not eliminate stress, it does augment ability to develop coping strategies.

People who enjoy a satisfying life and good health tend to have more positive attitudes, higher levels of self-esteem, and are better able to cope with stress and frustration than are people who are not satisfied with their lives, who are in poor health, and/or who have low self-esteem. A satisfying life includes not only the person's life at work but also his or her life away from work. A full, satisfying life away from work is good protection against the effects of work-related stress. Hobbies and other interests that provide outside motivation are important for coping with stress.

Physical Fitness. The number of physical fitness centers and health spas has escalated greatly in the past ten years. People are turning to amateur sports and other forms of exercise to work off frustration and stress as well as to improve health.

For those who do not feel comfortable participating in strenuous exercise, aerobic exercise has become an important alternative. Aerobic exercise reduces anxiety and strengthens the cardiovascular system so it is better able to handle stress.

"Research has shown that individuals tend to not progress to the last stages of dysfunctional stress if they exercise at least three thirty-minute periods per week."[9] Exercising and maintaining optimum health enhance a person's ability to cope with work-related stress, to prepare mentally to face tough mental tasks, to resist fatigue, to improve self-esteem, and to reduce muscle tension.

People who exhibit effective coping characteristics also have been found to be in optimum health and to practice preventative health behaviors. Many people have become more responsible for their own health and maintain health through preventive measures.

Proper Nutrition. Exercise is only one aspect of physical fitness. Good nutrition is another. In fact, the U.S. Surgeon General has reported that overconsumption of fat is still a major national health problem, with fat

---

[9]Veninga, Robert L. *Human Side of Health Administration.* New York: Prentice Hall, 1982. p. 112.

representing 37 percent of the caloric intake of Americans—exceeding the 30 percent level recommended for good health. Based on this and similar information, people have become more concerned about their diets; lower fat, caloric intake, and cholesterol are important to almost everyone. Estimates indicate that about 40 percent of consumers look for the information on the fat and caloric contents of the groceries they buy.

The finding that self-esteem and self-responsibility for health were effective in reducing work-related stress and increasing life satisfaction has had a significant impact on the choices people make today. Many people have joined wellness programs that include positive thinking, regular exercise, and healthy diets. Many companies support wellness programs for their employees, including hiring exercise trainers and equipping exercise rooms in their buildings. These companies have found that their wellness programs have reduced work-related stress and improved employees' self-esteem.

Educators should encourage students to take advantage of wellness opportunities and to make wellness a life-long pursuit. This will help provide the United States with a healthy work force; and a healthy work force is a productive work force, ensuring success for the organization as well as for the employees.

PERSONAL DEVELOPMENT FOR WORK PLACE SUCCESS

Formal education and employee training provide desirable knowledge and skill for job performance. Yet weaknesses in interpersonal skills may hamper the chances for success for students who are otherwise well prepared for the careers they seek. Attitude, common courtesy, and business etiquette are among the qualities that affect the success of interpersonal relationships. Even though educators generally agree that attitude and knowledge of etiquette are important qualities, specific attempts to develop them are frequently missing or glossed over in the effort to cover the more concrete elements of business courses. Conscious efforts by those who plan curricula, programs, and courses can decrease the negative impact of these elements of the hidden curriculum.

Attitude. The nebulous concept of attitude that is so often identified as a contributor to failure on the job is difficult for educators to explain and develop. Attitude is a state of mind—a characteristic of the human mental condition that affects communication and every aspect of interpersonal relationships. It is one's mental reaction to encounters with surroundings— people, events, objects, situations, organizations, and climates. Employees, as well as students, assume positions as they react to stimuli (people, objects, situations) in their environments.

Attitudes evolve; they are not taught. Therefore, the totality of educational and life experiences provides the filters through which students and employees react to stimuli. Every element of the curriculum can contribute to attitude development. Specific attempts to develop positive attitudes among students may be incorporated into specific units in office procedures, cooperative work experience, and simulated business experience courses. However, every educational experience and every classroom environment offer an opportunity to contribute to the evaluation of individual student attitudes. Understanding the right blend of assertiveness, self confidence, skill, factual knowledge, and problem-solving ability for job success will evolve for some students only as the result of concerted effort to incorporate such development into the curriculum.

Educators and employers agree that attitude is a characteristic that affects success in school and on the job. Although evaluators of students and employees use attitude as a criterion against which to judge performance, this characteristic is difficult, if not impossible, to measure. In fact, its use as a formal criterion for evaluation is discouraged because of the variation in definition from one evaluator to another. While there is general agreement about its importance, there is little agreement about the method for its development.

If attitude is so important that it can result in losing one's job, how can "acceptable" attitudes be developed among students? What are the contributors to attitude development? What methods of instruction influence attitude development?

Rich[10] believes that student awareness of the importance of attitude can best be achieved through learning activities that concentrate on the past experiences of students, rather than predicting activities that students can expect to encounter in employment situations. This approach can be easily adopted for the classroom activities associated with cooperative work experience or simulated business experience classes. Role-playing, problem-solving, and team project activities in any class can draw upon students' observations in working environments, student organization responsibilities, or school projects. Rich[11] identifies five attitude problems that prevail in working environments:

1. It's not in my job description.
2. If it's different, it's bad.
3. The company doesn't own me.
4. Don't bother me with work while I'm doing my job.
5. Doesn't everybody know that?

Explaining these attitudes, identifying behavior that represents such attitudes, and planning strategies for overcoming them can be a part of the classroom experience.

Learning experiences that deal with attitude development should go beyond identifying and talking about them. Students can be directed through role playing and other opportunities to practice their interpersonal skill development, to identify the attitudinal elements of their own behavior, and to react to these behaviors among peers. If students' role models have demonstrated negative attitudes, lack of trust, or even deceit, substantial effort may be

---

[10]Rich, Grace E. "Attitude Problems: Can Your Students Relate to Them?" *Journal of Education for Business* p. 305; April, 1987.

[11]Ibid., p. 305-306.

required to develop the trust and openness toward others that is necessary for a positive attitude. Planning learning experiences that contrast positive and negative attitudes, damaging and effective attitudes, and effective and ineffective interpersonal communication skills are more likely to change student attitudes than lecture/discussion activities.

Common Courtesy. What is courteous behavior? Like attitude, the definition of courtesy presents a challenge. As with beauty, the definition may lie in the eyes of the beholder and may be different from one environment to another. Courteous behavior is that behavior that communicates respect and consideration. Since courtesy, to some extent, is defined by the interpretations of those exposed to human behavior, norms for courteous behavior may change from time to time. However, job success will be affected by the worker's acceptance or rejection in a specific environment.

Students need to be aware that their behaviors in the work environment are being judged—that other people will be interpreting their actions and judging their behavior. Since values are also involved, students should be aware that conforming to expected behaviors may require compromises they are not willing to make. Behaviors that suggest respect and consideration for other people contribute to communication effectiveness and foster trust.

Courtesy involves overt behavior, what one should feel compelled to do, as well as avoided behavior, the knowledge of what one should not do, in a working environment. Common courtesies can be associated with most subject-matter areas, and concerted efforts should be made to incorporate them into course content. The behavior of receptionists toward the public, telephone communication courtesies for every employee, responses to customer and client inquiries, and responsibility for informing superiors about deviations to standard procedure are examples of behaviors affected by courtesy. As is the case for many of the topics discussed in this yearbook, learning about this set of behaviors is something that may not find its way into the curriculum without a concerted effort.

Development of courteous behaviors among students is complicated by popular attitudes that business success is in some way associated with the number of people "stepped upon or over" in climbing the career ladder. Students must realize that courtesy involves right behavior. While linked to financially successful people, it guarantees neither success nor failure. Courtesy is related more to personal success than to financial success; it involves guidelines for behavior that go beyond job descriptions, procedures manuals, and instructions from superiors. This quality involves the unwritten rules and the social sensitivity that govern behavior—those generally accepted behaviors that students may not understand or develop without a concerted effort in the classroom.

Business and employment courtesies are really forms of business etiquette or manners.

Business etiquette. Etiquette carries courtesy a step further, assuming some authoritative interpretation of right and wrong behavior. Businesses depend upon authorities who offer advice about the appropriateness of behavior in business-related social activity. Social etiquette in the past was influenced by authorities such as Emily Post and Amy Vanderbilt. Swings in the popularity of self- or otherwise-appointed authorities can be observed. Recent years have brought an increased reliance upon such authorities. Contemporary social etiquette is influenced by persons whose work and breadth of experiences with social behavior have enabled them to become authorities. Letitia Baldridge and Judith Martin are examples. Baldridge's[12] guide to executive manners has become a best seller that greatly influences business etiquette.

Without question, the advice of etiquette authorities is debatable. The advice may change from time to time, and it is not always consistent from one authority to another. At best, it represents expert opinion. However, works such as the Baldridge guide are based upon extensive research and probably represent a consensus among business people at all levels regarding appropriate behavior. The popularity and respect for these authorities is indicated by the number of professional journals that publish their work. Publications such as *Fortune*[13], *The Wall Street Journal*, *Management Review*, and *The New York Times Magazine*[14] frequently include columns and articles related to business etiquette.

A 1983 survey by *USA Today*[15] revealed widespread interest in the following ingredients in programs to help business decrease discourtesy:

1. Returning telephone calls
2. Answering letters
3. Avoiding putting people (telephone callers) on hold
4. Reviving the words *please, thank you,* and *pardon me*
5. Avoiding "getting instantly familiar with people"
6. Keeping one's word
7. Meeting deadlines
8. Being on time
9. Honesty
10. "Civil" behavior.

These qualities can be incorporated into any class, but they are especially appropriate for capstone courses in program series and in any course where student etiquette greatly impacts peers in team efforts. They should be reiterated in preparation for field assignments in cooperative work-experience programs.

While etiquette guides probably should be standard classroom reference books, specific units of instruction on this topic may be developed or procured from state departments of education. Newspaper columnists regularly include

---

[12]Baldridge, Letitia. *Letitia Baldridge's Complete Guide to Executive Manners*. New York: Macmillan Publishing Company, 1985.

[13]Dumane, Brian. "Miss Manners On Office Etiquette." *Fortune* p. 155; November 6, 1989.

[14]Brown, Patricia Leigh. "The Business of Etiquette." *New York Times Magazine* p. S8; May 21, 1989.

[15]Spangler, Douglas, W. "Reviving Common Courtesy." *USA Today* pp. 28-29; May 23, 1983.

business etiquette topics. These materials provide topics for discussion and ideas for classroom activities, particularly for students who interact with the business community through cooperative education programs and student professional organizations.

The following list contains topics that will be addressed in such publications:

- Anti-company behavior
- Putdowns by colleagues
- Rumor mills
- Reactions to criticism and dismissal
- Introductions, including titles and remembering names
- Hugging and kissing
- First names and nicknames
- Romances in the work place
- Dressing for work
- Meetings
- Invitations and forms of address.

Refraining from sexist communication and other sexist behaviors may be associated with business etiquette. Business law or management courses can draw parallels between business etiquette and legal requirements that employers avoid discrimination on the basis of sex. Such materials raise the consciousness of students to sexist behavior and the difference between intentional and inadvertent sexism.

Accepted behaviors in one country may constitute inappropriate behavior in another country; therefore, international business etiquette becomes important. The global nature of most business organizations today and the blending of cultures as more and more foreign firms move operations to the United States require U.S. educators to focus attention on international etiquette.

International etiquette. Employees, from clerical workers to top executives, are being exposed to multiple cultures and are becoming involved with multinational transactions at increasingly higher rates. Such exposure is no longer limited to employees who travel abroad for their employers. Satellite communication, teleconferencing, international electronic mail, joint ventures, foreign visitors to this country, and foreign acquisitions of American enterprises are examples of experiences that require international and intercultural etiquette in business dealings. Large organizations are likely to provide training for employees who need to learn international etiquette. However, the exposure is not confined to large organizations. All business students are potential international ambassadors for their employers, as well as their country.

The 1991 Gulf War provided unprecedented American exposure to foreign cultures and social practices and their effect upon allied service personnel. Similar differences exist for the business community when business firms of multiple countries are involved in projects and trade.

The discussion that follows does not attempt to suggest content for teaching students about business etiquette in other countries. Rather, it attempts to provide awareness for the need for such instruction and examples of topics for that instruction. The major objective for business students is an awareness that etiquette varies among cultures. Practices that are accepted standards in one country may be frowned upon in another country. Employees who find themselves involved in international communication should feel compelled to learn something about the other country—its people, culture, customs, and practices.

Students should know that libraries contain materials about other cultures and that other sources exist. Employees who have experienced relationships with people in other countries are excellent sources. Publications about foreign cultures, published lists of essential phrases for communicating in the languages of other countries, and lists of religious influences and taboo behaviors are helpful to employees who are preparing for international experiences. They also are valuable teaching materials for classrooms where international etiquette is being considered.

Practices such as the following can be identified and discussed for the purpose of pointing out differences in business etiquette among countries:

1. The importance of translating business cards into another language on the back side of the English version.
2. Customs regarding meals, tipping, and gifts when dealing with Chinese associates.
3. Restraint with regard to attempts at humor with representatives from other cultures.
4. Bowing and refraining from physical contact when being introduced to the Japanese.
5. Special customs and observances associated with funerals and religious holidays in other countries.
6. Variations in sensitivity to time in other cultures. Adherence to schedules is not a concern in Egypt or some South American countries, for example, but it may be extremely important in Sweden.

Successful classroom experiences involving international etiquette will convey the concept that cultures vary, that employees who deal with multiple cultures must appreciate and respect the differences, that restraint is a virtue, and that study and observation are essential.

WHERE IN THE CURRICULUM?

Self-esteem, stress, politics, lifestyle, and personal development content deserve attention in multiple courses because few students take all business courses, and time is not sufficient for a separate course devoted to these topics. Some of the ideas presented in this chapter deserve attention in every course. Every teacher should be aware of the signs of low self-esteem and possible steps to improving students' self-esteem. Every teacher should recognize the sources of stress in the classroom and the probable sources of stress in the work place. They should attempt to help students deal with the inevitable stressful situations. Activities that will improve students' attitudes toward work, peers, and superiors can be a part of every course.

Attitude development, courtesy, and business etiquette are especially related to courses and student activities requiring students to work together in teams or to simulate working environments. Guidelines for business etiquette should be stressed in every course involving direct student contact with the business community or with the public.

Curriculum planners for individual schools tend to rely too heavily upon textbook content for course content. Unless there are specific plans for course content and classroom experiences, the topics discussed in this chapter are likely to be overlooked or minimized. Department heads in individual schools, system-wide supervisors of business education, and state supervisors can jointly assume responsibility for attention to the elements that have been presented here.

Specific topics can be added to course content by state curriculum guide developers. The need for attention to conditions such as stress, company politics, and lifestyle can be addressed by those who plan professional development activities for educators. Specific assignment of responsibility or voluntary acceptance of responsibility for getting these elements into the curriculum is an essential ingredient.

CHAPTER 15

Education for Employment

CLAY V. SINK and SANJIV DUGAL

University of Rhode Island, Kingston

Ask employers what the highly coveted business graduates entering today's marketplace lack and they'll give you the traditional answer of a deficiency in language skills and computational skills. More recently, computer literacy skills have been added to the list of deficiencies. Employers know that they cannot compete without a workforce that has sound basic academic skills. For example, workers spend an average of one-and-one-half to two hours per work day engaged in reading forms, charts, graphs, manuals, and working at computer terminals. Writing remains the primary form of communication for transmitting policies, procedures, and concepts. Computation is used daily to conduct inventories, to report on production levels, and to measure machine parts or specifications.

Of course, these academic skills are important and are usually determined before one is employed. They are even more necessary in a society where the need for technology updates can make a person incompetent overnight. All learning builds on these basic skills. However, there is another issue that surfaces when employability is viewed from a long-term perspective. That issue is, what are the knowledges and skills that enable a person to maintain employment? Many career counselors call these skills *lifelong learning skills*. The purpose of this chapter is to show that education for employment requires more than training for the necessary routine mechanical operations. Education for employment is also an integration of knowledges and skills that enables a person (1) to develop skills for working with others (including those from diverse cultural backgrounds), (2) to contribute toward and function in a legal and ethical work environment, (3) to develop a commitment to the organization, and (4) to prepare for career changes.

SKILLS NEEDED IN THE WORKPLACE

The Carnevale study (1989), conducted under the auspices of The American Society for Training and Development and the U.S. Department of Labor, showed that employers want employees who can learn the particular skills of an available job; that is, who have "learned how to learn." Employers want employees who will hear the key points that make up a customer's concerns (listening) and who can convey an adequate response (oral communications). Employers want employees who can think on their feet (problem-solving) and who can come up with innovative solutions when needed

159

(creative thinking). Employers want employees who have pride in themselves and their potential to be successful (self-esteem); who know how to get things done (goal setting and motivation); and who have some sense of the skills needed to perform well in the workplace (personal and career development). Employers also want employees who can get along with customers, suppliers, or co-workers (interpersonal and negotiation skills); who can work with others to achieve a goal (teamwork); who have some sense of where the organization is headed and what they must do to make a contribution (organizational effectiveness); and who can assume responsibility and motivate co-workers when necessary (leadership).

Learning is now a fact of life in the workplace. Competitive pressures compel employers to shift employees between jobs and responsibilities, putting a premium on the ability to absorb, process, and apply new information quickly and effectively, whereas an educational environment often is so structured that students are not allowed to explore options or alternatives in problems. Other examples may be assignments that do not allow for flexibility, where thinking is not required because predetermined answers are considered correct; collaboration among students and team efforts are not encouraged; and information is prematurely supplied instead of forcing students to read manuals and search for the needed information. When educators spend so much time and emphasize so much the importance of following directions they often forget directions may be nonexistent or incomplete in the workplace. Students may need assignments where they are not given directions, or are given incomplete directions. Thus, a diagnostic approach to learning can take place. The important questions of "What is the problem?" and "What do I have to do to solve it?" would become a common denominator of the learning process and, it is hoped, transfer to lifelong learning skills. This approach to learning would help with developing competencies in being able to integrate all the skills needed for workplace success.

SELF-MANAGEMENT

In the workplace today employees need to manage themselves. In a society where authority comes as much from knowledge of work and procedures as it does from hierarchical positions, self-management is a must. Close supervision is an indication that workers are not able to manage themselves or are not being given the opportunity to manage themselves. Some would say this means that employers have a lack of trust in employees. Also, employees may not have adequate training; therefore, close supervision is a necessity. Costs are associated with a need for close supervision. For example, high turnover results because employees never develop the concept of being responsible for their own actions. Employees leave because they do not like someone looking over their shoulder all the time. Also, the supervisor's time is underutilized because it could be better spent in other developmental tasks for the organization. In other words, the supervisor becomes a taskmaster rather than a facilitator of work.

Learning self-management begins in the educational environment as self-managed persons take responsibility for their own actions; however, they function according to the authority given them and within the legal and ethical ramifications of the position as defined by the organization and by themselves. What takes place in the educational process from grade school through higher education can have a positive or negative effect on self-management. Educators may want to have students participate in developing the goals of an assignment and in determining dates and time frames. Too often assignments are teacher-dominated rather than student-oriented. Thus, the student is not given the opportunity to practice the concept of self-management. Grades often are a reflection of whether a student knows the content of the assignment and not a reflection of whether the student can practice self-management. Employers are thus sometimes misled by the grades students receive. Teachers should encourage students to seek help and ask questions but, at the same time, encourage students to develop self-management by finding needed information and processes without becoming dependent on the teacher. Industry would say that this is a way to develop competent subordinates. Educators should be saying that this is a way to develop competent students who will be able to function with a minimum of direction.

FOLLOWERSHIP QUALITIES

Success in most entry-level positions requires the employee to be a follower before becoming a leader. Students should know the importance of being a good follower. Good followers are able to think for themselves, to exercise control and independence, and to work without close supervision. To follow requires commitment! Students need to understand that commitment means they believe in what they are doing. Teachers will make sure students are committed to assignments by using participative practices and goal clarification before work begins on the assignment. The job of teachers is to acknowledge the qualities and effectiveness of their students and praise them for their good work. Part of being a follower is to accept the concept of corrective action. Good followers are receptive to constructive criticism that leads to corrective action.

PERFORMANCE EVALUATION

Many students, especially high school students, are not prepared for performance evaluation in the workplace. The concept of testing in an educational environment is not necessarily the same as in a business employment situation. Both testing and evaluation can be used for corrective action. Failure on the job usually means unemployment, whereas failure in an academic environment usually means that the course has to be repeated. In the workplace one is often told to do it again, to revise, or to take corrective action. In the academic environment, students are often not required to do it again or to revise. A "D" or a "C" is considered passing. In the workplace, anything less than 100 percent is unacceptable. This management concept

161

is not one of punishment, but one of taking corrective action and thus improving the work and the skills needed to be a competent employee.

In addition to task dimensions of job performance, performance evaluation includes those hidden skills that are often taken for granted—interpersonal skills and working cooperatively with others. Testing in an academic environment often overlooks this aspect of evaluation; thus students may not be prepared for a comprehensive performance evaluation. A performance evaluation usually will look at a set of human-relations variables, such as:

- Maintains and facilitates harmonious relationships with the most disagreeable supervisor, co-worker, customer
- Commands high respect by nearly all supervisors, co-workers, customers
- Maintains composure in difficult situations and is polite to those entering the departmental space
- Treats the majority of persons with courtesy and resolves minor conflicts that occasionally arise between staff members
- Exhibits somewhat superficial politeness with a tendency toward curtness when under stress
- Exhibits frequent unprovoked rudeness that occasionally, but significantly, impairs job performance
- Does not get along well with others and is a significant source of low employee morale and poor relations with other departments.

A consistently low rating over a period of time on any one of these variables will certainly jeopardize the person's standing in the organization even though the person may not be dismissed. Other behavioral observations that become a part of the job evaluation are such things as:

- Manages work time efficiently
- Promptly meets work/project deadlines
- Helps meet deadlines by aiding with the work of others
- Is willing to work overtime and weekends when necessary.

In the academic environment an effective grading procedure would incorporate these variables.

WORKPLACE CULTURAL DIVERSITY

Students should be made aware of performance evaluations and they need, also, to be made aware of the challenges and problems associated with a multicultural work environment. Often this topic is discussed as if cultural diversity is something that compares one country with another. In fact, cultural diversity in the workplace should be viewed as an in-house comparison. Several demographic forces will shape the workplace in America before the year 2000. These forces will cause some concern for those entering the workplace for the first time. Because people are living longer and because of a scarcity in the number of qualified entrants, America's work force will be comprised of more older persons. Are our students prepared to work with, for, or among older adults? Several questions emerge as one considers

America's aging workforce. What happens when a younger person supervises an older adult? What happens when a younger person is paid more or about the same as an older adult just because the company must pay market demands to get younger workers who have the skills that older workers may not have? How many of our young teachers have had a course in methodology for teaching adults? These situations are real, and young workers should be sensitive to them.

Another change in the workplace is that women will make up two-thirds of the new entrants, representing 47 percent of all workers before the year 2000. Some class discussion should pertain to managing a home under circumstances where the head of the household must share or be totally responsible for childcare/eldercare. Do students think of this when making job/career choices? An educational environment that does not address this issue is not preparing the student for employment. Case studies of what adults have done and how they have managed under unusual circumstances such as finding childcare/eldercare, managing as a single parent, or existing on public assistance should be a part of education.

Our society is diversifying. Immigrants will represent the largest share and increase in the workforce by the year 2000. By then one in three Americans will be a minority. Do our students know this? In fact, since many of our classrooms comprise some minorities at present, teachers need to discuss and have assignments that address working relationships with those who are different. Perhaps more group assignments where students are encouraged to work together would help demonstrate some problems associated with work in an environment where cultural differences exist. Further, teachers should include both male and female students in team activities. Daryl Smith, in a recent issue of *Academe*, made the point that our educational institutions need to reframe our conception of the relationship between the institution and the student, especially when we consider the goals of the emerging multicultural society. The experience of women, adult learners, those with learning and physical disabilities, and people who belong to minority groups is too often one of alienation. Students who are seen as different often experience racism, discrimination, stereotyping, and isolation. Often, individual failures of minorities are perceived as failures for the entire group, with individual successes often overlooked. Teachers and students working together can overcome this misconception. Students need to be prepared to face some of these same realities in the workplace. What does one do when confronted with racism, discrimination, stereotyping, and isolation? In the workplace, when conflicts arise, conflict specialists tell us that the best policy is to confront it openly and honestly.

DEVELOP A VALUES CLARIFICATION SYSTEM

The temptations to commit wrong in the workplace are evident. Those who have a system of values are perhaps less prone to commit unethical or illegal acts in the workplace. The superintendent of a high school recently said that students are coming to school unprepared to be educated, unable to follow directions, and unable to have a clear understanding of respect for authority, for someone else's property, for another individual and that person's rights. The basic goal of teaching values is to get students to make choices about themselves and their behavior based on a series of facts and options. The standard approach is Socratic, using stories, questions, and open discussion to prompt students to examine moral and ethical concepts. Values include honesty, kindness, courage, justice, tolerance, freedom and respect. These traits transcend ethnic and racial differences. An example of teaching values occurred in the Moon Area School District outside Pittsburgh, where every elementary school has a "theme of the month." One month it was "How Can I Be a Star?" Suggested answers including being kind and courteous, paying attention, being on time, saying "please" and "thank you." Also, during a reading exercise a teacher might ask how a particular character in the story could have been kind or courteous. In a writing exercise, students might be asked to write a paragraph about a good choice they have made. Certainly students are better prepared for employment and to face society when they have participated in a values-clarification program.

WORKPLACE ETIQUETTE

Ralph Waldo Emerson reminds us that "Your manners are always under examination, awarding or denying you very high prizes when you least think of it." Education for employment should prepare students for workplace etiquette. A student who has the qualifications for a position may be asked for a lunch interview—an opportunity to stand out from all others. Students should show that they know how to conform to the dress code, to accept graciously the seat offered, to laugh but keep it mild, to leave the table for personal grooming, to excuse themselves when leaving the table and keep their absence brief, and to avoid resting a purse or attache case on the table. Do students know to lay their napkin on their lap, how to handle a knife and fork, how to eat and hold a conversation at the same time? Students should be reminded that the way they act at lunch will be the way an interviewer or employer will judge their behavior should they interact with clients, customers, or colleagues. A wise investment is an etiquette book. Teachers can give assignments, especially case assignments, where students must apply the rules of etiquette.

Russ Hogg, former chief executive officer, Mastercard, Inc., suggests to students that the way to improve chances of getting a job is to prepare for the interview. He suggests: dress appropriately; speak clearly (use accepted English); prepare to ask questions; research the company before the interview; get a good night's sleep before the interview; and make no obvious etiquette violations.

PHYSICALLY FIT WORKERS

Education for employment includes awareness of physical fitness, which means doing all one can to remain healthy. The February 1991 *Providence Journal* gave results of a study completed at Brigham Young University by Larry Tucker. This study of 8,300 adult men and women employed at 35 corporations across the country found those who were the least fit had an absentee rate that was 2.5 times higher than employees who were most fit. The scope and nature of corporate concern for employee well-being in the 1990s will include mental health as well as physical health. How many of our students and teachers participate in health-awareness programs? Nutrition and adequate rest and relaxation contribute to a healthy worker and student. In our classes we can have students complete keyboarding exercises or case problems where nutrition and diet, exercise, and adequate rest are the subject area.

BEGINNING A NEW JOB

Getting off to a good start is important when beginning a new job. Beginners can use the following tips:

- Participate. Join in the activities. Many places of employment have receptions for newcomers. Go! Introduce yourself. Be easy to meet.
- Don't wait around for others to approach you. If you are shy, introduce yourself to one or two people at a time.
- Treat all employees with equal respect. While it is important to be friendly to everyone, avoid being too friendly too fast. We all notice the gadflies who perk up when the boss is around and act bored with everyone else.
- Be confident, solid, and strong. Honor those in positions of authority with respect, but avoid being obsequious.
- Take directions willingly. Every employer values the employee who respects the requests of supervisors.

LIFELONG LEARNING QUESTIONS

In a typical learning environment, either classroom or workplace, several questions need to be addressed by the learner. Teachers should review these with students:

- What effect do I have on my co-workers/classmates?
- What have I contributed to make this a better workplace/class?
- Why am I here in this workplace/class?
- How is this job/class going to help me with my career plans?
- Have I have been receptive to change in this workplace/class?
  Note: "Changephobia" in a day and age of technology will certainly lead to worker displacement because of deficiencies in using technology.
- Have I taken advantage of educational/training programs offered by my company/school?

Note: Many schools and companies offer after-school or after-work courses. Many in education think that the only courses one should take are courses that give credit, but taking noncredit courses is one of the best ways known to update skills. In fact, some of the pressure for grades is removed.

- How many times in the last month have you asked "What can I do to help?"

CONCLUSION AND IMPLICATIONS

Business educators can help prepare students for employment by addressing the issues presented in this paper, which are summarized as follows: (1) Be receptive to learning; (2) Be academically sound; (3) Practice self-management; (4) Learn to follow before trying to be a leader; (5) Be receptive to performance evaluation; (6) Be prepared for a workplace of cultural diversity; (7) Develop a values system; (8) Practice workplace etiquette; (9) Practice physical fitness; (10) Know the basics of beginning a job; and (11) Continue to ask some lifelong questions. Career information can be easily integrated into most business classes via assigned readings and commentaries, thus creating a hidden curriculum.

Part III

STRATEGIES FOR MARKETING THE HIDDEN CURRICULUM

CHAPTER 16

Teaching the Hidden Curriculum in Technology Courses

JAMES F. CLARK

Fulton County Board of Education, Atlanta, Georgia

JUDY D. WINZURK

Milton High School, Alpharetta, Georgia

While there are many worthy objectives in the hidden curriculum, this chapter will concentrate on what the authors consider to be three of the more significant ones: developing high esteem; developing analytical thinking skills; and developing lifelong learning skills. The first part of the chapter revisits those three objectives and makes a case for their importance and relevance. The second part of the chapter provides a treasure-trove of teaching suggestions—not suggestions to apply with rote efficiency, but suggestions that will help get the creative juices flowing and reward teachers and students with the fruit of their labors.

DEVELOPING HIGH SELF ESTEEM

In the hit movie "Pretty Woman," Julia Roberts portrays a prostitute who is turned into a lady by Richard Gere's character. The transformation takes place because he treats her as a lady and convinces her that she *is* a lady. In Grimm's fairy tales, Prince Charming did the same thing for Rapunzel. Remember, Rapunzel was beautiful in reality, but the detaining old witch deceived her into believing that she was ugly. That imagined ugliness kept her imprisoned. It took the winning exhortations of the prince to get Rapunzel to believe that she was beautiful and to let down her hair for the rescue.

Like the "Pretty Woman" character and Rapunzel, all persons—teachers, parents, and students—behave not as they are but as they *think* they are. As Henry Ford asserted (Ekeren, 1988), "Think you can or think you can't; either way you will be right."

There is ample evidence that many of the ills that afflict society—the crime, the drug use, the abuse of spouses and children—can be traced directly to low self-esteem. This is pointed out by the California Task Force to Promote Self Esteem and Personal and Social Responsibility (1990):

Statistics on drug and alcohol abuse and the myriad other problems related to them are staggering, and getting worse. Though substance abuse is too complex a concern to be tied to any one causal agent, the data are clear that low self esteem is a significant contributing factor. It is also evident that enhancing self esteem so as to affect abuse behavior, requires a deep change in one's sense of self.

When young people fail to find acceptance and affirmation, a sense of belonging, and a significant part in decision making, many of them seek those human necessities in gangs. People need to know that they matter—to be able to experience the personal accomplishment of making a difference. When these opportunities are not available in positive endeavors and relationships, disappointed and frustrated people often pursue them in ways that are both personally and socially destructive.

Unfortunately, a teacher may believe that he or she can't make much difference—that there are just too many students, too many problems, and too much lack of respect. But if the teacher is the spark that helps set just one student on the right path, to that one student the teacher has made all the difference in the world.

One teacher who did just that a few years back arrived as an import at a small Deep South high school. He filled one of the vacancies created when the previous year's eighth grade class created such turmoil that most of the staff departed. The school board may have had in mind that his heft would help hold down the rambunctious students who were now feeling their oats as ninth graders. But V. J. Gause seemed to have in mind as his mission the freeing of young human beings from the bondage of rural isolation. By placing high value on all his charges, by using positive words with them, and by helping them picture a successful future for themselves, he urged them onward. Backing up his words with actions, he stayed with the members of that class throughout their high school career. Almost single handedly he worked a miracle. More than teaching students to appreciate Shakespeare or to write a decent composition, he taught them over those four years to have confidence in themselves—to believe that they could reach for the stars and have a good chance of grabbing onto one of them. While only an occasional member of previous graduating classes sought the opportunities provided by higher education, many of that class did so, and 10 percent of that class went on to earn doctoral degrees.

Think of what a difference it would make in the lives of individual persons, maybe even occasionally in the course of world history, if all teachers played such a major role in helping their students succeed by having confidence in themselves. Think, too, of what that kind of success with students would do to teachers' self esteem.

Developing analytical thinking skills. As teachers confront a future filled with technology, they must ask how they can best help students meet the challenge of a rapidly changing environment. That challenge is complicated by the realization that many educational institutions are not able to keep up with the changes in technology.

The technology will change, but the ability to use reason and logic to make decisions about why and when to do tasks will not. Thus, teachers not only need to be teaching the technical skills, but also (and more importantly), need to be teaching students to be thinkers and decision makers. Teaching analytical thinking skills equips individuals with the power to deal with a changing environment through informed choice and decision making.

Hidden within the business education curriculum are many opportunities to develop and encourage critical and analytical thinking skills as opposed to teaching memorization. Lessons and units should be structured to encourage students to use their technical knowledge to think through procedures, to make decisions regarding appropriateness of equipment and software, and to select methods of completing the task at hand.

Teachers can start by giving students limited chances to analyze situations and to make decisions based on their conclusions. Gradually, as students mature in their analytical and critical-thinking development, greater and more significant opportunities should be given them.

The Policies Commission for Business and Economic Education (1989) states, "Technology provides opportunity for selecting alternate solutions to problems. For example, there may be more than one way to complete a task, but students need the decision-making and problem-solving skills to be able to decide the best solution for a given situation. Their success in the workplace may be measured by how well they apply these skills."

Not only should teachers be concerned about developing individuals who possess the ability to think through situations and make informed decisions, but also they need to be concerned about the ability to transfer what they have learned in the classroom to the workplace. As previously stated, society exists in a dynamic environment, and it is going to take critical thinkers to be successful in applying skills learned in the academic setting to the work setting.

Developing lifelong learning skills. In rapidly changing society, students must realize that education is a lifelong activity. They should know that graduation from any type of educational institution—whether it be high school, technical school, junior college, or college—is not the ultimate solution for success. Today's work environment no longer allows a person to remain in one job for life. Several different careers are the norm. Success is no longer dependent on one set of skills but on the ability to adapt to a constantly changing technological environment. Persons must be able to meet the demands and changes they face in the workplace. Business educators must encourage students to be open-minded and flexible as they master the basic technological skills.

Teachers must show students not only where to go for information but also how to find and extract the information once they get there. Teachers need to encourage students to be proactive to the changing environment as opposed to being reactive to its dynamic state. This can be done by teaching students that they have control over many areas of their lives. They can exercise more control by planning for the future, using logic and common sense, and making informed decisions. Within the business education curriculum, emphasis should be placed on preparing students to learn throughout life, not just on learning enough to graduate.

TEACHING AND TOUCHING WITH TECHNOLOGY

The first part of this chapter reviewed three of the important hidden curriculum objectives—developing self-esteem, developing analytical thinking skills, and developing lifelong learning skills. While there is little argument with the validity of these objectives, they are meaningless if they remain abstractions. On the other hand, they almost become living, breathing beings once they are bequeathed with concrete teaching methodologies and learning activities. Therefore, this second part of the chapter presents a bank of ideas whose application can do much to teach the hidden curriculum's objectives. While the bank does not contain deposits of all the great ideas that can be tried, regular withdrawals from its assets will certainly buy much.

The first of the following subsections gives suggestions for implementing the hidden curriculum in the general management of classes related to technology and telecommunications. The remaining sections give ideas for word processing/keyboarding, database, spreadsheet, telecommunications, and graphing classes.

Building with technology management. The way a technology classroom is managed can be either a builder or a basher. Everybody needs to feel like somebody, and that need can be either fed or famished by how the teacher structures the environment in which students work. While many of the following suggestions are second nature to good teachers, they bear review. Others may be new to the reader. While the first group of suggestions has application in any class, the second group deals exclusively with the management of computer-oriented classes.

The teacher should learn the names of students immediately and always call them by name. Nicknames should never be used, regardless of how innocuous they may sound. Even the most innocent nickname may be very unpleasant to the student on whom it has been pinned. Even if students seem to like the nickname, they frequently "pretend" for self defense after sensing they can't stop the name's use.

Each student should be personally acknowledged at least once during each class period. The teacher can stand by the classroom doorway and speak or make eye contact as students come and go. Or the teacher can make eye contact with students as individual assistance or class instructions are given. Paper returning time represents an opportunity to speak to students, finding a positive statement to make to each.

Students should be acknowledged as valuable humans at all times, not just when they accomplish something. After tests, the review of results should be done in as positive a manner as possible. It should always be done without reference to low grades or who made them. The positive should be accentuated, with students pictured as having long-term success. Dale Carnegie emphasized this in the following quote (Ekeren, 1988):

Tell a child, a husband, or an employee that he is stupid or dumb at a certain thing, that he has no gift for it, and that he is doing it all wrong and you have destroyed almost every incentive to try to improve. But use the opposite technique; be liberal with encouragement; make the thing seem easy to do; let the other person know that you have faith in his ability to do it, that he has an undeveloped flair for it—and he will practice until the dawn comes in at the window in order to excel.

170

While the preceding ideas work in any setting, there are others that apply specifically to classrooms in which computers and computer software are used.

When using stand-alone computers with diskettes for storage, putting students' names on the storage diskettes rather than just numbering them can provide acknowledgement and a sense of ownership. The small price paid for a few extra disks and labels can provide a large return in growing self esteem and shrinking behavior problems.

In a networked classroom, students' names should be used in their log-on identifications. When a student logs on as "Carolyn Carney" or "CARNEYC," as opposed to something generic like "STUDENT12," she is acknowledged as a person, and her self esteem grows, even if ever so slightly. When networks can do it, they should be set up to address the student by name, such as responding to a log-on with "Good afternoon, Sam Brown." Also, students should choose their passwords when using a network; it conveys to them that they are trusted.

The approach to class assignments can help make students more like automatons or can help them practice analytical thinking skills and lifelong learning skills. While some of them are disarmingly simple, they all have potential.

Students should decide when it is appropriate to print documents. They can be prompted to think through the criteria to use in determining when the need exists—is the work complete, has it been proofread, can a printed copy help make proofing and revision easier?

After students have been introduced to several different types of software—such as a word processor and a spreadsheet program—guides can be provided to help them decide the criteria that should be used in selecting the program most appropriate for the task at hand. They then make their own decisions as to which program to run, including selecting between brands if more than one is available.

Instead of being given specific due dates for each project, students with several projects over a time period can set their own due dates for each. They can be helped in development of a methodology for deciding if it is advantageous to do certain projects before others.

Using applications for more than mousing around. This section contains ideas related directly to the content of technology-oriented courses.

Keyboarding/word processing. The teaching of keyboarding or word processing provides many opportunities for creative activities that reinforce the technical skills of the student while subtly working on self-esteem and analytical thinking.

Students may regularly complete compositions at the keyboard. Emphasis should not be on just the topic, but on punctuation, spelling, and proofreading. Possible starting points for compositions include: (1) How do you see yourself one year from now, five years from now, and ten years from now? (2) Describe three of your best qualities; (3) If you could be anyone, who would you choose to be and why? (4) What characteristics of that person do you admire? (5) How could you have those characteristics yourself?

Similarly, students can compose an essay/paragraph on their favorite outside interest and share the results with other students. An activity of this sort allows students to get to know others in a new light—outside the typical school environment—and helps confirm each student as a unique human being.

With random grouping of pairs of students, each may write an essay on one quality that is admirable in the other member of the pair. Though they may be hard to find at times, everyone has good qualities! Upon completion of the compositions, the students swap papers and walk away feeling good about themselves and their quality that stood out.

Progressive papers not only create enthusiasm in keyboarding or word processing, but also allow each student to become an integral part of the group. This exercise begins with students starting a fictional composition on their computer. They each input for approximately two minutes. When time is called—even if they're in mid-sentence—the students rotate to the next computer in their row. Enough time is allowed to read what the previous person wrote. Then the recipients make their own contribution to the story. This rotation process can be repeated as many times as desired. After stories are finished, students rotate one more time to a user who edits the final product, correcting punctuation, spelling, and grammar. Completed stories can be printed and used for proofreading exercises or for inclusion in a class publication. This exercise creates a feeling of teamwork among classmates, a feeling some students have never experienced.

In word processing, the process approach to student composition works well. This involves getting an idea of what to write about, gathering data, outlining the topic, writing the rough draft, revising through sentence combining and the addition of modifiers. Ask students to save the first rough draft and then compare it to the finished product to see improvement.

Database. Students can create their own database of information related to colleges or technical schools they may be interested in attending. They can use database functions to rank the colleges on various criteria such as costs, admission standards, geographic desirability, etc. They can then use the data with word processing mail-merge to request information from desired schools.

Using either database or spreadsheet software—they decide which and why—students can enter each course and grade they have taken, with the quarter/semester and year in which taken. They can then do various analyses, such as: In which subject areas do they make the best grades? Why? In which subjects do they make the worst grades? Why? Have grades in general become worse or better over the course of their school career? Why? Is the grade trend consistent with the goals developed in earlier exercises? Are they satisfied with the grade point average? Why? If they want to improve their grade point average to a particular level, what grades must be made in the future?

Spreadsheet. Students can picture a successful future for themselves by bugeting for the projected job, income, and situation they would like to have after one year and five years. Let the spreadsheet show the expected growth.

By graphing the results showing change in percent of income devoted to necessities vs. desires as income changes, students can get a better picture of how they can control their lives. This activity can then be tied to a composition on how the students perceive themselves.

It is very eye opening to students when they plan a budget for college or technical school, to show sources of income as well as various expenses. They can then use research skills to find sources of scholarships to cover expenses. The potential scholarships can then be entered in the spreadsheet.

Another way students can work on lifelong learning skills is to investigate trends in career opportunities and job demands for careers in which they may have an interest. They can be shown how to look for appropriate sources of data, then do the actual research themselves. They can decide what spreadsheets and graphs are appropriate for communicating the information they have gathered.

The opportunity costs of further education as opposed to dropping out or stopping after high school can be shown with spreadsheets and graphs produced by the students. After research to find relative income levels for different levels of education, they can turn the decreased income of lesser education into concrete realities that they may dislike, such as "no Corvette" or "no season tickets to pro football games."

After using research as described in the preceding paragraphs, students can better map out plans to reach their career goals, showing expected income and costs at each step of the way. They can plan which high school courses are most appropriate to help them reach their goals; courses can be mapped out using word processing, spreadsheet, or database software.

Telecommunications. Students should use telecommunications services such as *Prodigy* or *Dialog* to locate the information for many of the compositions, spreadsheets, and database activities previously suggested.

Arrangement of computer communication with students in distant schools or even other countries can broaden the horizons of students and help them understand the global environment in which they live. Among the kinds of information that can be shared are complete biographic information on students and their environment with an emphasis on typical life styles, educational requirements, job requirements, earnings, and health care. Then swap this data with a partner school. Data can be analyzed and compared through the use of database or spreadsheet software. Special programs provided by telecommunications companies can significantly reduce the cost of a communications venture.

Desktop publishing. Once students have been taught basic desktop publishing skills, they can create a newsletter or some type of publication that showcases articles written by various students. Class members can select the role each student will play in the overall publication, such as reporter, graphic artist, copy editor, layout editor, and so forth. Upon completion of the publication, it can be shared via written form or telecommunications with a partner school. The newsletter can be published on an ad-hoc basis with students rotating to different roles each time. Ideas for publication content might be short essays about admired people or feature items related to the advantages of staying in school and continuing your education.

Hypermedia. A hypermedia program such as *LinkWay* or *HyperCard* can be used to complete cooperative learning projects. For example, a database class could put together an application to help a small business owner select the best database software to purchase. When the owner uses the hypermedia project, he is asked to mark which of many capabilities are required in his business. The application then can compare those requirements to the features of various commercial database packages and recommend those that best meet the needs of the business. The planning and creation of such an application would require much teamwork from the class. Various duties would be delegated to students. Some students could develop the list of requirements the business might have; others could research the features of commercial database programs; and others could work on the planning of the actual pages of the application. The success of this project depends on each student's performance. Thus, the success of each student becomes an issue of importance for the others. This teamwork approach also fosters each student's pride of ownership in his or her particular part of the project.

Using hypermedia software gives a teacher many chances to place decision making in the hands of the students. Whether students are completing group or individual applications, they can decide the kind of project they are going to complete as well as how they are going to organize it and what types of additional media (speech, pictures, etc.) they are going to bring into their application. This places trust in their decisions, and it forces them to think. Teachers can become their sounding board as they consider the best way to present their content using multimedia, while allowing their projects to be just that—THEIRS!

Whatever hypermedia projects do come out of the efforts, the power of sharing should not be overlooked. If students complete worthwhile applications, they should be shared with other teachers in other disciplines as well as other schools. This may not just enhance other teachers' instruction, but more importantly, it is enhancing the students' self esteem by acknowledging their accomplishments and allowing others to share in them. Letting students know up front that good projects will be shared may also become a motivating force and encourage them to do their best work—after all, who knows where it may end up?

Many activities and topics could be easily integrated into other classes students are taking. For example, if most of the students are in an economics class, the economics teacher can help identify topics that can be addressed in some way through word processing, spreadsheet, database, or graphing activities. After all, all teachers are playing in the same game. The door to technology can be opened for students as well as other teachers while strengthening student self-images, improving their analytical thinking skills, and preparing them for lifelong learning.

By using the kinds of activities discussed in this chapter, teachers can foster in students the kind of thinking exemplified by former tennis star Althea Gibson. In her book, *I Always Wanted To Be Somebody,* she insists that,

174

"I was determined that I was going to be somebody too—if it killed me."
Just as that kind of attitude made the difference for Ms. Gibson, it can make
the difference for students today.

REFERENCES

California Task Force to Promote Self Esteem and Personal and Social Responsibility. Toward a State Of Self Esteem. Sacramento: California Department of Education, 1990.

Ekeren, Glenn Van. *The Speaker's Sourcebook.* Englewood Cliffs: Prentice Hall, 1988.

Gibson, Althea. *I Always Wanted To Be Somebody.* New York: Harper, 1958.

Policies Commission for Business and Economic Education. "This We Believe About the Impact of Change Due To Information Technologies." Business Education Forum, October 1989.

CHAPTER 17

Youth Organizations and Their Role in Enhancing Elements of the Hidden Curriculum

LINDA J. NEWTON

Escambia County School District, Pensacola, Florida

Much has been written about the workforce of the year 2000 and the educating and/or retraining of workers during the 1990s. Kermeta "Kay" Clayton, president of the American Vocational Association, notes that occupational success will increasingly depend on an agile mind rather than on skilled hands or a strong back.[1] Research indicates that employers want workers who can think critically, solve problems, communicate effectively, work as a team member, and perform basic skills that are prerequisites to working productively.

Numerous research studies indicate that business educators are doing an excellent job in equipping students with technical skills. As one report notes, however, "But an alarming number of these students are discharged from their jobs because they have poor interpersonal relationship skills, poor attitudes, exercise poor judgement, and are unwilling to adapt to change brought on by new technology or shifting market needs."[2]

WORKPLACE SKILLS

As part of a major research project examining the skills needed for work, the report, "Workplace Basics: The Skills Employers Want," identifies the skills most desired by employers. The seven skills groups identified are (1) learning to learn; (2) listening and oral communication; (3) competence in reading, writing, and computation; (4) adaptability: creative thinking and problem solving; (5) personal management: self-esteem, goal setting/motivation, and personal/career development; (6) group effectiveness: interpersonal skills, negotiation, and teamwork; and (7) organizational effectiveness and leadership.[3]

Educators today must deal with what some term infusion overload. As the number of topics recommended or mandated to be taught in the schools

---

[1]Clayton, Kermeta. "Leadership for the 21st Century." *Vocational Education Journal* 66:8; January 1991.

[2]Wentling, Rose Mary. "Employability Skills: The Role of Business Education." *Journal of Education for Business* 62:314; April 1987.

[3]Carnevale, Anthony P.; Gainer, Leila J.; and Meltzer, Ann S. *Workplace Basics: The Skills Employers Want.* Washington, D.C.: U.S. Department of Labor, Employment and Training Administration, 1989. p. 9.

mounts, teachers are asked to integrate the new topics into the existing curriculum. Business educators must search for ways to ensure that students not only develop the needed technical skills but also acquire the workplace skills desired by employers. Beyond the basic reading, writing, and computational skills that have always been recognized as critical, educators must ensure that students will be able to use these skills on the job. Students must be able to summarize information received, to monitor their own work, and to use analytical and critical thinking in applying the basic skills on the job.

THE ROLE OF VOCATIONAL STUDENT ORGANIZATIONS

Many of the desired workplace skills are not specifically included in the curriculum nor adequately addressed in most textbooks. Educators are faced with the problem of how to integrate into their classrooms the skills needed by all students for success in the workplace. Vocational student organizations provide a logical means to acquire these skills. A 1982 National Advisory Council on Vocational Education resolution recognizes that "students are given the opportunity to develop, expand, and test the limits of their self-confidence, self-esteem, and motivation through vocational student organization activities."[4] The Policies Commission for Business and Economics Education states that vocational student organizations "provide business students with opportunities for leadership training, personal development, and social responsibility, as well as further development of specific business skills." The Commission states that vocational student organizations serve "a cocurricular purpose, with projects correlated closely to classroom instruction."[5]

Because vocational student organizations are cocurricular, it is difficult to differentiate between curricular classroom and vocational student organization activities. As the instructor begins to integrate the vocational student organization activities into the classroom, the correlation between the course curriculum and the activities of the vocational student organization becomes apparent. For almost every segment of the curriculum, the instructor will find a matching vocational student organization activity.

Human relations skills that cannot be as easily learned from a case study in a textbook or in a classroom activity can be acquired through vocational student activities. Critical thinking, effective communication, problem solving, and the effective use of basic skills are best learned in applied situations that are meaningful to the student.

Membership in a vocational student organization provides students with many opportunities to develop into business leaders of the future. Motivating students to do their best, recognizing achievement, and developing competent, aggressive business leadership are the basic goals of the vocational student

---

[4]Policies Commissions for Business and Economic Education. "This We Believe About the Role of Student Organizations in Business." *Business Education Forum* 37:10-11; October 1982.

[5]Ibid.

organizations. Students are provided an atmosphere in which they can develop their self-confidence, self-esteem, and motivation. Through participation in the organization, students can attain the skills, attitudes, and values necessary to succeed in school and in the workplace. These skills are essential for secondary, postsecondary, and collegiate students.

A doctoral study by Dr. Edward Miller, president and CEO of FBLA-PBL, concludes that student employees who are actively involved in FLBA are more likely to get ahead on the job because of personal traits they develop through their experiences in the organization.

The study, which surveyed 200 small businesses in Arkansas, presented nineteen statements defining personal traits and characteristics contributing to job success. Employers were asked to indicate the degree to which FBLA and non-FBLA student employees, both past and present, exhibited those traits.

The results of the study illustrate the competitive edge attained by the students in FBLA. In the areas of salary and advancement the study found that more than 80 percent of the FBLA student employees had an above-average chance of advancing in rank and that 82 percent were likely to receive salary increases as compared to 40 percent and 39 percent respectively of the non-FBLA student employees. Eighty-three percent of the FBLA student employees received above-average ratings for their ability to handle problem situations without needing to be coached or supervised while the same was said for only 31 percent of the non-FBLA student workers. This would seem to indicate that the students were able to acquire problem-solving skills through their participation in FBLA activities that were not available to the students who were not members of a vocational student organization. The study found that 91 percent of the FBLA student employees willingly accepted duties and responsibilities while only 50 percent of the non-FBLA student employees were willing to do so. The importance that FBLA places on dressing and acting in a manner that brings respect to the workplace was evident by the above-average rating given to 95 percent of the FBLA student employees.[6]

Although this was only one study, remarks from numerous nationally known corporate executives and from successful vocational student organization alumni lend credence to the statement that experiences in vocational student organizations pay off in the workplace. Mark Provine, a stockbroker with A. G. Edwards & Sons, Oklahoma City, and former national FBLA treasurer, credits both vocational education and FBLA in helping him to break out of his shell, meet people, and develop the self-confidence needed for career success.[7]

Recruitment. The opportunity to acquire skills necessary for success in the workplace begins with the very first vocational student organization activity, recruitment. Recruiting for the organization provides members an opportunity for creative thinking, artistic expression, and cooperative teamwork. Colorful bulletin boards have long been the basic recruitment tool. Such an activity requires planning and teamwork. Since the bulletin board will be on display for others to see and will represent the organization as a whole, students

---

[6]Miller, Edward. "FBLA Members Receive High Marks from Arkansas Employers." *Tomorrow's Business Leader* 20:34-35; March 1989.

[7]Stewart, Kelly. "How the FBLA-PBL Experience Pays Off in Business." *Tomorrow's Business Leader* 19:18; March 1988.

can develop a sense of pride in the product they are producing. Computer graphics in the form of posters or banners have become more prevelant with the use of computers and provide students with an opportunity to display their skills in using a computer graphics software program. Brochures, flyers, and pamphlets utilize and further develop word processing/desktop publishing and reprographics skills as well as the ability to communicate effectively through the written word. Videos and slide shows developed and produced by the students provide for the discovery and development of the creative talents of some members. Promotional articles for the school or local newspapers and radio/TV spots offer additional opportunities for improving writing and speaking skills.

Through their recruiting activities, students can experience a feeling of accomplishment and pride in their efforts. Initially, membership in a vocational student organization provides students with a purpose—something to which they belong and a place where they feel needed. As the year progresses and students realize that they are expected to contribute ideas and talents, to serve as committee members or committee chairpersons, to help with projects and activities, to serve as officers, to compete in events, and to be an integral part of the organization, they develop a sense of responsibility. They also have a feeling of pride in their chapter's accomplishments. Both contribute to increased self-esteem on the part of students.

Elections. The election of officers provides an opportunity for the development of leadership skills on several levels. Certainly the potential for leadership is evident in those students who choose to be candidates for an office. The willingness to get involved and the willingness to accept responsibility are already present. The ability to plan a campaign, to organize and work with a group of supporters, and to speak before a group are characteristics that can be developed within the vocational student organization. Chapter members should have the opportunity to prepare posters, bulletin boards, or flyers in support of their candidates. The election should be publicized in the school newspaper, giving students the opportunity to enhance writing and word processing skills.

The leadership skills developed by serving as an officer in a vocational student organization may be further enhanced through a leadership training conference held at the local or regional level. Intensive leadership training is combined with the opportunity to interact with leaders from chapters in other locations.

Participation in elections at the regional, state, and national levels gives both the candidates and the delegates at the conferences a greater insight into the election process. Attendance at a leadership training conference for state or national officers is an opportunity to develop the leadership skills and poise that will enable students to become business leaders of the future.

Officer Installation and Member Induction Ceremony. One of the first formal activities of the year is the officer installation and member induction ceremony. The event is similar to that of many professional organizations and gives students insight into the more social aspect of the business world. If possible, this occasion should be used to enable students to interact with business leaders in the community. Inviting a guest speaker or special guests to attend will increase community awareness of the organization and its purpose. Social awareness and communication skills can be increased by having students issue formal invitations requiring an RSVP. Plans for the ceremony, refreshments, and cleanup activities must be determined. The program must be printed—another opportunity to reinforce communication, word processing, and reprographics skills. All of the planning and organizing for the event requires teamwork and taking responsibility for the assignments accepted.

Recognition/Awards. The success of the vocational student organization is based upon the active participation of all members in the programs and activities. The organization draws its strength from the diversity of its members, and each member is equally important. Without every member working together to make the program succeed, the organization cannot meet its goal of preparing members to function at their best in the business world or achieve the goals for the year set by the membership. Every member has something to contribute and should receive recognition for that contribution.

Recognition can take the form of monthly awards, for outstanding achievement, for accomplishment of an individual or club goal, or for participation in a club activity or placing names on a hall of fame bulletin board or a formal presentation of awards at an end-of-the-year ceremony or banquet. The important factors are to help each student realize his or her own worth and to give public recognition for accomplishment.

Competitive Events. Recognition of students at the local level can help build the self-confidence needed for participation in competitive events at a higher level. A hall of fame to recognize students' achievements and awards may be the boost needed to motivate a student's participation in a competitive event. Regardless of the level at which the student participates—local, regional, state, or national—the events are designed to allow students to demonstrate their abilities in various areas of business. Events range from accounting to word processing and from individual to team and chapter competition and recognition. The variety of events allows for the participation and success of a large number of students.

Students should be allowed to select the events in which they will participate but should also be encouraged to expand their horizons into new areas. Competing at the local level gives students the opportunity to test their skills against others and to see how they will do in actual timed competition. For some students the recognition received through the local competition may be the first time they have been noticed and made to feel important. The experience and success achieved will help build self-confidence for those who wish to compete at higher levels.

Competition at any level usually involves people from the business community who serve as judges for events requiring interviews, job description manuals, speeches, or parliamentary procedure demonstrations. Such exposure can provide these individuals with insight into the type of skills the students are learning and can provide the students with contact persons in various businesses or professional organizations.

The competitive events offer unlimited opportunities to help students develop the traditional skills employers want in addition to the skills frequently mentioned in recent surveys—the ability to use critical thinking, effective communication, problem solving, teamwork, and basic skills to reach a desired objective. Whether at the local, regional, state, or national level, competitive events require self-motivation, self-discipline, commitment, and dedication.

Individual events encourage the student to strive for excellence and require that the student do some goal setting. Although the student generally participates in an event for which he or she is well prepared educationally, such events are usually highly competitive at state and national levels and require additional preparation. Because vocational student organizations are co-curricular, the teacher has an excellent motivational tool to use in integrating the organization activities into the classroom. Team and chapter events also require goal setting, and members must be encouraged to work as a group to achieve their common goals. Overall, competitive events help students to improve occupational skills, to work together cooperatively, and to develop self-confidence in their own abilities. Participation in vocational student organization competitive events allows for recognition in a way that is not possible in the classroom and further enhances the education of students for success in the workplace.

For students who do not wish to compete directly against their peers, some vocational student organizations sponsor awards that recognize success achieved through reaching personal goals or preset standards. The Torch Awards sponsored by the Business Professionals of America, for example, offer recognition for achievement in a wide variety of activities.

Projects. Employers look for productive employees who provide quality performance through self-motivation and pride in their work. The success of projects and activities in the vocational student organization is dependent upon the self-motivation, cooperation, and willingness of its members to participate. The members must believe in the project or activity, and they must take pride in what they have set out to accomplish.

The list of activities that vocational student organizations can perform as a service to the school or community is almost endless. These events provide students with many opportunities to plan, organize, schedule, budget time, coordinate, publicize, cooperate, and evaluate as they work toward a common goal. Some possible activities are visits to hospitals and nursing homes; participation in charity walk-a-thons and type-a-thons; food and clothing drives; adoption of a needy family; volunteer clerical work for nonprofit organizations; and assisting at school events.

Every fund-raising activity requires research, long-range planning, goal setting, publicity, budgeting, handling money, organization, sales, public relations, problem solving, and group interaction. Students assume responsibility for carrying out all of the tasks necessary for the success of the project.

The initial decision to conduct a fund-raising project is usually the result of problem solving by the students about how to raise funds to accomplish a previously agreed upon purpose. Fund-raisers may range from selling products, labor, or services to entertainment or participation events.

Whatever the activity or project, a chairperson should be elected to coordinate the event. The willingness to get involved is a characteristic of both leaders and followers. Both are integral parts of an organization or business, and time and energy should be expended to develop followship as well as leadership skills. An article by Robert E. Kelley in the *Harvard Business Review* discussed the concept of corporate success and failure based on the development of followers. Mr. Kelley concluded that both leaders and followers are essential to the successful operation of an organization.[8]

Meetings/Social Activities. The normal daily activities involved in managing a successful vocational student organization chapter require both technical skills and workplace skills essential for success in the business world. Meetings must be planned and conducted using basic rules of parliamentary procedure. Agendas, minutes, reports, and correspondence provide a means of reinforcing skills taught in the classroom. Actual experience in handling money and in preparing budgets and financial reports makes concepts and skills taught in the classroom more meaningful. Inviting speakers from the business community to chapter meetings enables students to receive up-to-date information on current trends in technology and employment and helps to develop career awareness.

Social activities for the chapter should be flexible enough to appeal to all members. For many students membership in a vocational student organization is their first involvement with any school organization. The interaction with other members at social events can help students develop poise and self-confidence in social settings. Social activities promote social awareness and a camaraderie not achieved through classroom activities.

Conferences. Conferences at the regional, state, and national levels provide opportunities for members to travel, to meet other people, and to participate in activities that are structured to provide both personal and professional growth. Competitive events, election campaigns, general sessions, keynote speakers, banquets, exhibits, tours, and award presentations are combined to make the conferences memorable events as well as valuable learning experiences.

CONCLUSION

Vocational student organizations enhance the curriculum taught in the classroom by bridging the gap between the classroom and the business world. When students use skills taught in the classroom to successfully complete chapter activities, they gain knowledge and skills that will benefit them both personally and professionally. Whether the chapter is a local organization or affiliated with a national association, vocational student organizations play an integral part in the education of tomorrow's business leaders.

As educators search for ways to ensure that students not only develop the needed technical skills but also acquire the workplace skills desired by employers, vocational student organizations are the logical means to enhance elements of the hidden curriculum.

---

[8]Kelley, Robert E. "In Praise of the Followers." *Harvard Business Review* 66:142; November-December 1988.

CHAPTER 18

Education and Work Partnerships

DONALD K. ZAHN
University of Wisconsin-Whitewater, Whitewater, Wisconsin

VICKI A. POOLE
Wisconsin Department of Public Instruction, Madison, Wisconsin

Preparation for productive employment in our modern economy was included in the educational reform goals proposed by President Bush.

> President George Bush called the nation's governors together for an Education Summit in the fall of 1989 because he believed the time had come . . . to reverse the declining performance of our educational system . . . but he and the governors also understood the growing importance of education in the modern, technology-based workplace. . . . The connection between education and work, or more broadly, between an educated workforce and America's international economic competitiveness, was therefore much on the minds of the leaders who gathered in Charlottesville, VA, to discuss education reform.[1]

This goal is easier to state than it is to accomplish in today's technologically sophisticated culture. It is commonly understood that schools need to be restructured if this goal, and others, are to be achieved. How to achieve this goal is less commonly understood or agreed upon.

Proposals for restructuring education typically include recommendations for lengthening the school day, strengthening teacher preparation standards, testing student aptitudes and knowledge prior to graduation, promoting school choice, and increasing business and education partnerships. Regardless of the methods proposed, virtually all of the national efforts to improve the public education system have as a goal increased student performance and school accountability.

Many of the people requesting improved student performance are employers. Businesses produce well defined products and have, as a bottom line, a profit motive. Profits are easily measured, and there are financial incentives for employees to produce. Quite often, employers expect schools to be able to produce the same "bottom line." In contrast, schools can measure reading and math achievement levels, but the "products" that schools produce vary considerably. Even right from the beginning of the process, schools do not have the consistent, uniform raw material available that businesses do—consider, for example, the differing IQs, economic and cultural backgrounds,

---

[1]Cavazos, Lauro F. "Building Stronger Bridges from School to Work." *Partnerships in Education Journal* 4:10; November 1990.

values, social experiences, and physical characteristics of students. Employer expectations of the finished products also vary, depending upon the needs of individual businesses. While it would be nice if schools could be restructured to be as accountable as businesses, in reality, this will probably never occur.

Recognition of the variety of skills that employers desire leads to an understanding of the difficult task that educators face—not only does the raw material vary considerably, most classroom student/teacher ratios simply do not allow for the amount of individualization that is needed to meet the diversity of employer expectations. If education is ever going to succeed in producing graduates who possess the skills and knowledge needed by employers, business must be willing to become full partners in the effort.

IDENTIFY SKILLS NEEDED

Before effective education and work partnerships can be developed, a list of the competencies most employers generally consider necessary prior to high school graduation must be identified. First and foremost, most employers demand strong reading and math skills, both of which can be objectively measured and taught in a structured educational environment. There are other skills needed, however, that cannot be as easily taught in the classroom alone.

Businesses vary considerably in the job specific skills needed, depending on the nature of their business. No common list would accurately portray the collective needs of employers. Development of these skills is best accomplished through specific training plans and agreements, tailored to meet the needs of individual students and employers.

A third set of skills needed by business, but not easily defined, is often referred to as "employability skills." These skills are often considered by employers to be as important as reading, math, and job specific skills. However, they are not easily taught or measured. Before consideration can be given to the best method of teaching these skills, it is important to define them.

Employers typically agree that the following categories and components represent the employability skills needed by all graduates:

Personal development

1. evaluate own work
2. understand personal characteristics
3. establish personal and professional goals
4. accept authority and supervision
5. develop good self-esteem and a positive self-image
6. demonstrate emotional stability and patience
7. display honesty in personal work situations
8. practice good personal hygiene
9. dress appropriately
10. demonstrate mature behavior.

184

Human relations

1. recognize difference in value systems
2. accept constructive criticism
3. work cooperatively in teams
4. display a friendly and cooperative spirit
5. demonstrate tactfulness in difficult situations
6. become aware and accepting of cultural differences
7. respect the rights and property of others
8. display leadership qualities
9. understand different management styles
10. exhibit appropriate assertiveness.

Work ethic

1. demonstrate reliability and dependability
2. observe all organizational policies
3. show interest and enthusiasm in the job
4. exhibit loyalty to the organization and to its employees
5. strive to improve job performance
6. display care for tools and materials
7. seek new assignments when time permits
8. complete assignments in a timely manner
9. possess a commitment to quality.

Reasoning and problem solving

1. integrate creative and innovative ideas
2. synthesize and process job components
3. adapt to changing demands of the job
4. reason and make objective judgments
5. understand rules, procedures, and employer expectations
6. apply basic skills
7. organize work and manage time efficiently.

Communication

1. question appropriately
2. demonstrate clear, effective written and oral communication skills
3. demonstrate good listening and responding techniques
4. develop appropriate telephone skills
5. use correct grammar and spelling
6. follow oral, visual, and written directions.

Job seeking and getting skills

1. prepare applications and resumes

2. conduct career/job search

3. learn job-application letter-writing techniques

4. demonstrate effective interviewing skills

5. become familiar with benefits and payroll programs

6. understand career ladders and advancement

7. access career information

8. understand need for career flexibility and adaptability.

Some of the tasks needed to prepare students to become contributing members of society can be developed by educators. Others, such as job-specific technical skills and most employability skills, need education and business working together. Employability skills, in particular, are not easily defined, taught, or measured. Yet most agree good employability skills are essential for success at both school and work. In order for students to develop competency in the skills previously listed, the collective efforts of business and education are essential.

WHY PARTNERSHIPS?

Business and education partnerships are needed today more than ever. The United States is confronting major demographic, social, economic, and technological changes along with a changing work environment. Many schools are not prepared to meet the demands of an increasing population of at-risk, multicultural, and economically disadvantaged students (not to mention the multiple language barriers that exist). Even if student profiles were not changing dramatically, most schools would still not be prepared to teach the skills needed for highly technical occupations—the cost of equipment and need for continuous teacher retraining would be prohibitive. It should surprise no one that the gap is widening between the preparation business wants in graduates and the quality of graduates that schools are producing.

Albert Shanker, president of the American Federation of Teachers, noted in his Sunday, October 16, 1988, column in *The New York Times*, "Business needs an informed and seasoned insider to get involved in public education if business is to survive, and educators need an outsider—one with a clear commitment to public schools—to help jar them into new ways of thinking if public education is to survive." A common thread found in most proposed solutions to school reform is the need for school-business-community linkages. Schools simply cannot be expected to solve all of society's ills in isolation. Large urban centers are reporting astronomical dropout rates and truancy figures. As disenfranchised youth continue to escape from traditional school structures, it is clear that more alternatives are needed to engage the interest and attention of youth. This fact is increasingly recognized by business and educational leaders. As a result, community-wide collaborative efforts are expanding.

Businesses must keep close to their customers, study their needs, and look for ways their product can better meet customers' needs if they are to remain competitive. It is no different for schools. Our products (students) must match the expectations of employers and the community in order to satisfy our customers (taxpayers) and produce future leaders, business owners, and employees. Educators cannot possibly meet the needs of their customers without communicating with business leaders and involving them in educational planning and delivery strategies.

PLANNING TECHNIQUES

Effective partnerships need honest, open communication and a clear understanding of each other's expectations. Businesses must be willing to offer professional skills and resources to improve the quality of the school experience and, in the end, to create a better work force. They must understand their commitment needs to be ongoing in order to be effective. Educators must be willing to talk with representatives of business without becoming defensive. They must listen to what business leaders are saying and aggressively pursue strategies to change the quality of the school experience for all students. Successful partnerships require a genuine commitment, a long-term relationship, and dedication of resources.

Create awareness. Building community and school awareness is an important first step in creating successful partnerships. The catalyst for a partnership (superintendent or teacher) should contact a local community or business leader and jointly develop strategies to make others within the school system and community aware of why partnerships are important and how the community can become involved. One way to accomplish this is to develop a shared presentation that can be made to local service organizations and school personnel.

Form a steering committee. Once community awareness has been accomplished, a steering committee must be formed. Partnerships will not be successful unless, from the very beginning, planning becomes a shared effort. There should be equal representation of both business and education membership on the steering committee, and the chair of the committee should be from the business community. Although it is important to include a representative cross section of people, it is equally important to keep the steering committee small enough to be manageable. A committee of 10 to 15 people typically meets both criteria. Members who have respect and credibility within the community should be selected. Good human relation skills are also essential to build the level of trust and communication needed for success. Educational administrative representation and commitment, as well as representation from local company presidents, are also critical components in building successful partnerships. Without enthusiasm from those in command, most partnerships do not survive long enough to truly make a difference, no matter how dedicated staff members are.

After the membership of the committee has been determined, it is important for business and educational representatives to jointly plan the agendas. Too often educators believe they need to have everything organized and planned before involving business and community representatives. This is a mistake.

187

In order for a partnership to be successful, all parties involved must have ownership in the planning process.

Assess needs. Clear goals must be set in order for partnerships to succeed. Before goals can be set, a variety of factors need to be considered—local demographics, student profiles, community needs and interests, and the potential resources of both the community and the school. Business people need to know what they can expect from the school, and school personnel need to know the types and level of commitment they can expect from the community. By jointly assessing community/school resources and expectations, both parties can potentially expand each others' ideas by providing an independent outside perspective.

Start small. Once community/school needs are identified, it is beneficial to initially adopt small, manageable partnerships specifically targeted to a particular age group or clientele. It is equally important to match available partners with the right partnership activity. Starting on a smaller scale and providing careful management greatly enhances the chances of the partnership succeeding. After creating positive beginnings, future partnership efforts can be expanded based on assessing the strengths and weaknesses of the initial efforts.

Consider school/community benefits. Schools typically have limited staff and few monetary resources to share. Businesses, on the other hand, are often viewed as avenues for human and financial resources. It is very important for schools to understand that many businesses are also operating on a tight profit margin and may have limited human and financial resources, particularly small businesses that employ a very small number of people. Likewise, business representatives need to understand the limited time available to school personnel who often serve as community liaisons, coordinators, and coaches (along with teaching 125 students per day). Both school and business representatives must be realistic about the level of services and financial commitment each has to offer. The benefits that can be derived from partnership arrangements need to be discussed early in the planning process.

While there are obviously many ways that schools benefit from partnerships, there are also ways that schools can reciprocate in a partnership arrangement. Some examples include (1) allowing for the business to occasionally use the school facility for training and meetings, (2) providing teachers to conduct on-site training for businesses (such as in the area of basic skill improvement), (3) extending use of the school gymnasium or pool for the recreational pursuits of some company employees, (4) giving complimentary tickets to school functions, and (5) experimenting with after-school day care arrangements that benefit working mothers and fathers.

Business can offer time, talent, knowledge of community resources, and a pool of caring adults to a partnership arrangement. In addition, while some businesses cannot offer financial resources, there are many that do. Benefits to businesses from school/community partnerships may come in the form of some tax deductions, but the real benefit is measured in more than financial terms. Employees benefit from the personal feelings gained when they invest their time and talent in youth and are able to watch them prosper and learn.

Other benefits include building positive community images and developing potential future employees who understand the free enterprise system and the skills and attitudes needed to be successful.

Investing the time and financial resources needed to build a more productive work force sometimes may seem overwhelming, but the benefits of school/ community partnerships far outweigh the potential costs. Consider this quote from the November 7, 1988, issue of *Fortune* magazine (p. 46): "If you think education is expensive—try ignorance. It costs some $14,000 a year to keep a prisoner in jail; 62 percent of all prison inmates are high school dropouts. Welfare families drain the government of an average $4,300 a year; dropouts head more than half of them."

BUSINESS EDUCATION COLLABORATIVES

Business educators have a long history of using collaborative partnerships to teach the academic and behavioral curriculum students need for entry into employment. There is evidence, however, that some of these partnerships are not as successful as possible. Many states are experiencing a decline in both the number of vocational courses offered and student participation. Perhaps it is time to set the past aside, critically evaluate the components of business education partnerships, and add the ingredients needed to rejuvenate the partnership concept as applied to curriculum in business education.

Advisory committees. One of the collaborative partnerships business teachers have been using for many years is the advisory committee. All too often they have been underutilized or not used at all. Advisory committees received an emphasis when they were included in the vocational legislation as a requirement for funding of vocational programs. Too often teachers did not know how to use this vast resource—and many still are not using them effectively.

The advisory committee should be an integral part of any business program (funded or not). It should include a representative cross section of the area business community. Business persons can provide the business teachers help with identifying worker deficiencies, support for equipment and material requests to the board of education, and legislative advocacy. Business advisory committees can also help with program evaluation by providing feedback, based on the needs of business, on programs and courses that need to be added, changed, or dropped.

Simulations. Projects and activities that simulate real-world offices are often incorporated into business classes. These projects may include selecting candidates for positions (requiring students to formally apply through job application and interview procedures), "employee" (student) evaluations, and interaction with other "offices" (classes) located in different parts of the school building. Project IN/VEST is an example of a flow-of-work simulation that started in California and is an instructional partnership in other states as well.

In Wisconsin this activity has existed for 15 years in partnership with the Independent Insurance Agents of Wisconsin (IIAW). IIAW provides classroom quantities of all forms and manuals that are needed to run the simulation. In addition they provide workshops during the year on topics of interest to teachers. Each school works closely with a local independent agent who may help with classroom instruction, provide financial assistance, help place graduates of the program, serve as a resource person in conducting mock interviews, assist with student organization activities, and become a liaison to the local board of education.

Cooperative education. Business education's most familiar partnerships are cooperative education programs. With the implementation of the 1963 Vocational Education Act, schools formalized and expanded programs that placed students in jobs in the community that matched students' identified career objectives, interests, and aptitudes. A school coordinator was assigned to supervise the work experience and provide regular in-school instruction. Other components of cooperative education included a home visitation by the teacher, teacher release time to visit students at work, and prerequisites for students to be admitted.

In recent years, the number of cooperative education programs has diminished. Reasons cited by teachers and administrators include decreasing student enrollment, increasing costs of running the program, and declining federal funds. Although there may be legitimate external forces that are causing the decline, it is important to examine objectively internal operations to see if changes are needed to make the programs more viable and cost effective.

For example, business education cooperative programs place an inordinate emphasis on prerequisites for admission. Students who can benefit most from the instruction are sometimes not admitted because they can't satisfy all of the prerequisite requirements. Also, many students no longer have time in their schedules to complete the prerequisites because of increased requirements for graduation in mathematics, science, English, and social studies.

Cooperative education is still an excellent instructional method. By retaining the components that are integral to the quality of the program and modifying others, business education can once again demonstrate one of the most effective partnership arrangements that has ever existed.

Personnel development. Employers can provide business educators with specialized instructors, resources, and training in areas such as job delegation skills, time management, goal setting, teamwork development, and performance assessment. This use of outside resources adds a sense of realism to the curriculum that is often missing. Business teachers are given real-world business examples they can, in turn, use when instructing future employees.

Curriculum development. Do business educators really ever call upon business partners to assist with curriculum development? Too often, the answer is probably no. Businesses may assist schools by:

1. offering summer externships/jobs to business teachers to expose them to new business developments—including technology and business practice
2. inviting business teachers to attend training seminars with the corporation's employees
3. providing speakers and business experts when the business teachers are covering special curricula

4. examining course content to determine whether or not it is relevant in light of workplace expectations.

Models and mentors. Role models and mentors play a significant role in training people for executive development in the corporate environment. Similar relationships that could exist for business teachers, students, and corporate employees include:

1. business representatives making classroom presentations explaining career opportunities and advancement techniques using personal experiences
2. local businesses providing employees as tutors
3. human resource staff from an area business conducting student seminars on job hunting, job application—completion skills, interviewing skills, and career options.

TYPES OF PARTNERSHIPS

The variety and types of partnerships are infinite. At first glance, some of these may not seem appropriate for business educators. But by examining different models, new ideas and extensions can result to strengthen and build upon the partnerships typically found in the business curriculum. Here are a few ideas that communities and schools can adapt to meet local needs:

Mentorships. Research confirms the need for all children to have at least one positive adult role model in their lives. Unfortunately, in today's society there are far too many children who lack the stability of a positive adult role model and are not exposed to future career opportunities through such a relationship. Mentorships are typically one-on-one experiences between a youngster and an adult, designed to provide the child with an opportunity for an ongoing relationship with an adult that can broaden horizons and assist the child in adopting more ambitious career goals than he or she may initially have.

The previous United States Labor Secretary, Elizabeth Dole, delivered comments at the National Mentoring Conference in Washington, D.C., on March 28, 1990. During her address she stated that mentors "are not writing educational policy or becoming part of a bureaucracy. They are not required to know or teach 'new math' or computer skills. When needed, they simply share their wisdom and experience. They ask about homework. They tell young people of the connection between staying in school and getting a good job. They serve as a successful role model pointing out the pitfalls and potholes on the road of life. And they make a difference."

Corporate volunteers. Corporate volunteers can be brought into the classroom to participate in a variety of activities. Some ideas include tutoring students in basic skill areas, serving as classroom assistants and guest lecturers, reading special stories, training students in the techniques of public speaking, and serving as translators for foreign students. These volunteers can also assist with administrative functions such as coordinating tax levy and bond campaigns; helping with fund-raising activities; and contributing professional expertise as accountants, attorneys or medical advisors.[2]

Decorate storefronts and showcase businesses. A good public relations tool for schools to use is to get permission to use empty storefronts for displays of students' work. Likewise, employers can be invited to showcase their business in trophy cases at school, and special assemblies can be held inviting a business person to speak on what it is like to run a business.

Senior citizens. Senior citizens are the fastest growing segment of our economy, and they tend to vote in greater numbers than other age groups. Consequently, it makes good sense to develop activities that can both utilize the talent of this group and also provide them with some services. Following are just a few examples:

- Make school hallways available to seniors for morning and evening walks.
- Have some coffee available for them and have students help them home if the weather causes slippery conditions.
- Encourage seniors to use school libraries.
- Provide free tickets to seniors for school events.
- Invite seniors to share stories with classes on what life was like when they were growing up.
- Host a grandparent day.
- Sponsor a senior-citizen prom.

Dr. James Leary, Superintendent of Adrian Public Schools in Adrian, Michigan, has incorporated into his school system many community outreach activities that target senior citizens. As a result, Dr. Leary has reported that in Adrian, senior citizens overwhelmingly vote in favor of school issues!

Apprenticeships. The apprenticeship system in Europe is frequently looked upon by American educators and policy makers as a system with potential for adaptation in American school systems. In this system, school learning is merged with workplace learning. As a student matures, increasing amounts of time are spent in part-time work (and less time in a structured school setting). The Germans have been perfecting their system of apprenticeship since the Middle Ages. As a result, they are able to produce more goods for export than any other country in the world (even though they have only a fourth of America's population). Several arguments can surely be made against the German apprenticeship system—the most frequent negative comment made is that the system perpetuates sharp class differences because the vocational track is usually started at a very early age in a student's life. While the American society would probably not tolerate such a formal apprenticeship arrangement, it does appear that some features may have relevance for our nation's public school system. For instance, the National Academy Foundation has high school curriculum and work-study arrangements in manufacturing, public service, travel, and tourism.[3]

---

[2] O'Connell, Carol. *How to Start a School/Business Partnership*. Fastback 226. Indiana: Phi Delta Kappa Educational Foundation, 1985.

[3] Mann, Dale. "Bridge from School to Work: Warning—Dangerous Crossing." *Partnerships in Education Journal* 4:7; November 1990.

Teacher internships. Teacher internships with employers can achieve a variety of objectives:

1. Participating teachers are better able to give students accurate and timely information on career opportunities

2. Teachers' competence and motivation are enhanced because internships give teachers direct contact with current research and practice in the real world

3. Businesses can be provided with qualified and reliable part-time employees

4. Barriers between schools and other institutions in society begin to dissipate as people interact with one another.

Teacher internships can be both informative and refreshing. They can also help teachers recognize the things they like about teaching—autonomy within their own classrooms and daily opportunities to influence the lives of the young.[4]

EVALUATION COMPONENTS

Without evaluation, partnerships cannot be revised and improved. One of the easiest ways to develop criteria for evaluation is to study the objectives of the partnership and ask two fundamental questions, "Have the objectives been met?" and, if not, "Why not?" Other, more general questions that may be asked include:

1. Are there ways to enhance communication between partners?

2. How might the partnership be improved?

3. Are there areas of the partnership that could be eliminated and still achieve the same objectives?

4. Should the partnership be continued? If yes, for how long?

5. Should different business partners be recruited?

6. Are the targeted students appropriate participants for this particular partnership, or should a different group of students be included?

Other information that should be collected as part of the evaluation tool includes the number of volunteers needed; the number of hours served by participants; the attitudes of students, teachers, administrators, and volunteers; student absenteeism; and student achievement levels. Partnerships should be evaluated by teachers, administrators, students and buisness people. A good evaluation will identify both strengths and weaknesses and serve as the basis for improvement. Other outcomes of evaluation include an opportunity to gain additional community support and to facilitate future planning.

Evaluation should not occur only at the end of the year. Successful evaluations should occur at the beginning, middle, and end of partnership activities. By doing so, partners can be alerted to changes that need to be made before a partnership activity becomes negative or misguided.

---

[4]Gold, Gerard G. "A Reform Strategy for Education: Employer-Sponsored Teacher Internships." *Phi Delta Kappan* 68:384-387; January 1987.

RECRUITMENT, RETENTION, AND RECOGNITION

Recruitment. To ensure an adequate number of volunteers for partnerships, recruitment must be an ongoing effort. Once small, manageable partnerships have been successfully implemented, the size and scope can be expanded. The best recruiters of new partners are people who have been enthusiastic participants. Business partners should be encouraged to contact other business people and explain to them what a partnership entails, what the benefits to business are, and why the experience can be mutually satisfying and enjoyable.

Retention. Partners feel more committed when steps are taken to ensure a systematic involvement of influential school, business and community representatives. Ongoing activities for the partners themselves should be a component of any partnership activity. For example, some partnerships recommend tours and orientations at each other's facilities. A typical orientation includes introductions, information about the partner, a brief history and description of the business, and a tour of the partner's facilities.

Retention is the art of keeping partners involved with school improvement year after year. Partnership programs usually retain their partners and attract new ones if they

1. provide staff development opportunities and train school personnel to work with business and community partners,
2. show the partners concrete evidence of how they have made a difference in the schools,
3. allow the partners to have a variety of responsibilities and contact with different people, and
4. let the partners know that they are appreciated.[5]

Recognition. Public recognition is a key element in showing appreciation and keeping partners involved. While there are a variety of ways to demonstrate recognition, some of the more popular methods include giving plaques, holding end-of-the-year banquets to honor participants, submitting feature articles to the local newspaper, nominating the business partners for awards, and sending letters of appreciation to the partner's employers.

CONCLUSION

"We can shift from an America of muscle to an America of mind. Doing so will involve reforming, reshaping, recreating, retooling or replacing the public school. And business has a big stake in that."[6] Both businesses and school systems acknowledge the need to collaborate and share resources in order to shape the future strength of our nation. Collaborative activities can range from counseling and mentoring partnerships to more specific job

---

[5]*Education for Employment: A Resource and Planning Guide.* Wisconsin Department of Public Instruction, Bulletin No. 9160, 1988. p. 31.

[6]Mann, Dale. "Bridge from School to Work: Warning—Dangerous Crossing." *Partnerships in Education Journal* 4:7; November 1990.

training partnerships. Because of the racial, social, ethnic, and economic diversity of our nation, these activities work best when they are developed and implemented at the local level.

Academic skill development must address the need for literacy, math, science, and communication skills; but, just as important, attention must be paid to development of the employability skills that provide for the work ethic, leadership, and problem-solving capabilities needed to succeed and advance in today's economy.

Business and education must work together and establish goals by consensus. Such goals must be positive, specific and measurable, or they will become mere philosophical statements.

"Will we build an American school-to-work bridge? The availability of the technologies is less of a problem than the will to begin."[7] There is no single correct partnership model, but all programs must revolve around the vision to produce a better educated, more productive America. Education, in isolation, cannot possibly produce this vision alone. Only through school-community-business linkages will real change occur. Many students need a combination of social services, adult role models, and classroom adaptations to meet a variety of different learning styles before they can begin to succeed in school and work.

When communities band together and partnerships begin, it is important not to place blame on any one institution when attempting to determine "why Johnny can't read." Pointing fingers and placing blame is counterproductive and only defeats the objective of developing the harmony needed to work together in behalf of kids.

> There will be no place on the agenda for school bashing. The objective is to turn people on, not off. Education's past successes will be acknowledged and validated. Everyone's attention will be focused on a new shared vision and the difficult new challenges. In this cooperative endeavor, business and education will be seated at the same side of the table. With shirt sleeves rolled up.[8]

Business educators, once again, have an opportunity to lead in this new venture by adapting old cooperative models, adjusting curriculum to meet the needs of students from different cultures, venturing into partnerships with younger pupils, and providing community leadership that combines technology with the need for increased social and economic services.

---

[7] Ibid., p. 27.

[8] *Labor Force 2000 Corporate America Responds.* Allstate Forum on Public Issues, 1989. p. 19.

CHAPTER 19

Networking Telecommunications into the Business Curriculum: Activities and Student Objectives

DENNIS LABONTY
Utah State University, Logan, Utah

CHERI A. JIMENO
Western Montana College, Dillon, Montana

Telecommunications has the potential to change the classroom just as it is changing the work environment. Educators and students can expect exciting variations in distance learning through computers, as well as new instructional delivery methods using televideos, television, and telephone services within the next decade. Some states are already increasing their resources in telecommunications to link information infrastructures. All of this comes at a time when many teachers feel unprepared to use telecommunications, let alone teach or introduce it to students.

Learning to use the technologies related to telecommunications is becoming the responsibility of all business personnel. Business educators who are on the cutting edge of technology should be teaching and using on-line services, networks, and telecommunications. Studies tell us that more educators are using personal computers in their classrooms or for personal use and that the average student to computer ratio (30:1) has been getting smaller and continues to shrink each year. Also, public perception suggests that secondary schools should be placing *more* emphasis on computer training and applications. Additionally, more computers are being linked together, and by 1999 it is estimated that 85 percent of the microcomputers will be networked. Businesses, too, are recognizing telecommunications as being more than just an ancillary service—it is the artery of communication.

While much is being said about telecommunications, there are few suggestions about how to teach it or how to incorporate it into the secondary business curricula. What is being dubiously omitted and avoided is: How can telecommunications be applied and taught?

The twin intentions of this chapter are to create an interest in using telecommunications and to furnish activities with objectives that allow telecommunictions to be introduced into business courses. These activities do not tap all the possibilities nor do they exhaust all of telecommunications' potential, but these strategies should stimulate creative thoughts that could lead teachers to utilize new technology in their classrooms.

The last part of this chapter suggests some useful teaching tips and suggestions for integrating telecomputing into business subjects.

WHAT IS TELECOMMUNICATIONS?

Telecommunications is an accurate and electronic or electromagnetic exchange of text, data, graphics, or voice between two or more points. Various transmission methods, media, equipment, and services exist that expand the dimensions used to describe this term. Like an amoeba that changes within its environment, electronic applications change for economic survival. Satellite relays, fiber optics, laser technology, and networks are opening new doors of discovery and potentials that affect the interpretation and meaning of telecommunications.

Keeping abreast of current terminology may seem impossible, and business teachers can get dizzy just distinguishing the spiral of tele-terms that have been generated. Words like *telephone, television,* and *telegraph* are recognizable; but words like *telecommuting, teleconferencing, telemarketing, telecomputing,* and *teledemocracy* are new. Adopting the necessary terminology is a prerequisite to effective utilization and understanding of new technologies. The telecommunication nomenclature is growing with the technology, and business educators, if they are to remain current, must incorporate these terms into their business subjects.

PLANNING A TELECOMMUNICATIONS UNIT

An effectively integrated unit including business courses and telecommunications requires meticulous planning to assure quality and student motivation. Four fundamental ingredients must be molded together when connecting computers and on-line services for student activities.

First, an inventory of on-line services is necessary. A variety of on-line services needs to be investigated to match properly the needs of the class, computer enthusiasm of the users, budget for the business department, long-distance rates, and geographical location of schools and on-line service access cities. On-line vendors can be grouped into five basic services: information utilities, bibliographic, after-hours, full text, and numeric.

Second, appropriate classes for integration must be identified, although telecommunications is pliable enough to be molded into most business courses. Some possible classes are consumer education, word processing, keyboarding, general business, economics, marketing, business communications, office procedures, and business law.

Third, special attention must be rendered to props (e.g. computers, software, modems, telephone lines, and on-line services). Any one of these components, when operated incorrectly, can prevent a successful connection. Coordinating a phone line, modem, and on-line subscription is no simple task. Therefore, properly tested equipment, reliable communications software and services, and rehearsed navigation commands can assure that students will enjoy an electrical journey to new discoveries.

Lastly, students should have a basic understanding of the operations of telephone systems and data communications. Since computers and telephone technologies are interrelated or coincide, it appears that a communication foundation regarding telephone services is necessary. With an understanding of on-line services, courses, equipment, and telephone services, a telecommunication unit can effectively commence.

INTEGRATED STRATEGIES

Many of the following strategies are described using the information utility *CompuServe*. Other on-line information utilities and bibliographic, after-hours, and full tax services are available. Subscription rates for these services vary and can influence the potential for different strategies.

New Products

Student
Objectives: To explore an electronic store that provides many product options
To compare the effects that consumers have on pricing and related expenses
To appraise stores, products, and procedures that are provided in the electronic mail

An effective teaching unit could be initiated by combining materials in a consumer education, general business, or marketing class with *CompuServe's* electronic mall. *New Car Showroom* is one electronic store that permits the customer to make choices about new cars. For instance, there is a narrative that contains information about the price, standard features, and special options for just about any type of new car. Students could make changes like selecting an interior of velour or leather, or they could choose a three-liter, fuel-injected engine and watch the price escalate—instantly! This demonstration gives students a realistic view of the cost of new cars and the changing value that special features impose. A follow-up could include comparing the insurance costs that are not available on-line to determine if they escalate too.

This activity could teach students how to make an on-line connection, effectively use their on-line time, and how to exercise a download function. Their downloaded results to their data disk could be printed after they hang up. A decision about the "best" car or "best" features could then be discussed.

Economics & World Events

Student
Objectives: To plot stocks on an on-line service that provides up-to-date quotes
To distinguish the relationship between the U.S. economy and world events
To design events that would have positive or negative effects on the U.S. economy

Students could vividly witness the immediate impacts of national and world events on the economy. One discernable characteristic of telecommunications is that everything is current—NOW! Plotting stock quotes is always an enlightening activity, and a connection with an on-line stock service could prove very illuminating. A similar activity could include tracing stock price changes during major world events. What differences occurred in blue chip stock prices when the PanAm jet was bombed over Ireland, or when the Berlin Wall was opened, or when Iraq invaded Kuwait? These events and their effects could be closely watched or charted right from the classroom.

Electronic Stores

Student
Objectives: To classify the variety of stores and products available on-line

To describe the marketing principles employed by on-line stores

To compare electronic telemarketing techniques

This activity could be used in a marketing class. Students could visit these stores in the electronic mall: Speigel, Coffee Anyone, Alaska General Store, and Rent Mother Nature (on CompuServe). This sampling of stores could lead to a discussion about the advantages and disadvantages of on-line shopping, products, marketing strategies, and ordering by computer. Students could participate in marketing simulations, discussions, and activities related to electronic shopping, while they "shop 'til they drop" using electronic bits.

A business communications class could be enhanced using the electronic mall in *CompuServe* or *Prodigy*. Students could explore the variety of shops and compare prices to local stores; and they could prepare oral and written exercises describing topics like their electronic experiences, interesting stores, different methods that stores use to market products, shortcuts, or unique qualities about stores. Students could (through a simulation) design their own store and electronically market their own product. Since *CompuServe*'s products are described in text, students could learn to write product descriptions and share those descriptions to assess the accuracy and conciseness of their writing style.

E-mail

Student
Objectives: To demonstrate the advantages of using private computer-based message systems

To identify assorted computer menaces (i.e. invasion of privacy, ethics, and viruses)

To develop communications with other students in other regions or countries

Learning to use electronic mail services can be helpful in writing or keyboarding classes to demonstrate composition and formatting skills that are increasingly necessary for survival in business. Correspondence is more than just dictating, keyboarding, and editing—with electronic mail all of these skills happen at video game speed, and students can practice and perfect composition and writing skills while electronically corresponding with another student.

Ethics and security are important business subjects, and telecommunications certainly encompasses these concerns. Computer literature is full of articles about viruses and electronic sabotage. These subjects could fill a unit in business law. Additionally, telemarketing practices (i.e. telephone calls on Sunday afternoon from someone selling metal house siding) could keep a business law class in active discussion. These activities do not need any on-line capabilities, but ethics is a topic that spills into telecommunications.

On-Line Libraries of Databases

Student
Objectives: To define research skills that are available through computer technology and on-line services
To create electronic searches for research
To compare the features of on-line bibliographic services

Some students don't often consider library research exciting. However, the power of electronic searches could make students' eyes sparkle. Business communications courses could benefit from bibliographic and database searches. These searches could be from on-line services like *DIALOG* or *BRS* or from CD-ROM technology at a public or university library. *KNOWLEDGE INDEX* and *BRS's AFTER DARK* are affordable alternatives to expensive on-lines databases.

The drudgery of manual searches could be reduced to a few descriptors and, within an electronic blink, the screen fills with selected references. Writing term papers has never been a favorite assignment, but with electronic searching, the first hurdle for beginning writers could become a positive experience rather than a toil of labor.

A demonstration of *CompuServe's Executive News Service* (ENS) could fascinate students. This service captures up-to-date news articles and stores them in an electronic folder. This handy method of catching current information about a topic (without searches or indexes) could pique students' interests as the computer searches the newspaper while the students' energy is directed elsewhere.

Telecommuting

Student
Objectives: To recount the changing work environment of information processors
To assess production of information processing personnel
To compare a current work environment with a traditional work environment

The office can be located wherever someone can tie into a telephone outlet. The modern automated office produces and absorbs information, and communication of that information is central to the theme of telecommunications. Therefore, it is not peculiar to find information processing being conducted outside the walls of the office and workers transforming into telecommuters.

The office procedures class could (1) experiment with uploading and downloading file transfers and (2) equate the advantages of working at home to the advantages of arriving at the office. This activity could expand further into flex-time, employment benefits, release time, and required skills for modern information managers. Classroom discussions could center around controversial questions such as: Will employees produce more? Who will supervise these workers? How will projects be completed and supervised?

Electronic Bulletin Boards

Student
Objectives: To devise methods of sharing information and things with other people
To catalogue interesting ways to communicate to a small or large group of readers

Electronic bulletin boards are available on most on-line services, and they are provided on most private networks. Posting an electronic note on a community bulletin board is as unnerving as making a public speech. Therefore, preparing a message to appear on a public bulletin board requires communication and keyboarding skills alike.

In a course like keyboarding or business communications, many students practice communicating through letter writing. An enhanced communications activity could involve preparing a written piece to be shared with hundreds or thousands of readers on an electronic bulletin board.

Students could choose to prepare a message from the following suggestions:

- Describe an item to trade or sell.
- Make a short biographical sketch of your school to share with other schools (e.g. mascot, history, memorable graduates or events, etc.).
- Poll other schools about school rules, homework, activities, computers, or shopping.
- Compose an electronic newspaper about your school.

These activities would emphasize both effective communications and the power of electronic bulletin boards. Concepts like uploading, data transmission, and private or public messages could be featured using this activity.

Telecommunications for administrators

Teacher
Objectives: To persuade school administrators to join in the consolidated campaign to incorporate telecommunications both in the classroom and for the school
To catalog various on-line services that could benefit other teachers and administrators
To evaluate services, equipment, software, and other telecommunications-related accessories

Distance learning has numerous capabilities. Some colleges and universities are focusing on electronic learning and electronic teacher support. Also, some states are vigorously augmenting their capacity to extend educational services through telecommunications to rural schools or schools that do not have equipment or personnel to teach certain subjects. Administrators in these locations may expand the school's offerings through electronically delivered courses such as advanced math, science, foreign language, journalism, or agriculture.

Schools could improve their instructional opportunities by linking themselves with collegiate education departments. Elementary and secondary teachers could request assistance in lesson plans, library materials, and field-tested activities. School leaders could belong to database services that track current legislation or highlight current events affecting education. In Montana, for example, this service is provided by Big Sky Telegraph at Western Montana College.

A SHOPPING LIST FOR A
TELECOMMUNICATION UNIT

The following points could be considered before venturing into a telecommunications unit.

- Upgrade any current equipment to allow telecomputing or networking. The equipment needs to be a computer (minimum 8088 processor), an internal or external modem (consider 2400 baud), communications software, and an overhead projection panel. A telephone-line connection and money for long-distance telephone calls are necessary. At most schools it is impossible to expect a computer and modem for each student. Not only would such an arrangement be financially prohibitive, but telephone security and access is a major consideration and often requires outside expertise.
- Become a subscriber to at least one national network (i.e. *CompuServe, Prodigy,* or *Dow Jones New/Retrieval*).
- Develop contacts with individuals knowledgeable in telecommunications. Later, these contacts could become guest speakers.
- Develop some creative simulations and activities.
- Ask questions of technicians, vendors, and telecommunications enthusiasts.
- Test any new knowledge by explaining it to someone else.
- Keep at it! Soon you will have an exciting new unit ready for your class.

TEACHING SUGGESTIONS

When teaching a telecommunications unit, educators might consider two defined areas—information transmission equipment and local and wide area networks.

Information transmission equipment. New terminology needs to be introduced in this area. Introduction of terms such as *analog* and *digital signals* leads to the use of and discussion of different types of modems. Various types of media such as twisted-pair, coaxial cable, fiber optics, and lasers can be introduced. Demonstrations can be effective. For example, most telephone companies usually have some twisted-pair and fiber optic cable they will donate. Any business that has a computer system connected via an Ethernet-based LAN will have some coaxial cable available for exhibits.

Microwaves must be transmitted in a straight line between two points. A good deal of the analog signals that we receive daily (such as television and radio) are broadcast through the atmosphere as microwaves. Microwave transmission via satellite is used to transmit data on a worldwide basis. Therefore, students could create a visual depiction (using string or cable) of analog signals being sent through the air as microwaves.

Many network services like *CompuServe, Telenet, TYMNET, DataPak,* and others have telephone access numbers that can be connected with a local phone call. Since not every city in every state has an access number, other cities and towns in that state must pay long-distance charges. It is helpful for students to understand that on-line services may have long-distance charges; therefore, it becomes necessary to identify the cities that have access numbers. One way to demonstrate the connectivity of cities is to require students to make signs for each access city and connect *CompuServe* cities with red yarn, *TYMNET* cities with blue yarn, *Telenet* cities with brown yarn, etc. Soon the room becomes a large string-art diagram of node sites. This demonstration entails the use of many telecommunication terms, and turns a weary lecture into an effective learning experience.

Another demonstration to help students visualize fiber-optic cable is to describe the information transmission as an electronic worm crawling down a glass tube. By using a few props and some imagination, the worm could be a laser light, moving in nonometers, traveling through a fiber-optic cable.

Local and wide area networks. The philosophy behind networks is that all types of input/output devices can be connected to one system for sharing and exchanging information. Local area networks (LANs) link various types of equipment used within a building or several buildings within the same geographic area. LANs can be expanded into extensive networks that enable individuals to send information from city to city, across the nation, and to other countries throughout the world, i.e. wide area networks (WANs).

The LAN component in a telecommunication unit could include demonstrations of accessing common databases, file sharing, or the sharing of expensive output devices such as printers or facsimile machines.

Electronic mail is the subject of a good LAN or WAN activity. Students could send messages around the school, to people from all over the United States and/or internationally without using envelopes or telephones. How about finding local, national, or international "electronic pen pals"?

CONCLUSION

Descriptions about equipment, software, and services should be presented cautiously to allow for query and discovery. Also, a slow baud rate (300 baud) when accessing on-line services displayed through a projection panel could maintain students' interest over a longer period of time. A slower transmission rate translates into a slower reading rate. A 1200 baud rate jumps on and off the screen so quickly, and while the transmission saves some long-distance costs, it often jams the students with too much information—or information overload!!

Using a projection panel is essential. A Y-connector or box that connects the CPU, monitor, and projection panel is helpful. By arranging the panel facing the overhead screen and the monitor facing the overhead screen, the teacher can face the students and follow the monitor. Not only is student eye contact maintained, but the teacher is in a more comfortable teaching position.

Costs can be reduced by using simulations. Vendors are marketing affordable simulations that duplicate on-line services with no network subscription costs. An economical unit could include accessing the U.S. Department of Education's research database (a free service) using *ProComm*, a shareware, communications software. By demonstrating uploading/downloading and other related activities, basic telecommunications concepts can be demonstrated at minimal costs.

The conclusion of a telecommunication unit could relate to something about the future. Within our lifetime, it is likely that voice communications will replace keyboards, and video telephones will transmit routine phone calls. Pass around a fiber optics cable; future telecommunications applications are as endless as the imagination of the students who touch that cable.

Creativeness is the key to teaching telecommunications. Hands-on activities will help change imagination into reality and allow students to explore new ways to electronically communicate ideas.

REFERENCES

Grunwald, P. (October, 1990). "The New Generation of Information Systems." *Phi Delta Kappan, 72*(2), 113-114.

McLeod, R., Jr. (1990). *Information Systems.* New York: MacMillan Publishing Company, 11.

Ray, C. M., Palmer, J., Woh, A. D. (1991). *Office Automation: A Systems Approach.* Cincinnati: SouthWestern Publishing Company, 216-255.

Rosen, A. (1987). *Telecommunications.* San Diego: Harcourt Brace Jovanovich, Publishers, 4.

Weinstein, S., & Roschwalb, S. A. (October, 1990). "Is There a Role for Educators in Telecommunications Policy?" *Phi Delta Kappan, 72*(2), 115-117.